RIDING HOME

RIDING HOME

THE POWER *of* HORSES TO HEAL

TIM HAYES

ST. MARTIN'S PRESS NEW YORK

www.stmartins.com

The Library of Congress Cataloging-in-Publication Data is available upon request.

ISBN 978-1-250-03351-2 (hardcover)
ISBN 978-1-250-03352-9 (e-book)

St. Martin's Press books may be purchased for educational, business, or promotional use. For information on bulk purchases, please contact the Macmillan Corporate and Premium Sales Department at 1-800-221-7945, extension 5442, or write to specialmarkets @macmillan.com.

First Edition: March 2015

10 9 8 7 6 5 4 3

For Mom and Dad

Thank you.

I love and miss you both.

CONTENTS

FOREWORD

Horses have been a part of my life for as long as I can remember. My first time on a real horse was when I was five or six. Granted, it was only in the pony-ride ring, but it was instant love. This bighearted animal moving me along like it was the most natural thing in the world.

But that's the thing about horses. They connect in ways that often words can't capture but hearts can. It's powerfully emotional for both human and horse. In *Riding Home*, Tim Hayes brings this forth with the force of a great storyteller blessed with passion for his subjects, horse and human.

Through my early teens, my relationship to horses was always on horseback, and along with my friends during those days, riding had a decidedly show-off, wild quality to it. It wasn't until I found myself in Estes Park, Colorado, at fifteen, where I spent days grooming and caring for horses to earn my keep, that I developed a true connection that went far beyond riding horseback.

This simple emotional connection is at the heart of Tim Hayes's stories, which is ironic, as most of the people he features are considered to have very complicated challenges. I've always been drawn to the truth and simplicity inherent in nature. And that's why I believe Tim Hayes is really onto something here.

Therapy. Equine therapy. The power of nature—horses—and its connection to the human spirit are front and center at every turn of the page in this important book. And it is manifest in the experiences of everyone from autistic children and brave veterans—coming home with everything from PTSD to paralysis and the loss of limbs—to prisoner inmates and troubled teens who've endured way too much in their young lives.

In most cases, nothing else had cracked the code of their suffering or their myriad challenges. And somehow, the majestic horse entered the picture, sometimes by chance, sometimes as a last resort, and suddenly there was hope for the first time in as long as anyone could remember. I think this is what drew me to my 1998 film, *The Horse Whisperer*, along with a portrayal of ranch life out West that was fast disappearing. At the heart of the story is a man and a horse and healing not only for the man but also for those around him.

There's something meditative about communicating with horses, something instinctive where you eventually have to merge into one in order to move forward together. I think maybe that simple notion is why we are seeing such widespread success in the horse's ability to break through where nothing else has worked, and we're just left with a form of healing. Tim Hayes has made this his lifework, and the world is a better place for it.

Tim says that in his natural horsemanship classes, he brings students along by looking at the horse-human relationship from the horse's point of view, and in so doing, makes the focus understanding and compassion rather than force and intimidation. As a society, we can learn much from the clear simplicity of this notion.

The lessons you'll take away from this beautiful volume of healing and love between man and nature will stay with you for a long time. And who knows? Maybe it will open a door to healing for you or someone you love.

—Robert Redford

RIDING HOME

INTRODUCTION

For thousands of years, one animal has been unequaled in its contribution to human survival. It has been a source of food, a means of transportation, a provider of physical labor, and an instrument of war. This amazing creature is the horse. Throughout human history, people have loved, owned, and ridden horses. Horses fascinate us; they silently speak to our hearts.

That fascination also goes beyond riding. Millions of people—horse owners and non–horse owners alike—have discovered the amazing abilities of horses to help us heal from disabling physical and mental conditions, such as cerebral palsy and muscular dystrophy, by participating in what is known as equine therapy.

In the last few years, something new, and quite extraordinary, has been discovered about the ability of horses to help humans. Men, women, and children afflicted with severe emotional damage are healing and making dramatic recoveries by receiving the simple love, understanding, and acceptance that comes from establishing a relationship with a horse.

In the following pages, what I hope to pass on is twofold. On an individual level, I will endeavor to explain why horses have this remarkable ability to heal and positively transform emotionally wounded men, women, and children. On a societal level, I wish to offer a call for increasing the awareness, support, and expansion of those equine programs that are now accomplishing the healing many institutional organizations that rely on traditional psychotherapy and pharmaceutical medication have often been unable to achieve.

Readers will also discover both how and why horses help people become better human beings and have better relationships, and show us the qualities we need to become more loving and compassionate. Horses connect us to the power of nature and of living in the moment. Something unimaginable and profound occurs when a human begins a meaningful, emotional, interactive relationship with a horse.

However, one's epiphanies do not come from riding on a horse's back. Remarkable human psychic breakthroughs originate and are manifested with horses when a person creates a relationship on the ground. Not only are the results both transformational and lasting, but they occur with amazing speed.

In the Wild Horse Inmate Program (WHIP) at the Florence, Colorado, correctional facility, prisoners who have never before seen a live horse come face-to-face with a one-thousand-pound snorting, biting, and kicking wild animal. Under the direction of the U.S. Bureau of Land Management, prison inmates are taught to gentle wild horses and make them safe for public adoption.

But what began as an attempt to manage the free-roaming

American mustang by utilizing cheap prison labor became something no one could have ever imagined. Gentling the horses caused the WHIP prisoners to unwittingly experience profound emotional transformations. Even more surprising, when WHIP inmates were released back into society, their recidivism rate, compared with that of prisoners from the general population, was drastically lower.

State-of-the-art equine recovery programs are also found in therapeutic schools and adolescent wilderness retreats. For some of today's young men and women, often referred to as either "Youth at Risk" or "at-risk youths," horses are significantly helping to prevent troubled teenagers, high school dropouts, and children from divorced, alcoholic, or abusive families from turning to drugs, becoming pregnant, ending up in hopeless incarceration, or taking their own lives. Many a heartbreaking yet universal story becomes a testament and a further example of this remarkable capability of horses to heal and change human beings.

The natural ability of a horse to give unconditional acceptance to a troubled teen who is revealing his true self creates a feeling of self-worth extremely hard to obtain with traditional rehabilitation methods. Through simple yet meaningful interactions with horses, young adults gain profound insights into their own lives, attitudes, and relationships. With increasing frequency, the most successful therapy at many of these rehabilitation institutions is the horsemanship program.

The most cutting-edge example of a recent equine therapy program is Horses for Heroes. What began as a method of equine physical therapy for wounded soldiers with paralyzed or missing limbs miraculously became a source of emotional recovery as the horses unintentionally began to heal veterans suffering from the devastating effects of PTSD. And just as with the equine therapy programs for troubled teens, horses were remarkably able to succeed where traditional talk therapy and prescription medication had often failed.

For close to two decades, I have had the good fortune to do what I love: teaching humans how to create a meaningful, emotional, and interactive relationship with a horse. I have worked with and studied the nature of hundreds of different horses as an Idaho cattle ranch cowboy, a New York State dude ranch trail guide, a trainer at a multimillion-dollar state-of-the-art equestrian center in New York City, and a visiting instructor for the animal science departments of the University of Connecticut and the University of Vermont.

Today what I teach is referred to as "natural horsemanship," a methodology that involves looking at the horse-human relationship from the horse's point of view. Books and movies have called it "horse whispering."

Whether I'm instructing university students or conducting international clinics for horse owners and their horses, what I'm sharing is how to create a more positive relationship with a horse by using understanding and compassion, as opposed to force and intimidation. Now I wish to share how an equine relationship can go even further and heal the deep wounds of what could potentially be millions of men and women.

Being with horses changes people. To have an interactive relationship with a horse is to discover and know yourself, other humans, and the environment with more truth and compassion than perhaps you could dream of or imagine.

But must we wait until a teenager drops out of school, becomes pregnant, turns to drugs, or goes to prison before he or she is provided with the opportunity for healing and transformation that comes from creating an interactive relationship with a horse?

I believe we live in the age of partial attention. Not only do smartphones, e-mails, texts, computers, and 24–7 activities depreciate our human connectedness with others, they erode our relationship with ourselves and remove us from the natural world.

Horses reconnect us to the truth of our irrefutable yet fragile collective humanity. A great many members of our human family may look different from one another on the outside, but that which resides hidden inside all of us and which is most personal is always the same. Horses have the ability to instantly remind us that, just like them, we inhabit the same planet, share the same fears and desires, and, more than anything else, all desperately desire to get along with one another.

Horses help us discover hidden parts of ourselves. They cause us to become better people, better parents, better partners, and better friends. They teach us that when we're not getting what we want, we're the ones who need to change; either what we're doing or who we're being. A horse can be your greatest teacher, for as you will see, a horse has no ego, he never lies, and he's never wrong. It is this amazing power of horses to heal our emotional wounds and teach us about ourselves that I now share with you.

1

WILD HORSES—WILD MEN

They call it supermax, "Alcatraz of the Rockies," a place for the hopeless, the worst of the worst, transfers from other prisons, killers of guards or fellow inmates, sitting among a complex of nine state penitentiaries and four federal prisons. It is a fortress of concrete and steel on six hundred acres of Colorado grasslands—a silent, lonely structure surrounded by mountains of grace and splendor rising too far away for anyone to notice.

I sat in the back of an old rusted-out yellow school bus as it moved down an empty gravel road, bouncing in and out of potholes. We were going deep into a world of guard towers, fences topped with razor wire, and tough-looking men in jeans and denim work shirts. The bus stopped in front of a gray stone building, its sides framed around windows of broken glass and caked with mud. A guard opened the bus door and told me and the seventeen other men to get off. He led us around the building to a large rectangular wooden corral, had us climb up the side, and told us to sit on top of the fence rails.

All was silent but for the wind blowing whirls of dust, which moved across the middle of the corral, then stopped and disappeared. As we sat on the fence, our legs hanging down, a sound like rumbling thunder moved toward us. A metal gate at the end of the corral swung open, and fourteen wild horses came barreling past our feet, snorting, kicking, running, trying to escape the terror that burned in their eyes.

I was sitting next to a tall, muscular black inmate named Morris. On the bus he'd told me he was "doing fifteen to twenty-five for manslaughter." He said he was a member of the West Side Crips of Los Angeles. His troubles began when he broke the arm of a rival gang member, snapping it over his knee like a stick. When the guy pulled a knife with his other hand, Morris put the man's head in the space between a car doorframe and its open door and kept slamming the door until the man's skull was crushed. Morris was twenty-three and had been in the gang since he was fourteen. He'd never been out of South Central Los Angeles. He'd never seen a live horse.

The Wild Horse Inmate Program was originally set up by the U.S. Bureau of Land Management (BLM) to assist in managing the country's thousands of free-roaming wild horses. Prior to any government regulation, America's wild horses were gradually being left to the mercy of slaughterhouses. This practice, if left unregulated, could have led to the permanent extinction of one of our country's most revered icons: the wild mustang.

In 1973, the government stepped in with legislation that would permit any U.S. citizen to obtain and own a wild mustang as long as they had enough land and the proper facilities to care for it. The BLM then created a program called Adopt a Horse; the agency would make the animals available in various regions, and for a fee of $125, anyone who qualified could permanently "adopt" a wild mustang. This, however, created an additional challenge. Most of the people bringing home the wild horses were not experienced enough to safely handle them. Without professional training prior to adoption, the mustangs were too dangerous.

To safely gentle thousands of horses would require many experienced horsemen and be enormously expensive. In 1986, BLM officials came up with what they believed was an ingenious solution. The concept was simple: if prison inmates could be used as cheap labor and taught to manufacture license plates, why not teach them how to gentle wild horses?

Having recently heard about WHIP, I had now come as an observer to see it firsthand. I had worked on cattle ranches, on dude ranches, in fancy equestrian centers, and at every type of local or backyard barn. For years I had taught people about horses—not only how to ride them but how to understand them, communicate with them, control them, and care for them. Countless times I had witnessed the self-awareness and emotional connections humans could experience by forming relationships with horses, but I was not prepared for what I was about to see in this prison.

Although the gentler methods of "starting horses," with communication—as opposed to "breaking horses," which uses force—had already begun in the mid-1990s, some of the old-fashioned traditional methods were still occasionally being used. Today, the Cañon City, Colorado, prisons, as well as other BLM

WHIP programs in Kansas, Oklahoma, Nevada, and Utah, start their wild mustangs using methods of kindness, communication, and understanding—otherwise referred to as natural horsemanship.

At the end of my first day, I'd learned that new members like Morris are assigned to small groups of experienced inmates who have, over time, become proficient at the skilled process of gentling and then training wild horses. Being in WHIP is a privilege. Inmates first have to volunteer, then qualify, satisfying requirements involving both a personal conduct history of good behavior and recommendations from superiors.

Once in the program, if they follow the rules, they acquire a small amount of additional freedom and a sense of purpose unique to prison life. If they mess up, they are returned to the general prison population. Therefore, all the inmates in WHIP, both old and new, are highly motivated to try hard to succeed and do their time working at their newfound vocation of "gentling" horses.

As I sat on the fence next to Morris, a cowboy wearing a white straw hat rode into the corral on a chestnut horse and moved slowly toward the fourteen mustangs. One by one he separated each horse from the herd and sent it into an adjoining pen, which prevented it from returning.

When there was but one horse left, the cowboy drove it into a metal chute, trapping the fear-drenched animal. Once locked in the chute, some horses freeze in terror; others go crazy, desperately trying to escape. This one stood on his hind legs, towering ten feet in the air, frantically striking at the metal panels with his front hooves.

It was the middle of July and about ninety degrees. Most of the prisoners had been told that they could take off their shirts, which they'd done, revealing iron-pumped arms with multiple tattoos. The cowboy yelled out to Morris and two other new inmates to watch the experienced old-timers go through the gentling process with this new horse. The horse in the chute had dropped his front legs and was now standing on all four feet, frozen with fear, nostrils flared, eyes wide as if waiting for death.

An old-timer named Swifty slowly put his hand between the metal bars of the chute and ever so gently began to stroke the horse's back. For a new inmate, this action most likely appeared insignificant. For a wild horse that has never seen a human, much less been touched by one, it was terrifying. Swifty gently stroked the horse's withers, stopped and took his hand away, then began stroking again. Slowly the horse began to relax.

The most pleasurable place one can stroke or pet a horse is the area between the neck and back known as the withers. It is the first place a mare will nuzzle her newborn foal to nurture, calm, and relax it. The gentle nuzzling of a horse's withers causes a release of endorphins and a lowering of the heart rate, both of which serve to produce feelings of safety and well-being.

After about twenty minutes the cowboy told Swifty to leave, pointed to Morris, and said, "You, jump down and stand over there by the fence." Then he told one of the old-timers to explain to Morris how to put a halter and rope on the horse's head without getting his arm broken or bitten off.

I watched, keenly aware of the two biggest differences between these horses and the domestic horses most people encounter: the mustangs' freedom in their natural environment to run anywhere, at any time, and their total lack of exposure to people. Not only had these horses never had any type of confinement experience, they had also never seen a human being.

The horse is a prey animal; the human is a predator. Predators eat prey. All horses are born knowing this. Domestic horses are raised around humans. They learn to get along and not to fear people; otherwise, they could never be ridden. People often think of the horse as a "flight animal," one that would rather run from danger than fight. That's true most of the time for domestic horses, but not for wild mustangs. These horses can kill a man in the blink of an eye. More than once they have.

Morris hung over the top panel, his hands wavering, and barely managed to put the halter over the horse's head. Next he cautiously attached a soft fifty-foot cotton rope to the halter, stepped back down to the ground holding the rope, and walked backward about twenty-five feet. The cowboy, still sitting on his horse, yelled for five other inmates to join Morris and take their places along different sections of the rope. Then he rode to the chute, unhooked the latch, and swung the gate open.

At once the mustang bolted out of the chute, running for his life. He smashed into the gate, cutting his front right pastern—I could see blood just above his hoof—and raced toward the other end of the pen. I watched as all six men held on tight and pulled at the rope as the horse desperately tried to escape—imprisoned humans fighting wild animals like ancient gladiators battling lions. The cowboy now wanted the inmates to begin what was called the gentling process.

As this began, I stayed focused on Morris. He not only needed to show the animal he was in control, he needed to do it in a way that would gain the horse's trust. I could hear an inmate they called Stucky, a skinny kid from somewhere in Ohio, muttering to himself: "He ain't never gonna get near that animal."

To understand how much it takes for a wild horse to trust a

human, imagine you have gone to visit a remote village where one hundred years ago the natives practiced cannibalism. No one speaks English. One of the natives makes a motion indicating that he wants you to go with him into his hut. Even though he and his relatives haven't eaten human flesh in over a hundred years, would you go with him without a second thought?

Would you go if he began to look annoyed and frustrated when you hesitated and said, "No, thank you"? Even though you knew it was their custom to show friendship by sitting and eating with you, how would you react if he and five of his native friends began to physically move you into the hut? Would you feel trusting and easily go in or stand your ground and insist, "I said no!"? What was happening now in this prison corral was similar. It didn't matter that the visitor was a horse.

The horse stood frozen, his body shaking, staring wide-eyed with horror at six tattooed predators dripping with sweat. It was a tug-of-war, wild horse versus wild men. The cowboy yelled for the men to pull the horse's head to the left. This caused the animal to move his feet, turning his body to the left. Next, they were told to pull the head right, which moved the horse's feet to the right.

Head left, then right. This went on for about a half hour. As it continued, it took less and less effort to move the horse. With increasingly less resistance from the mustang, the cowboy told one of the inmates, then another to leave the rope and return to the fence.

Horses, whether they are born in the wild or on a million-dollar Kentucky breeding farm, live their entire lives motivated by three factors, which are valued in the following order: survival, comfort, and leadership. First, they will always run or fight until they feel no threat of being eaten by a predator. Second, when they feel a hundred percent safe, they will do whatever is necessary to be physically and emotionally comfortable—that is, rest, eat, drink, sleep, and remove themselves from anything stressful.

Finally, when they feel both safe and comfortable, they will seek their place in the leadership pecking order of the herd. Knowing one's place in the herd's pecking order eliminates disputes, which can cause fights. Eliminating fights prevents injuries, reduces stress, and makes daily life more comfortable.

Horses obtain their leadership positions by participating in contests of physical dominance. It starts when one horse challenges another with threats of kicks or bites. The horse that moves away from the confrontation first loses the contest. The horse that stands its ground is the winner and thus the leader of the two. The entire herd participates in these contests until there is an "alpha," or herd leader, and every horse knows its place in the herd.

Being the alpha brings with it the responsibility for the safety of the herd. It also brings privileges such as eating first. Although contests can get rough and threats of bites or kicks can rapidly escalate to physical contact, the object is never to seriously hurt or be hurt. While it can take two days or more for a herd to accept a new horse as an additional member, most pecking-order contests are resolved quite quickly. Eighty percent of the time this is accomplished with nothing more than threats expressed by ear pinning or head swinging. In fact, horses think of this method of deciding leadership roles as play.

However, because it can be extremely rough, if people engaged in similar behavior it could easily result in unintentional physical injury. For humans, most often children and teenagers, this type of behavior is not only considered dangerous, it has appropriately come to be referred to as "horseplay." (Swimming pools often have posted regulations that include "No horseplay.")

When all three of horses' primary needs—survival, comfort, and leadership—have been satisfied, their next most lasting and fervent desire is to just get along with one another and anyone or anything that enters their world. These natural qualities of acceptance and tolerance have allowed horses to endure for millions of years while thousands of other animal species have perished.

Of all the invaluable attributes of another species that could benefit the human race, I have often thought that none could so powerfully make a difference for the future of our planet than if humans would simply emulate these two humble character traits of our equine friends.

It was late afternoon in the prison corral and the sun was slowly moving west, bringing a warm breeze that helped dry the sweat of both man and horse. The mustang, having initially squared off against six inmates, thinking they were going to eat him, had not only realized that he was still alive but had repeatedly been made to move his feet in a contest much like one he would have had with another horse.

It had become more comfortable for him to move than to resist. Because he'd been moved with less and less physical effort, he was in fact losing the contest and was now facing only one man: Morris. The cowboy told the inmate to move up the rope, approach the horse with his hand outstretched, and allow the mustang to smell him.

The former South Central L.A. street-gang member moved closer, extending the fingers of his right hand, and stopped about three inches from the horse's mouth. Morris was powerful and dangerous-looking, and though he'd never seen a live horse, he, like the rest of the inmates, had arrived here believing that all horses were like the ones on TV or in the movies: easygoing, submissive, and respectful of men, especially tough men. He was wrong.

With lightning speed the mustang reared up, and Morris fell backward, hitting the dirt hard. He immediately jumped up and backed away as the horse came down, pounding his two front hoofs into the ground. The cowboy yelled at Morris to try again.

The mustang's first strike had hit the ground short of its mark. I could hear Morris yell out that he was lucky the horse missed, but I knew he was mistaken. The horse was sending Morris a warning, as if to say, "If you don't move away, the next time I strike I'll make contact and I'll hurt you." If a horse strikes or kicks and wants to make contact, he never misses. This was another example of the many noble qualities of horses: they're just, they almost always start with a warning, they mean what they say, and they never lie.

If they want you to move, they'll start by asking you to move using their body language. They'll pin their ears back and kick the air in your personal space. They do not begin by making physical contact. Just as they would with another horse, they give you a warning, which lets you decide how you want to respond and allows you the dignity of choosing your answer.

If you still don't move, they will tell you that you should have listened and respected their request. They'll tell you this by kicking again, but this time they'll make contact, sometimes with deadly accuracy.

Morris began to repeat what he had done, but I could see that something about him was different. It was the look on his face. Something in Morris, I was soon to discover, had shifted. The cowboy yelled out, "That's enough for today." He rode over to Morris, took the rope, and led the mustang to his herd mates.

The next time I saw Morris, he had been working with that same horse for three days while being mentored by some of the old-timers. I could see from his physical manner and gestures that he had begun to acquire a slower, gentler approach as he moved around the horse.

Now when he took the mustang into the pen he could touch the animal all over its body. He could put a blanket and saddle on the horse's back. He could pick up all four hooves and clean them as the horse stood quietly. The only thing he hadn't done was ride him.

Getting on a horse's back for the first time is the most challenging moment in creating a relationship between horse and human. No matter how much prior trust has been established, having a meat-eating predator climb on top of a plant-eating prey animal is enough to instantly cause an explosive equine meltdown. In a flash, a horse will take off and run for his life. He'll buck and rear, sometimes so violently that he'll tip over backward and fatally crush his rider.

At the same time that new inmates like Morris were learning the process of gentling wild mustangs, they were also being taught to ride older, experienced, "saddle-broke" horses. By the time an inmate sat on a wild horse, he knew how to ride.

As Morris gently put his leg over and sat down on the mustang, I saw the same look in his eyes I had seen at the end of his first session. He settled his weight, leaned forward, and gently stroked the mustang along his neck. Morris made a kissing sound, squeezed his legs, and the horse slowly began walking. They walked together around the pen for about ten minutes, then stopped in the center, and Morris quietly got off.

I walked over to Morris as he stood stroking the side of the horse's head. I asked him what he had learned in the past few days about horses—creatures he had never seen and might never see outside of prison for years to come. Morris spit in the dirt, looked at me, and slowly began to speak:

"They say they're dumb . . . they ain't dumb. They could damage you with all that power, but you could put an eight-year-old kid on 'em and know it's okay. I know 'cause I seen it in movies and TV. The horse thinks you're goin' t'hurt 'im. They get angry and try to hurt you . . . and they could. They don't understand what you're tryin' to do. They act tough, but I think they just scared. Yeah, they ain't mean . . . just scared. I think maybe once you get to trust 'em, they trust you."

It was amazing; Morris had had an epiphany.

He went on to tell me that he saw in these horses something that he knew was also inside him, something he could never admit to himself or anyone else. Morris had been living his whole life in fear. If these powerful, tough wild animals could be afraid, maybe, he said, maybe he could say he had been afraid, too.

The inmates who participate in WHIP have committed every crime imaginable, some frightening or violent. They arrive at prison with a lot of swagger. Most are from gangs. In their world they see themselves as tough guys, dangerous, bad. The first time a wild mustang comes at them, their rock-hard attitudes crumble. The only way they know how to relate to almost anyone is with anger, mistrust, and deadly force, but now it's instantly apparent that their way won't work with these horses.

And just as with Morris, something happens to all of them. The inmates start to see that the mustang's violent behavior is caused by fear. The horses are just trying to survive. They act mean and aggressive, but in reality they are scared to death, just like the men. For the first time in the lives of these men, they are shown the undeniable truth about who they are.

They have learned and believed that being tough and vicious is their only hope of survival. But now—just like these beautiful, wild, violent, and unpredictable animals—the men can see that their motive had been fear. And maybe, just like the horses, they, too, can change.

Behind their violence, the mustangs are deeply afraid. The inmates identify with that. They see themselves. They begin to feel compassion, an emotion they have probably never known or felt before. They feel it for the horses, they feel it for each other, and they feel it for themselves.

America has the highest incarceration rate in the world. In 2010, according to the U.S. Bureau of Justice Statistics, 2,292,133 adults were incarcerated in U.S. federal and state prisons and county jails. A recent study by the bipartisan Commission on Safety and Abuse in America's Prisons reported that within three years of their release, 67 percent of former prisoners are rearrested and 52 percent are reincarcerated, a recidivism rate that calls into question the effectiveness of America's correctional system, which costs taxpayers $60 billion a year.

According to the Colorado Department of Corrections, the

recidivism rate for inmates from the Wild Horse Inmate Program is half the national rate of 67 percent. The horses of WHIP have helped prevent more than 780,000 former inmates from returning to prison. Not only does the public get to adopt safer horses, the rate of prisoner recidivism is drastically reduced.

Many inmates from the WHIP program leave prison and become productive members of society. Remarkably, the relationships created between inmates and horses achieve a level of human rehabilitation that billions of dollars and hundreds of years of traditional systems of incarceration have never been able to attain.

I had come to this prison to study the wild mustang and learn what effect, if any, working with horses might have in the practical rehabilitation of hardened inner-city criminals. What I saw was a miraculous transformation I don't think anyone could have imagined. I certainly hadn't.

The inmates were trying to gentle the horses, but in truth the horses were gentling the inmates. The process of gentling wild horses to fit into human society was simultaneously gentling "wild" humans to fit back into the same society. I had not only watched the use of cheap prison labor save a great American icon, the wild mustang; I had witnessed the unintended healing of lost souls.

2

THE NATURE OF HORSES—THE NATURE OF HUMANS

To understand why and how horses not only have a unique ability to interact with humans but possess the extraordinary power to heal those of us afflicted with such varied emotional wounds, we must first know the horse with the same understanding we have of humans. Wild by nature, the horse most people come into contact with has been domesticated for the convenience of humans. People see, judge, often misinterpret, and, when in doubt, anthropomorphize everything a horse does. The vast majority of what people expect from horses is often that which is most unnatural for them.

A perfect example is riding. The enormous size, power, and speed of the horse developed over millions of years as a result of natural selection. These three enhanced survival characteristics evolved solely to improve the horse's ability to escape from its natural enemies and not to enable it to pull or carry things on its back. If riding a horse were natural, we would see horses riding other horses. Humans are the only animals that ride other species.

It is truly remarkable to comprehend the level of transformation that human domestication has had on the horse. Today horses are flown to other countries to compete as Olympic athletes in events televised and watched by billions of people throughout the world. The modern cowboy and his ranch horse engage in sophisticated teamwork enabling them to control thousands of cattle, many weighing eight hundred pounds or more, on millions of acres of solitary land. Police horses partner professionally with police officers to control dangerous and rebellious crowds of thousands on the streets of great international cities.

All of these extraordinary capabilities come from an animal originally the size of a small dog that appeared millions of years ago with a singleness of purpose: to survive, flourish, and run free in an environment surrounded by nature and untouched by the human mind or hand.

Unlike humans, horses have no need for prepared food, shelter, clothes, beds, phones, doctors, police, computers, weapons, or money. To survive any attack from animals that consider it food, horses have two chief time-tested defenses: their enormous speed, which allows them to escape, and, if they're trapped, their massive physical power, which makes them a formidable opponent in a fight.

The modern domestic horse, with an average size of seven feet long and five feet high at the withers, exists improbably yet comfortably among the ultimate predator: humans. Many live much of their lives inside a barn, with long periods of confinement in small wooden stalls. What theoretically should be a traumatic experience for an animal that feels safe only if it has endless geography on which it can escape becomes not only tolerated but willingly accepted.

Imagine the reverse situation: that you're trying to survive (not to even mention live comfortably) in the wilderness, without food, shelter, weapons, or any means of communication and at the mercy of bears, mountain lions, and wolves. The average person, even one of superior intelligence, would most likely perish.

Is it any wonder that what separates humans from every other species and has enabled us to thrive, despite our inferior strength and speed, is the ingenious yet unnatural world we have created with our brainpower? The magnificence of the human brain is responsible not only for the extraordinary creations of modern-day life but for our nearly absolute power over every living organism on the planet.

However, the same brain that has been the source of our evolutionary omnipotence has also contributed to our separateness from one another. And some, when contemplating the future, believe that it will eventually lead to our extinction.

The fact that humans and horses have such a magnificent history of partnering in so many varied and productive relationships is truly astonishing when one realizes that these two species are genetically hardwired to not get along. The horse is often considered the ultimate prey animal. It does not kill anything to eat, nor does it kill other horses. Its sophisticated social skills, which might even be described as enlightened, have been at the core of its epic fifty-five million years of survival.

By contrast, *Homo sapiens* has been present for only about two hundred thousand years and has evolved into the ultimate predator of all species. We not only kill anything we want, including each other, we hire others to kill for us. Killing is often our solution for anyone or anything we are unable to get along with.

As human technology, designed to master and improve our global existence, keeps advancing at breathless warp speed, I often think human survival would stand a better chance if our species would simply adopt some of the characteristics naturally inherent in the society of horses.

Completely apart from riding, learning how to communicate and interact with a horse on the ground is similar to creating a relationship with someone who speaks and understands only a different verbal language, e.g., English versus Chinese. The language of the horse is body language. In fact *everything* a horse does with its body means something.

Knowing this when interacting with a horse allows us to instantly understand how they feel about who we are and what we're doing. This is the basis for how humans can learn to communicate with horses in *their* language, which, in turn, is the basis for what is today known as natural horsemanship.

For example, when interacting on the ground, if a horse is comfortable with you and what you are doing, it will remain standing where it is. If not, it will move. Moving is the horse's way of communicating that although it acknowledges you and what you're doing, you need to change your attitude or intention or do what you're doing differently.

It's as if you were speaking to another person and they said, "Please repeat that again more slowly; I'm not completely sure what you said or want." They're asking you to change the way you're speaking so that they can understand, relate to, and connect with you.

The vast majority of the time, when a horse walks away, it's telling us that we need to move more slowly, be gentler, or be more relaxed. What the horse is saying is that it would be more comfortable staying with us if we acted less like a human/predator and more like a horse/prey. And just as with every man or woman who has ever tried to change another person only to discover that they can't, the only way to positively have or improve a relationship with a horse is to change oneself.

The dynamics inherent in these equine-human interactions become the initiator of human awareness breakthroughs, and these personal epiphanies are what lead to the emotional healing of equine-assisted therapy, whether with prison inmates, at-risk youths, autistic children, or war veterans with PTSD. Unable to teach a horse to speak our language, we can nevertheless teach ourselves to speak in their equine body language.

Why body language? The wisdom of body language, another evolutionary strategy to assure horses' survival, enables horses to communicate with other members of their herd silently, avoiding sounds that could fatally reveal their presence to predators.

Before the creation of our verbal language, humans, just like horses, communicated using body language. Human verbal language originated and continues to reside in the brain. Today, using our bodies to communicate in our relationships with others is generally not our initial preference. Nonetheless, our thoughts and feelings are unconsciously and continually revealed and expressed by our bodies.

At its core, the motivation for every decision a horse makes is always based on what is in its best interest in terms of survival. Nondomesticated (wild or feral) horses in their natural environment are always moving. They travel about twenty miles a day, migrating from one grazing area to the next. Because their survival is dependent on the ability to escape from predators, they are most comfortable knowing they can move anywhere at any instant.

Even equine eating behavior is based on providing optimum escape ability. Unlike the sorts of predators who are content to sit, eat a big meal, and take a nap, horses graze, eat small amounts, travel, then eat small amounts again. This prevents them from having a full stomach and keeps them lighter and therefore faster if they need to run. It also conserves the energy that would have otherwise been burned up for digestion and stores it to use when necessary for escape emergencies.

The ingredients of the horse's diet also reinforce its survival. Horses eat and thrive on vegetation that other animals consider inedible. This not only eliminates the necessity to fight for food, it provides an unlimited equine sustenance resource.

When a horse is confined to a stall and unable to travel and graze, its natural ability to maintain healthy teeth and feet is greatly compromised. These are only two of any number of negative side effects that result from the horse's relationship with humans.

It has been estimated that while traveling and grazing in its natural environment, a horse chews approximately forty thousand times a day. When domesticated, living in stalls and eating only two or three times a day, the average horse chews about ten thousand times fewer.

Over the years, this prevents the natural wearing down of the sharp ends that develop in horses' teeth. Consequently, it creates the need for regular equine dental work, or "floating," to eliminate these sharp points, which can cause painful lacerations in the delicate soft tissue of the horse's mouth.

Unfortunately, many horse owners either are unaware of this process or don't care about it and neglect to look after their horse's teeth. And just as with a person who never goes to the dentist, it results in endless discomfort or pain for the horse.

Sometimes, if a horse resists his rider's request, such as refusing to turn left or right, he is trying to tell that person that the left or right side of his mouth hurts. Since horses are unable to explain their discomfort to their riders, untreated equine dental problems can also show up as rebellious behavior issues such as bucking or rearing, with the uninformed rider blaming the horse for "misbehaving." If you were a horse with dental pain, how would you try to get your rider's attention to ask for help?

Horses that are not being ridden have no way to communicate with humans when they are experiencing mouth or dental pain. As the leader, the human is responsible for having his domestic horse examined periodically by an equine dentist.

The domestic horse's lack of daily long-distance travel also prevents the natural wearing down of their hooves. This creates the need to periodically trim their feet. In addition, traveling on hard ground or stepping on a stone can, as a result of the additional weight of a human rider, cause injury. This can create the need for horseshoes.

Domestic horses must also endure huge emotional adjustments to compensate for the loss of their freedom and their natural environment. When kept in a stall and unable to travel great distances on a daily basis, some horses will develop mental and emotional problems, much like humans who have been incarcerated. A person unable to adjust to or cope with being incarcerated will often turn to a crippling drug addiction or even commit suicide.

For horses, the emotional pain from stress is usually expressed physically. Examples would be head shaking, body weaving, pacing, wood chewing, and cribbing, or sucking in air. These are all coping behaviors horses engage in to reduce their anxiety and stress.

And just as with addictive behaviors in humans, some of these habitual neurotic patterns can stimulate the horse's brain to release endorphins, the same chemical that provides us emotional soothing. This is identical to the way some humans "self-medicate" their emotional stress and anxiety with compulsive behaviors like exercise, work, sex, or eating, any of which also serve to alter their brain chemistry.

Interestingly, all of these equine "stall vices" involve either a form of movement or a type of simulated eating, which may help replicate the natural travel and grazing that has been eliminated by domestication. For a prey animal like the horse to adjust to a world created and designed for the pleasure and convenience of human predators requires the ultimate in acceptance, tolerance, forgiveness, and trust.

Horses have one of the best memories in the animal kingdom. They not only remember everything, they selectively store what they remember in one of two categories: things that will eat me and things that won't eat me. To attempt to ensure their survival without this ability to remember and selectively categorize, a horse would need to run away from every potential predator, real or imagined. This would wastefully use up energy needed to run from actual life-threatening situations, drastically increase their vulnerability, and decrease their odds of survival.

In terms of the evolutionary design of the horse, their spectacular survival capabilities are undeniable. To this end, horses live their entire lives on alert. People are often amused or think it stupid when they see a horse react in terror at the sight of a plastic bag blowing across the ground. From the horse's point of view, this reaction not only represents the height of pragmatic intelligence, it's a matter of life and death.

Unless a horse knows with a hundred percent certainty that what he's seen is safe and harmless, he assumes that it's always best to run away to a safe distance first and investigate later rather than to stay, examine, and discover that the potential threat was only a plastic bag from the supermarket. This sensible decision makes it certain that the horse will live another day, no matter what he saw moving across the ground. Waiting to discover that it is not a plastic bag but a lone wolf can be an unnecessary fatal error in judgment.

Adding to the arsenal of hardwired equine survival capabilities is the possession of the fastest reaction time of any animal, prey or predator. Reaction time is the elapsed time between a stimulus (i.e., a sound or something that moves) and the response to the stimulus (i.e., kicking or running away). To survive, a prey species must have a faster reaction time than its predators do. And it must not only be able to run away, it must run instantaneously at an unmatchable high speed.

Two examples of the extraordinary speed of a horse's reaction time are regularly experienced by humans. One is the frustration of repeatedly and unsuccessfully trying to get close enough to put a halter on a horse that doesn't want to get caught, followed by the often surprising swiftness of its escape.

The other is the after-the-fact shocking realization of being kicked. No matter how observant, alert, or fast on one's feet, if a person is within kicking range of a horse who is intent on lashing out, there is no escape from the speed and accuracy of the horse's hoof. We will always get kicked, and we will never see it coming.

Whether they're on the plains of Idaho, in a local Ohio barn, or at the center of New York City's Times Square, once a horse feels safe from any predators, its next most important behavioral motivator is comfort, both physical and emotional. Unless they are engaged with other herd members in play—running, kicking, rearing, and bucking—or contests of physical dominance to determine a leadership pecking order, horses are usually most comfortable resting, relaxing, and mutually grooming each other. This not only feels good, it conserves their energy, which is in the best interest of their survival.

When it comes to humans, there are countless ingredients necessary for creating primary healthy, functioning relationships. In simple terms, it could be said that the basic core ingredient is love: love of oneself and love for another, the latter accomplished by two people mutually relating to each other in a loving way. I believe the same is true for horses.

For humans, one of the simplest yet most effective ways to express love to another is to find out what the other person loves and give, be, or do that for them without expecting anything in return and without compromising one's own values, principles, or dignity. Every time I watch two horses mutually groom each other, I am reminded of this.

When I witness the loving-kindness of one horse gently scratching the withers of another horse with its teeth, while the other horse is simultaneously doing the same thing, because neither horse can stretch far enough to reach its own withers, I think of an old yet often quoted parable of heaven and hell.

It is said that hell is a beautiful room with a giant table laden with the most delicious and wonderful food imaginable. Around the table sit twelve men and women, all holding three-foot-long forks. The forks are so long that the people cannot reach their mouths with the food. Try as they may, no one is able to eat. Heaven looks exactly the same: the same room, people, table, food, and three-foot forks. But in heaven everyone is eating, talking, and laughing, for in heaven, the people are all feeding one another.

It is only by giving love that we are loved. No other animal demonstrates this more powerfully than the horse.

Of all the unique evolutionary traits that have allowed the horse to develop, evolve, and survive for eons, two of them fortuitously turn out to be distinctive qualities that enable horses to assuage the suffering of humans in acute psychological pain. These two unique abilities give rise to the power of horses to heal our emotional wounds. The first is hypervigilance, empowered by superhuman senses. The second involves herd dynamics, established and practiced with the greatest principles of love.

HYPERVIGILANCE—SUPERHUMAN SENSES

To evolve and survive as a prey species, horses needed to develop and master everything that could keep them from being eaten by predators. What began millions of years ago as an animal no bigger than fifteen inches in length grew into one of the fastest and most powerful of any four-legged creature on the planet, yet one also deeply sensitive.

Not only did their power and speed enable horses to outrun and escape from all of their natural enemies, they also developed superhuman sensory organs. These allow them, at great distances, to detect the slightest sound, smell, or movement, any of which might indicate the presence of a life-threatening predator.

It is these superhuman senses that enable horses to be extraordinarily perceptive to both the presence and the current emotional state of all living creatures, as well as everything else in their sur-roundings. When interacting with their environment, it could be said that the hypervigilant horse is primarily "other-centered." Humans, it could be argued, most often tend to be "self-centered."

To be safe and survive as a vulnerable prey animal, the horse must see the world exactly as it is. As a self-aware, self-conscious, egocentric predator animal, the human invariably sees the world the way he or she is.

The horse has the largest eyes of any land mammal. They are set on either side of its head and can operate independently, look-ing in two different directions at one time. This is known as bi-lateral monocular vision and, except for two 10-degree blind spots (one in front of the animal's face, the other directly behind its tail), it allows the horse to see everything within 340 degrees while standing in one place, without having to move. This lets the horse constantly monitor vast panoramic areas for predators. A horse does have some binocular capability, though limited, in order to also see predators or objects directly in front of it.

Humans have binocular vision and, as with most predators, our eyes are set closely together, enabling us to see, focus, stalk, and kill our prey. The placement of eyes on an animal's head is one of the many ways horses identify predators.

A horse's vision can be both sweeping and sniperlike. While taking in great vistas, a horse can instantly see the slightest move-ment of leaves on a tree three hundred feet away, a warning of the potential presence of a mountain lion.

At the same distance they can hear the breaking of a twig, which might signal an approaching bear. Not only do horses have superhuman hearing, their ears can separately rotate 180 degrees.

As with their independent eyes, this allows them to operate and hear simultaneously in two different directions.

Most of the time, horses will listen in the same direction as they are looking, although their left ear and eye can be pointed in a different direction than their right ear and eye. This ability to simultaneously see and hear in two different directions is one of the most distinctive equine survival characteristics. People sometimes find it difficult to tell by looking at the animal's eyes if their horse is paying attention to them. The easiest way to know if your horse is paying attention to you is to look at his ears. A horse usually points his ears, whether together or separately, toward what he is looking at with his eyes.

Many horse owners think that the blustery gusts of a windy day are what cause their horse to become overexcited, frantically running around its paddock. In fact, it is the noise of the wind interfering with the horse's ability to hear potential predators that causes equine anxiety. Horses move when they're anxious. If they are standing still, they are usually relaxed.

Brilliantly designed for instantaneous escape, the horse is a hypervigilant walking time bomb wrapped in a defensive shield of sophisticated sensory radar, forever ready to explode into a run with the fastest reaction time of any animal on the planet. The simple fact of knowing this—seeing horses from this perspective and, most important, seeing life from the horse's point of view—is transformative. It allows for a level of relationship between human and horse, prey and predator, that would otherwise be impossible. Finally, it allows for compassion, the single most important ingredient in any mutually beneficial relationship.

The three other senses of a horse—smell, taste, and touch—are all greatly superior to those of a human, but it is their sense of touch, or feel, that has the greatest impact when horses interact with people. One of the most common misconceptions when people first begin to ride horses is how physically firm they need to be to cause a horse to move or halt, as evidenced in the "kick 'em to go, pull 'em to stop" method.

Many of these same people experience near epiphanies when reminded that they have most likely already witnessed how it takes no more than the touch of a fly to cause a twelve-hundred-pound horse to lift a leg, stomp a foot, or walk away. In fact, it is horses' sense of touch, their sensitivity to a physical feeling, and their distinctive body language that constitute the basis of equine communication. This is what must be mastered by humans who want to have a mutually effective and satisfying relationship with a horse, whether on its back or on the ground.

Horses are a hundred percent honest, which is to say that everything they express when communicating with their body language is the truth about how they are thinking and feeling at that exact moment. They never misrepresent themselves, give mixed signals, or manipulate with pretense. They never lie to each other or to humans.

It is impossible to deceive a horse. If a person is feeling angry or anxious, a horse will know it immediately from the person's body language. A person can hide negative emotions from another person by acting as if they are actually feeling happy and relaxed. This often works with other people. It never works with a horse.

In order to have survived for as long as they have, horses needed to acquire and build a mental library of thousands of bits of information on predators and their behavior. We may think we are acting calm and relaxed and disguising our anxiety, but our body language never lies. This evolutionary survival ability to read with flawless accuracy not just the behavior of others but their silent intentions is what gives the horse the psychological mirroring expertise of the most gifted human therapist. Psychologists define "mirroring" as the phenomenon that enables a person to see himself represented by his behavior as a reflection, or mirror image, in the eyes and/or behavior of another person with whom he is interacting.

As convincing as we may act to hide our true feelings, they always show up in our bodies, and a horse will instantly and without fail perceive all of them. For example, if a person says they're happy to see you but they have their arms crossed across their chest, their body language is saying the opposite, or at least something very different. Ralph Waldo Emerson wrote, "Who you are speaks so loudly I cannot hear what you say." His words could have easily been written by a horse.

This equine survival skill of external awareness through hypervigilance also exists as a symptom in humans suffering from PTSD. (For more on that topic, see Chapter 7.) It can be acquired by a soldier in combat or by someone who has grown up in an alcoholic or abusive family.

It is both the identification with and the attraction to what is familiar between a hypervigilant horse and a hypervigilant human victim of emotional trauma that constitutes the first of the two natural qualities that enable horses to dramatically help in the healing process of these wounded individuals.

HERD DYNAMICS

The second natural equine characteristic that gives horses their unique ability to heal the emotional wounds of humans involves herd dynamics. In order to increase their chances of survival, horses live in herds. When a mountain lion shows up, it's safer to be in a herd of fifty horses than be all alone. Any species that depends on living in groups in order to survive must be able to continually get along with all of that group's members.

Horses have textbook-perfect social skills. They must care about each other, help each other, look out for each other, and peacefully resolve conflicts without hurting each other. They are masters at getting along with their own species.

To promote social harmony and keep the herd together, horses possess a number of evolutionarily hardwired qualities. These include: being accepting, tolerant, kind, respectful, honest, fair, nonjudgmental, compassionate, and forgiving. It takes only two everyday examples from equine society, expressed in a horse's body language, to reveal some of these altruistic behaviors.

First, to witness acceptance, tolerance, fairness, and respect, one need simply observe two horses as they work through, resolve, and establish their herd pecking order. The more dominant animal, horse A, will pin his ears back, which will cause his buddy, horse B, to willingly move away and let horse A eat first. Since at some point horse B will have previously learned to respect the pecking-order superiority of horse A, he will know that horse A's ear pinning is his way of saying, "Please move away now, and if you don't I will kick you."

Second, to truly comprehend unequaled forgiveness is to marvel at the nonexistence of anger or resentment between the members of a herd after years of biting and kicking that have repeatedly transpired in the constant reestablishing of the herd hierarchy.

And whether presented to one another by a horse or a human, all of these character traits represent some of the essential ingredients inherent in the expression of love. They are instantly recognized in conscious or unconscious body language, usually reciprocated, and frequently lead to a horse-human relationship of authenticity, compassion, and self-acceptance unlike any other.

If one were to greatly simplify the emotional nature of the horse, it could be said that based on their hardwired evolutionary survival characteristics of hypervigilance and herd dynamics, horses live in a state either of fear or of love.

In fact, in 1890, Oscar Gleason, the author of *Practical Treatise on the Breaking and Taming of Wild and Vicious Horses* and one of the few historically referenced horse whisperers, said, "The two controlling passions of a horse's nature are love and fear." It could also be argued that when a human is asked to interact with a horse, they, too, immediately feel and therefore unconsciously exhibit some form of body language that expresses either love or fear.

Everyone has a reaction when they meet a horse. One person will be immediately attracted or drawn to the horse's quiet, gentle, and peaceful nature, a response that could be characterized as love. Another will feel insecure, anxious, or frightened, not knowing what to expect from such a massive, powerful, yet silent animal; this could be characterized as fear.

It is this instantaneous and simultaneous identification of either love or fear, experienced from either horse to human or human to horse, that creates an opportunity for compassion, true self-awareness, and, therefore, profound emotional healing that is not only extraordinary but unlike any other interspecies relationship on the planet.

Both love and fear exist in any number of subcategories. Fear can encompass anger, anxiety, frustration, resentment, aggression, and so on. The subcategories of love can be endless, but one oft-quoted description has always seemed useful:

"Love is patient, love is kind. It does not envy, it does not boast, it is not proud. It is not rude, it is not self-seeking, it is not easily angered, it keeps no record of wrongs. Love does not delight in evil but rejoices with the truth. It always protects, always trusts, always hopes, always perseveres. Love never fails" (1 Corinthians 13:4–8).

In all but a few places in this quote, "love" could be easily be replaced by "a horse."

One of the most wonderful and easily observable demonstrations of a horse morphing from fear into some aspect of love is the onset of its curiosity. Upon seeing a flag flapping in the wind (the movement of something unfamiliar), a horse will usually recoil in fear. If a person (either on the ground or on horseback) can support and reassure the animal to remain and not flee, in time—sometimes only a few minutes—the horse will become curious about the flag. It will begin to cautiously approach it, smell it, and eventually either touch the fabric with its nose or put some part of the flag in its mouth.

This process, discussed earlier in this chapter, enables the horse to compile information and remember everything it ever encounters, by filing each object in one of two categories necessary for survival: things that will eat me and things that won't eat me.

Emotionally, a horse shifts from fear to curiosity. Once the animal is convinced of the absence of predators, its curiosity is followed by feelings of safety, comfort, and finally acceptance, all ingredients contained in some of the most healing aspects of love.

Remarkably, this is the same process necessary for the emotional survival and recovery of humans who have experienced trauma. The emotional epiphanies that can occur when a person witnesses and then identifies this transformation in a horse are what contribute to the healing and recovery of the emotional wounds of PTSD. (For further information, see Chapters 6 and 7.)

When it comes to riding horses, fear is one of two issues with the biggest impact on a horse-human relationship. The other is time. Horses and humans experience fear and time in dramatically different ways.

If a rider makes a request or tries to control the horse and lacks the knowledge of this difference, he or she will most often resort to the counterproductive use of physical force. This only increases resistance and disharmony and keeps the person forever stuck in a limited old-fashioned "traditional riding" relationship with the horse, which will manifest itself in phrases such as "I kick the horse to go forward; if he doesn't, I kick harder. I pull on the reins to stop; if the horse doesn't stop, I pull harder."

Understanding the concepts of time and fear from the horse's point of view enables a person to replace force with understanding, communication, and leadership. This contributes to the creation of a powerful and intimate interspecies relationship based on mutual love, trust, and respect and leads to the best possible riding experience for both. Without it, the safety of both horse and rider is profoundly compromised.

Horses live in the moment and have no concept of what humans call time. They know if it's light or dark, winter or summer, and are acutely aware of patterns. However, they never worry about running out of time or being late.

Humans, on the other hand, invented time. We have schedules

and agendas; we are rarely in the moment and often in deep con-templation about our past or future. Thoughts of the past can create depression or disappointment; thoughts of the future can create fear or anxiety. Human emotions are not only expressed verbally, they are expressed physically, with our bodies.

If a person has an unmet agenda or is worrying about some-thing like being late, it can often lead to feelings of tension, anger, frustration, or disappointment. This, in turn, creates a rider who is anxious, aggressive, preoccupied, and tense. All of these distinc-tive human qualities are predatory in nature and are physically felt by the horse. Horses fear and do not trust predators. More impor-tant, horses fear predatory behavior.

When a horse feels the anxiety in a rider's body, it causes him to lose trust and confidence in the rider's leadership. The horse immediately becomes uncomfortable, resistant, and defensive. A horse may think, "If my rider is anxious, maybe I should be anx-ious. I may be safer asking my rider to get off me"—read: buck—"so I can run fast enough and far enough until I feel safe."

Riding a horse when a breakdown in leadership has occurred is not only unpleasant, it is dangerous. To ride and have a great rela-tionship with a horse, one needs to be happy, relaxed, and confi-dent. To ride safely and have fun, one must be totally "in the moment" with one's horse. Some might call it Zen-like or "the power of now." I call it being on *horse time*.

Whether you are riding or on the ground, having a relation-ship with a horse and being on horse time is not only safer, it's the most dramatically effective way to improve a human's patience, acceptance, tolerance, and awareness. Being on horse time, with-out schedules, agendas, or expectations, is crucial when training or teaching a horse something new. Horses, like humans, are all different; some learn faster, some more slowly.

What's important is to allow each horse the time it may individually need and not cause it to feel frustrated, criticized, wrong, or discouraged. In fact, I have often thought that an old cowboy philosophy for teaching a horse was equally appropriate when teaching a child: "Expect a lot, accept a little, reward often."

A domestic horse and a child share two major similarities. First, they both are very vulnerable. They are totally dependent on human adults for everything they need for survival, including food; protection; physical, emotional, and mental development; and, most important, love. Second, both a horse and a child (up to a certain age) are unable to communicate a great deal of crucial information to their caretakers: what they're feeling, when they don't understand, and why certain things are frightening. This brings us to fear.

Horse fear and human fear are profoundly different and greatly impact their relationship, whether the horse and human are on the ground or riding. Horses know they are prey animals and therefore food for predators. They are afraid of only one thing: being eaten.

To feel safe, they must be a hundred percent certain that there are no predators or anything behaving in a predatory manner within their flight zone. If not, they will always feel some degree of anxiety. A horse in this state is often referred to as "spooky."

Until they are completely convinced of their safety, any unidentifiable sight, sound, touch, or smell can be the cause of their fear. If they think there is even the slightest chance of encountering a predator, they run. A horse that believes he is running for his life is impossible to stop by anyone or by any means.

Fear is such a powerful equine motivator that it can cause a horse to run to its death from either exhaustion or from causing a fatal accident by mistaking an improperly attached saddle on its body for a horse-eating predator. Unless educated with good horsemanship, many riders are unaware of the potential life-or-death situation that can occur from simply not knowing how to properly saddle a horse.

When being saddled, most horses will inhale and push out (blow up) their bellies to prevent a tight-fitting cinch or girth from causing them discomfort. (The feeling is not unlike that experienced by someone whose belt is too tight.) Once the rider mounts and sits down on the saddle, the horse will exhale and return his belly to its normal, nonexpanded, more comfortable state.

At this point, should the rider lose his balance by any means—for example, an increase in speed, turning left or right, or if the horse accidentally stumbles—he can easily slip off to one side just far enough to be unable to get back on the horse's back. When this happens, the rider's only option is to jump off or be thrown off. Depending on how fast the horse and rider are going and what type of ground the rider will hit, this separation is potentially catastrophic.

But even when the rider has come off, the saddle still remains. It is either attached to the horse's side or has slipped underneath and is now strapped to the horse's belly. The belly is one of the horse's most sensitive and vulnerable body parts. It is the first place a predator such as a wolf or a bear will attack to rip open a horse's body and bring it down.

Feeling anything attached to its belly is both terrifying to and intolerable for a horse. They will instantly take off and run as fast as they can, in a harrowing attempt to dislodge and rid themselves of the saddle. Since it is securely buckled and attached, the attempt is usually futile, often resulting in serious injury or death for the horse.

Riding a horse is a high-risk sport, and just as with other dangerous activities, like skiing or surfing, it has the serious potential for many types of devastating accidents. However, it is the only sport where the risk of getting hurt is significantly increased because one's "equipment" can become nervous.

Horses, like humans, have left and right hemispheres in their brains. In a horse, the left side of the brain is the reasoning side. It allows for communication, curiosity, playfulness, and problem solving. It is only with the left side of the brain that a horse can learn or habituate to new or unnatural things or situations—including domestic human requests such as horseback riding.

Sometimes and in certain situations when a horse is using the left side of his brain, endorphins are released from the brain into his bloodstream. Just as with humans, these brain chemicals produce a sense of relaxation and well-being. When a horse is accessing the left side of his brain, his body is relaxed and his neck and head are level; this is where the expression "level-headed" originated. The look in his eyes is soft and often curious. He is said to be "calm, cool, and collected."

The right side of the brain is the instinctual side. It allows for immediate, impulsive, survival-at-any-cost, reactive responses while eliminating the need for thinking, which can require time-consuming logic and reasoning. It instantaneously and involuntarily puts the horse in the fight-or-flight mode. To survive, a horse will always choose to flee as a first choice, unless he is cornered or sees no possible ways of escape. In that case he will fight, to the death if necessary.

When the horse is using the right side of his brain, adrenaline is released into his bloodstream, providing additional power. This enables him to either run faster and escape from his enemies or fight harder, prevail, and live another day. When a horse is using the right side of his brain, his body is tense and braced, his head and neck are elevated, his nostrils are flared, and his eyes are fearful and opened wide, often exposing the white area around the pupil. It is the right side of the brain, with its lightning-fast instinct for self-preservation activated by the equine's superhuman senses, that has enabled the horse to survive for millions of years.

The left and right sides of the human brain, though far more sophisticated, have a major similarity with those of a horse. When a person is filled with fear or anger or is in a fight-or-flight situation, the right side of his brain will also be involuntarily activated. That person's decisions will be made instinctually, often without reasoning or logic, and completely focused on survival. He can be impulsive, nonrational, and uncommunicative.

When someone is blind with rage, you can't talk or reason with him; he's "lost it." Like a horse's, his body is flooded with adrenaline. In fact, anything you say or do to try to help him at that moment can often make the situation worse. It's at this time that a person who is reacting from the right side of his brain has to calm down, cool off, collect himself, and relax before he does or says anything. Like a horse, he must return to using the left side of his brain and become calm, cool, and collected.

He must take some time and do something—"take a walk around the block" is common advice—that will get him out of the right side of his brain. He must get off adrenaline and back to using the left side of his brain. It is only then that you can talk to, reason with, relate to, or communicate effectively with him. This is exactly the same for horses. Knowing this and what to do about it if you are riding a horse can literally save your life.

When a horse is afraid and ready to run, he is being directed by the right side of his brain. This means that if he wants to move, buck, rear, or run away at forty miles an hour, there is no human, no bit, no carrot; there is nothing that can stop him. Not only is this a life-threatening situation, but if a person tries to stop him with force or pain—for example, by pulling hard on a severe bit—it will usually be futile and, like pouring gas on a fire, make the situation even more dangerous.

A common and often dangerous mistake is a rider's belief that a bit is required to stop a horse. In fact, many riders believe that one of the purposes of the bit is for stopping the horse. If their horse doesn't stop, the solution is pulling harder or using a bigger bit. One only has to ask anyone who has ever been on a horse that did not want to stop to learn the terrifying truth about the nonexistent stopping capability of a bit. What one will usually hear is "Nothing I did could stop my horse. I'm lucky I'm alive and not in a wheelchair."

Further compounding this dangerous assumption is the belief that pulling a metal bit against the inside of a horse's mouth will create enough physical pain to motivate the horse to stop. Pain is useless as a motivator for stopping, or for any other request from a rider. Causing a horse pain will not only frighten the horse, it will motivate him to run faster.

The number one motivator for any horse in any situation is always survival. This is always accompanied by some level of fear.

Any time a human does anything that causes a horse to experience physical or emotional pain, it immediately creates fear. Anytime a horse feels fearful it will always run, sometimes dangerously fast.

There are endless horrific examples of terrified domestic horses running through fences, into walls, ripping their flesh, and running to their death, all driven by the right-brain irrational fear of an object or situation that in reality is completely harmless.

For the rider, there is nothing more important than knowing when your horse is beginning to exhibit right-brain behavior. It can show up in a number of different physical warning signs, such as the tightening of body muscles, a raised head, and/or snorting. The rider must learn how to recognize these signs and help the horse calm down before it's too late and the situation becomes dangerous. This can be accomplished by causing the horse to switch from his nonthinking right side of his brain to his thinking left side.

Dangerous right-brain survival-motivated behaviors such as running or bucking are instinctual and do not require a horse to think (thinking is a function of the left side of the brain). Left-brain behaviors, such as moving laterally, or sideways, by crossing his left legs over in front of his right legs, are not instinctual and require a horse to think.

When the rider feels his horse becoming anxious, directing the horse's hindquarters to step sideways, crossing one rear leg in front of the other, will help prevent the horse from slipping into to his fear-driven right brain and prompt him to remain in his more confident, reasoning left brain.

One of the most important steps in horse training is known as "groundwork." It is an indispensable preparatory component of riding that can vastly increase horse and rider safety by establishing the rider as the horse's respected and trusted leader before he gets on the horse's back.

Groundwork is non-mounted training. The rider is connected to the horse by a rope attached to a halter. By replicating the dominant body language of a herd leader or alpha horse the rider is able to influence and thus control the horse's ability to move or to stop. In natural herd dynamics, the horse that can control the movement of another horse is always considered the leader.

Groundwork exercises that are used to establish oneself as a horse's leader also provide tools and techniques that can be transferred to and used when riding. One extremely valuable method enables a rider to safely switch the horse from using the right side of his brain to his left side. Although it is not always possible for even the most skilled horseman to gain complete control of an out-of-control horse, learning how to execute what is often referred to as an "emergency stop" is one such tool that can potentially save a rider's life.

Ideally, in an emergency stop, the rider uses one of her legs to cue the horse to cross one hind leg in front of the other and thus move his hind end sideways (this is referred to as "the disengagement of the hindquarters"). At the same time, the rider uses one rein to bend and bring the horse's head around to the rider's foot. With much practice the emergency stop has the potential to cause the horse to switch out of his nonthinking, fearful right brain and into his more confident, thinking left brain. It stops the horse's out-of-control forward movement and causes him to turn in a safer and more controllable circle.

It is only then that the rider can reestablish communication with the horse, continue to have fun, and, most important, stay safe. In other words, to be a good horseperson, which always means first and foremost knowing how to keep yourself and your horse safe, you need to be able to know and recognize your horse's emotional state of mind.

One way a human can determine a horse's emotional state of mind and identify the presence of fear is to observe his feet. Unless playing with other horses or grazing, a horse that is relaxed will usually prefer to stand still. Once they know they're safe, horses are primarily motivated by physical and emotional comfort.

A horse that is anxious will usually move his feet. Since he must use his feet to run in order to survive, a horse will always test (move) them first to make sure they're working and ready if needed. If a horse becomes anxious while standing still, he will walk; if he is already walking, he will trot; if he is already trotting, he will canter; if he is already cantering, he will run.

Human fear, however, can often seem antithetical to horse fear. First of all, we are not afraid of being eaten. Most riders think of a horse that spooks at bicycles, cars backfiring, or flapping plastic bags as a dumb or stupid animal that is exhibiting completely irrational fear.

On the other hand, human fears include things completely irrelevant or nonexistent to horses—for example, running out of money, losing a job, and what others think of us. While we are riding, however, there are always two fears that are shared by both humans and horses: injury and death.

In a horse, these fears will originate the instant he senses any potential lethal threat within his environment, whether real or imagined. Often this can cause him to run, buck, or rear. Historically, this hardwired equine survival behavior has saved vast numbers of vulnerable horses. However, the perceived horse-eating predators encountered by most of today's domestic horse and riders are invariably nonexistent.

Unless one is riding in an area that is a natural home to equine predators such as mountain lions, wolves, or bears, the only predator that could threaten a horse is the one that is sitting on his back. However, it is not the actual sighting of a predator but the perceived predatory behavior that a horse is most aware of. A horse does not immediately fear or feel threatened when seeing a bear at rest. If the bear starts to come toward the horse, it is this predatory behavior that will cause the horse to run away.

The movement of a threatening mountain lion could easily be mistaken for the movement on the ground of something unknown, such as a plastic bag blowing across a riding arena. A mountain lion in a tree could be incorrectly perceived from the sound of rustling leaves created by two birds. There can be endless sensory stimuli that indicate the presence of an equine predator, both real and imagined. In order to survive, a horse will always run first and, if interested, investigate later.

Human fear while riding also comes from anticipating some type of potentially lethal threat. However, it originates not with the rider's environment but with the horse. When a horse becomes fearful, most riders become fearful. If the horse then starts to buck, rear, or take off, most riders grow even more fearful, imagining their own potential injury or death. Ironically, the lifesaving behaviors for horses become life-threatening behaviors for humans.

If a rider knows with certainty that there are no horse-eating predators around, then they know their horse is totally safe and only afraid of imaginary predators. And just as they would with a child who is afraid of monsters, they can immediately comfort and reassure the horse. They can gently stroke the horse's withers, which will release endorphins that will help him relax. They can refrain from forcing the horse to get closer to the perceived predator unless the horse becomes curious. They can breathe deeply and physically express feelings of calmness and safety in their own body. They can ask their horse to back up, turn in a small circle, or execute any simple request that takes the horse's attention away from the fearful stimulus and directs it back to the rider. This will help the horse relax and look to the rider as a brave, trusted, and confident leader.

When dogs play with other dogs, their behavior often harmlessly practices and replicates their predatory survival skills of biting and clawing. Not recognizing this as play can sometimes cause it to appear frightening to a human. Similarly, when a person is either riding or on the ground, a horse can naturally do something playful that any horse might do to replicate and practice his prey survival skills, such as bucking, running, kicking, biting, or rearing up. In other words, he might engage in horseplay. This, too, can frighten humans, though horses would have no idea why it does.

The natural fear of a horse reacting to a nonexistent predator is as unnecessary as the natural fear of a human reacting to a playful horse. When either of these situations occurs, one of the species is often baffled, doesn't understand, or thinks the other is being downright silly. The irony is that without this understanding or knowledge of each other, horses and humans are very often needlessly afraid of the same thing: getting injured or killed.

Humans know that loud noises, bicycles, and flapping flags cannot kill or injure their horse. They can also learn that if a horse runs, bucks, or kicks, it is either a fear-based survival response or an expression of the horse's natural play behavior. It is not an attempt to injure or kill the human. Since it is our superior human intelligence that allows us to understand this paradox, it is our responsibility to remove or manage the fears of both species.

The rider must teach the horse that he can't buck, kick, bite, or rear when the two are riding or interacting. She must also help the horse learn that he is safe from predators in his domestic human environment, become more self-confident, and look to the rider, his human partner, as a source of safety and reassurance.

Unlike many traditional riding methods, natural horsemanship always begins this process on the ground. It's a little too late to discover that your horse likes to playfully buck and rear once you're already on his back.

The key to the fun and exhilaration of riding a horse is knowing that you are safe. The key to safety is becoming a respected and trusted leader for your horse. When your horse willingly accepts you as his leader, he knows you are also keeping him safe. Therefore, he is happy to respond positively to all your requests. And should he become anxious or afraid, he is able to quickly regain his confidence with the understanding, support, and reassurance of his trusted human leader.

In the equine world, for a horse to become the leader, he or she must have and demonstrate superior survival skills. He or she must be more intelligent, confident, perceptive, and sensitive than the others in the herd. He or she must have acquired the most survival experience and therefore the most wisdom. This horse is thus the alpha. This is true whether it is a herd of one hundred horses or a herd of two, the horse and his human rider.

In a wild herd, the alpha is often an old mare. She has usually been there the longest, has seen it all before, and is looked to for her wisdom when survival decisions need to be made. In a herd of two, if the horse does not perceive his human as possessing these leadership qualities, he will not feel totally safe and therefore will not accept his rider as his leader. The horse will then rely on himself. He will be his own leader, constantly evaluating and sometimes challenging every request his rider makes.

If the horse thinks a rider's request happens to also be in the best interest of his survival, he will comply, creating the illusion that his rider is in control. If for any reason there is the slightest doubt, the horse will resist and attempt to do what he believes is more aligned with his best interest. Often one will hear a rider say, "I was on my usual trail ride today and suddenly, for no reason, my horse stopped and wouldn't go forward." To the rider this appears as resistance, misbehavior, or disobedience. To the horse who doesn't accept his rider as his leader and may have heard a noise his rider didn't hear, it's not only completely rational—it's a matter of life or death.

When a horse resists a rider's request, that reaction is usually prompted by one of the following four reasons: fear, disrespect, misunderstanding, or pain. When reduced to their origin, all four are based on and motivated by the instinct for survival. Although the rider's response in attempting to eliminate the resistance may be different in each of the four situations, all four responses are based on the knowledge and ability that come from the same source: leadership.

1. FEAR-BASED RESISTANCE

If a horse believes a specific request from his rider (e.g., riding somewhere unfamiliar) may jeopardize his survival, he will become fearful and will initially resist. However, if he looks to his rider as his leader, he will trust that his rider would never do anything to jeopardize his safety. He will then allow his rider to help him become more confident, overcome his initial fear, and follow his rider's request.

2. DISRESPECT-BASED RESISTANCE

When a horse does not respect his rider's horsemanship, he will not accept that person as his leader. He may then choose not to accept his rider's decisions, choices, or requests if he believes they are not in the best interest of his survival. His resistance translates into: "I don't respect your leadership, and my survival is my first consideration; therefore, I'll decide what's best for me."

3. MISUNDERSTANDING-BASED RESISTANCE

Even in human relationships where both partners speak the same language, poor communication can lead to misunderstandings. Although horses can be trained to respond to auditory cues, they do not speak, nor will they ever speak, English or any other verbal language. It's therefore the responsibility of the human to learn to communicate in the only language the horse knows and understands: body language, touch and feel. Force is not a language.

When we attempt to speak in the horse's language but are not completely clear, our horse can easily misunderstand what we are asking of him. If our horse does not acknowledge us as his leader and does not understand our request, it is safer for him not to comply, instead of potentially risking becoming more vulnerable. If our horse has acknowledged us as his leader and knows that our requests are also in the best interest of his survival, he will faithfully carry out what he believes we have asked for.

In this case, if we have not been clear in our communication, he may do something other than what we requested while believing that he is doing what we asked for. If, for instance, we are too firm with a leg cue when we ask the horse to go from a walk to a trot, the horse may think he is supposed to canter. When this happens, many traditional riders assume the horse is not listening or is misbehaving. They become annoyed and see the horse as the problem.

If, however, the rider knows that their horse accepts them as their leader, then what matters is not what they "said" to their horse but what their horse "heard." As the leader, such riders will objectively look at themselves, reconsider the quality of their communication, and make the appropriate change.

The rider can use less pressure with a leg cue when asking for a trot. When the horse complies by trotting, they can stop and let the horse rest for a moment. Rest is a reward for a horse that's being ridden and lets the horse know that whatever he just did was exactly what his rider asked for. If the rider is not getting the right answer, they may have to change the way they're asking the question.

No matter what a horse does, he must always believe that his response is the most beneficial to his self-preservation. It can be said with a hundred percent certainty, as originally stated by both the legendary horseman Tom Dorrance and his protégé Ray Hunt: "The horse is never wrong."

4. PAIN-BASED RESISTANCE

Horses, like many other animals, are amazing at tolerating physical pain. What else can they do? Horses are constantly telling us about themselves with their bodies, eyes, head, tail, and feet. They're either moving or still, standing or lying down. If we learn what they usually do when they're healthy, hopefully we'll be able to tell that something's wrong when they're not. If they're not eating, for example, something's usually wrong.

Before we saddle a horse, much less get on his back, it's important to check him out physically. We need to have him move to see if he looks comfortable and sound. We need to palpate his back and legs for soreness. Horses often hide their pain. It's a matter of survival. The weak or injured horse is usually the first choice of a predator. It is always our responsibility to make sure our horse is not in pain.

Whether it's based in fear, disrespect, misunderstanding, or pain, all equine resistance is initially motivated by survival. What the horse is telling us is: "I believe what you're asking of me is not in the best interest of my self-preservation. You must change your knowledge, attitude, and behavior so that I can understand, trust, and respect you. Then I will be happy to respond with respect, confidence, and enthusiasm."

Positive acceptance and execution of a rider's requests are possible only when the rider becomes the leader by earning the horse's love, trust, and respect. When the horse looks to his human as his leader and knows his rider is safeguarding his survival, a true mutually beneficial and willing partnership is formed. Then what makes riding truly safe also makes it truly fun.

Knowing and understanding the differences between horses and humans can be fascinating and invaluable for horse trainers and riders of all disciplines and abilities. In addition, the more one knows and understands about horses and what they are telling us through their equine body language, the more one's self-awareness, emotional insights, and potential for personal growth become possible. Serendipitously, however, the power of horses to heal our emotional wounds is also possible for someone who may have never even seen a horse before.

Often, in fact, the less one's thinking-based left brain knows about the nature of horses, the more that person's insights will be derived from their emotional, intuitive right brain, as they unwittingly identify and see themselves reflected back from the interspecies mirroring of the horse. In either case, a horse can often become one of a person's greatest teachers for self-discovery and personal development and, remarkably, a source of healing one's emotional wounds.

3

HORSES HEALING HUMANS . . .
BODIES AND MINDS

My first eyewitness exposure to the psychological impact a horse can have on a person occurred when I was invited to observe a unique equine program at a high-end health spa outside of Tucson, Arizona. Its name is Miraval, and it offers what it calls the Equine Experience, which was created and is led by a brilliant therapist and horseman named Wyatt Webb.

Unlike other equine health spa programs, which focus chiefly on horseback riding, the Equine Experience offers what it says is "a program designed to help participants challenge learned behaviors, correct false beliefs, and rediscover one's authentic self."

This is accomplished not only by interacting with horses without any riding but in short periods of time. It begins with a mixed group of six men and women each being asked by the program leader to interact on the ground with one of the program's horses.

Tasks are simple and range from getting a horse to walk from point A to B without the aid of a halter and lead rope to picking up and cleaning each of a horse's four feet. Since the participants have no prior experience dealing with horses, the way each person goes about these tasks instantly reveals profound information about their coping skills, learned beliefs, and personal relationship abilities.

A forty-year-old woman named Mary was asked to walk over to a horse named Daisy and pick up and clean all four of her feet. Mary tried everything she could think of—making noises, pinching the horse's leg, even verbal pleading—to get Daisy to lift up a hoof, but nothing worked. After about five minutes, Mary started to cry.

Mary was asked to come back and share with the group what she was thinking and feeling. She said, "I feel like such a failure. I hate myself for not being able to do this." The therapist said, "Mary, have you ever done this before?" Mary said, "No." The therapist said, "Why didn't you ask for help?" Mary said, "It's embarrassing." She stopped crying, thought for a moment, and almost absentmindedly added, "That's probably why I never try anything new."

The therapist asked Mary to share what else was occurring for her. Mary told the group that she thought her need to look perfect and not ask for help was probably something she had done her whole life, without thinking. She said this most likely prevented her from doing things she had always yearned to try, both personally and professionally.

The therapist asked Mary if she could now see how a lifelong attachment to what others thought of her and wanting to look good in others' eyes might have caused her to overcompensate by "playing small" and, consequently, robbed her of wonderful, untried life experiences. He also asked her if she thought exploring this insight with a therapist when she returned home was something she might consider. Mary took a deep breath, wiped her eyes, smiled slightly, and said yes. Her entire session had taken forty-three minutes. I was astounded.

Miraval's Equine Experience brilliantly demonstrates the natural ability of horses to instantly present a psychological awareness to a person that is not only insightful but, in many cases, transformative. From that moment on, my knowledge of the self-awareness that can occur for people interacting with a horse has profoundly improved my ability as a teacher of natural horsemanship. Although I am not a professional psychotherapist, I can now easily observe how a horse's behavior often mirrors that of his human partner and thus affects their relationship.

A horse's behavior is always motivated first by what is in its best interest for survival. In turn, this is followed by behavior that will provide the horse with the most physical and emotional comfort. Consequently, horses much prefer to get along in all their relationships and not be arbitrarily disagreeable.

Knowing this has allowed me to help my students immediately see that it was their own behavior and not that of their horse that created resistance problems in their relationship. Typically these problems are expressed in statements such as "My horse won't stand still when I mount him" or "My horse tries to bite me when I put on her saddle." And just as in their human relationships, if a student wants his partner (horse) to change, he has to change himself first. He has to either stop what he is doing or change the way he is doing it.

At some point in life, most people realize that no matter what they do, that can't get another person to change. This is one of the first enlightening, though often disappointing, revelations confronted by couples entering marriage counseling. Unfortunately for many horse owners, seeing themselves as the possible problem and changing their own behavior is often way down the list of possible solutions they consider when confronted by their inability to improve their relationship with their equine partner. Whether your partner is a horse or a human, the only way to get them to change what they're doing is to first change what you're doing.

Before my visit to Miraval, the only "therapeutic" use of horses I knew was one called hippotherapy (*hippos* is the Greek word for "horse"), and this I'd discovered completely by accident. Years ago I had been asked to conduct a natural horsemanship demonstration at the Thomas School of Horsemanship in Melville, New York. As I was setting up the sound equipment I would use for the event, I noticed an unusual wooden structure next to the riding arena where I was to perform my demonstration. Alex, one of the barn staff, said it was a wheelchair ramp for clients from HorseAbility, a therapeutic riding program that used the barn for something called hippotherapy.

Alex went on to explain the concept of therapeutic riding. She said that for someone with special physical needs, sitting on a horse as he slowly walks can move the rider's body in a way that partially replicates the healthy muscle movements of a person who is able to walk naturally. This, in turn, strengthens weakened muscles and bones, creating a beneficial effect in the body of the rider.

For many disabled people, the horse becomes the legs they don't have or can't use. Men, women, and children suffering from a wide range of afflictions, including multiple sclerosis, cerebral palsy, and muscular dystrophy, have all had and continue to experience significant improvements in balance, flexibility, and muscle strength from hippotherapy. There are emotional benefits as well.

Some participants find a new joy in going somewhere without a wheelchair. For many, it becomes an enormous confidence builder, inspiring them to try other things they had previously found too intimidating. Being with such a large animal is empowering. As a horse begins to feel emotionally and physically comfortable with his rider, he comes to accept them, along with their physical limitations, without judgment. When a disabled rider perceives and feels this nonjudgmental acceptance from their horse, it can often produce significant emotional healing for one's feelings of inadequacy or self-doubt.

For many children, as they grow older, their relationship with a horse provides them with additional feelings of self-esteem. Children with special needs realize they are different. Having a connection to a horse gives them something wonderful they know is special and just for them.

Hippotherapy originated in Germany in the mid-twentieth century and shortly thereafter was brought to the United States. Today it is one of a number of different equine therapeutic practices, all of which are referred to as therapeutic riding programs. HorseAbility, as well as many of these other programs, is part of a worldwide organization known as PATH International (the Professional Association of Therapeutic Horsemanship International) that assists in the rehabilitation of a vast number of human ailments. (For more information about PATH International, see the Appendix.)

At the time, I loved horses, had learned a lot about them, but had no idea they possessed such significant therapeutic capabilities.

Over the next few years, my interest in the use of horses as a method of healing for humans began to grow. I watched as horses were brought in to assist therapists in a number of varied human rehabilitation programs in what is now generally referred to as equine-facilitated psychotherapy, equine-assisted therapy, or sometimes simply equine therapy. In addition to how horses helped with physical ailments, I could see how humans with mental and emotional conditions were also experiencing profound healing effects from interacting with horses.

Even though they may lack any knowledge of equine behavior, many humans with certain types of emotional damage experience positive feelings of familiarity as they unconsciously identify with the two primary equine survival traits of hypervigilance and herd-dynamic-based social skills. These shared traits and interspecies identification can create mutual feelings of safety, acceptance, and compassion for both human and horse. In turn, this identification can lead a person to the self-awareness necessary for healing their emotional wounds.

The core of many of these emotional wounds often originates either in a past trauma or from one's damaged feelings of self-worth. The populations that most often suffer from these wounds are troubled teenagers, defined as Youth at Risk and war veterans with PTSD. Although autism is not classified as an emotional disorder, many autistic children have also found significant emotional healing from participating in equine therapy. (For more on this, see Chapter 8.)

Ironically, the shared equine trait of hypervigilance that can initiate the healing of an emotionally damaged person can sometimes unintentionally cause the very emotional wounds they are suffering from. Hypervigilance can facilitate the creation of unsettling negative associations by bonding stimuli that are frightening with those that are harmless. (See Chapters 6 and 7.)

One example comes from an emotionally wounded teenager named Dennis who was in treatment at In Balance Ranch Academy, a therapeutic boarding school. It involved a reoccurring anxiety-producing situation that was originally created from the harmless sound of water streaming out of a garden hose. (For more information about In Balance Ranch Academy, see the Appendix.)

As a six-year-old boy growing up with an alcoholic father Dennis got used to a certain pattern. Every night when Dennis's father came home, before he entered the house he would turn on the garden hose and water the plants in the window boxes. He would then come inside the house drunk and angry and yell at his son. Eventually Dennis would feel anxious any time and anywhere he heard the sound of a water hose being turned on.

As Dennis's "water-hose-triggered" anxiety continued to occur repeatedly in the early evening, his hypervigilance unconsciously made an additional association, generalizing and transferring his anxiety to this specific time of day. As Dennis got older, he became aware of frequently growing anxious in the early evening, but he had no idea why.

Years later, as a teenager, Dennis, with the help of a therapist, was able to heal his anxiety by revisiting his childhood. Together they discussed and emotionally processed the original source of Dennis's fear, his drunken, angry father. This enabled Dennis to disassociate his fear from the water hose and the time of day and emotionally return both of them to their harmless existence.

This condition is often referred to as "free-floating unidentifiable anxiety" and is one of the primary symptoms of adult children of alcoholics and abusive families. The hypervigilance that facilitated Dennis's water-hose-triggered anxiety could also cause a hypervigilant horse or a hypervigilant soldier in combat to form the same sort of association.

If a horse sees a hose and hears the sound of water shooting from it at the same time he is frightened by the smack of a rope on his butt from a handler attempting to get him to move forward into a wash stall, he will indefinitely associate the sight and sound of a water hose with something both fearful and physically painful. Once this association is made and unless he is repeatedly desensitized to the water hose, any time the horse sees or hears it, he will panic and attempt to run away.

A similar association could be made by a soldier at his outpost in Iraq who turned on a water hose to wash mud off his Humvee at the same instant his buddy, standing thirty feet away, stepped on a roadside bomb and got his legs blown off.

Both horses and humans are vulnerable to acquiring these cross-wired associations. They are created with what is referred to in psychology as "classical conditioning" and often show up as human PTSD triggers. They are sometimes referred to as "emotional baggage" and can often have a negative impact on a person's reactions and responses to others.

A classic example of equine emotional baggage is exhibited in the behavior of a head-shy horse. A horse that has, even only a few times, had his head hit or physically abused by a person's hand will from then on recoil whenever any person attempts to touch his head, even if it is to lovingly pet his face. Equine emotional baggage can most often be linked to some form of human abuse or aggressiveness.

Human emotional baggage can begin in similar ways. Consider, for instance, a little girl who is constantly scrutinized by her father. By relentlessly correcting her when she forgets to do something or if she makes a mistake, he can, over time, unwittingly instill in her painful feelings of inadequacy. When she is a married adult woman, if one day her husband lovingly says he closed the garage door for her because she forgot and left it open, she may overreact and angrily tell him to stop picking on her. She would have no idea why she was so annoyed, and he would have no idea what he did to make her so upset.

Humans are often unaware of their own emotional baggage. This can lead to repeated difficulties in their interpersonal relationships. A harmless comment from a loved one can unintentionally be a reminder of some upsetting situation from childhood and immediately trigger a painful feeling associated with that event. Witnessing an act of kindness between others can bring up feelings of loss or sadness for someone whose childhood lacked sufficient nurturing.

An affected person might say something like this: "Any time I see someone do something loving to another person in a movie or in a television commercial, I don't know why . . . but I always cry." Upon examination, the person's reaction can frequently be traced to some type of emotional wound acquired in childhood from the neglect, abuse, or abandonment by a parent or some other adult. If love was withheld when a person was a child, seeing it expressed by either human or horse when they become an adult can be deeply moving.

Whether it's a horse, a war veteran, or someone from an alcoholic family—all three can be hypervigilant in how they experience the world. Although this can help them survive, it can also create other problems—such as the unintentional association of the sight and sound of a harmless water hose with feelings of panic, fear, or anxiety. With humans, it can also activate the memory of emotional wounds from long ago.

All three share the survival trait of hypervigilance. Their ability to recognize it in each other is what can produce feelings of compassionate identification. As a result, when a wounded human interacts with a horse, this creates the experience of what the eminent American psychologist Dr. Eugene Gendlin calls "focusing" or using a "felt sense."

This process of focusing or using a felt sense, which was originally discovered as occurring between two humans, is exactly what transpires between a human and a horse in equine therapy: a nonverbal identification with the anxiety- or fear-based presence of another hypervigilant being. It is this simultaneous connection to what feels familiar, along with a shared feeling of compassion, that creates the unique power in horses to help humans heal some of their most debilitating emotional wounds.

In the words of Dr. Gendlin: "Focusing is a psychotherapeutic process. . . . It involves . . . an internal knowing which is directly experienced but is not yet in words. Focusing can . . . be used to become clear on what one feels or wants, to obtain new insights about one's situation, and to stimulate change or healing of the situation. . . . Once the person had accurately identified this felt sense, new words would come, and new insights into the situation. . . . The person would begin to be able to move beyond the 'stuck' place, having fresh insights, and also sometimes indications of steps to take."

The identification and sharing of the physical and emotional underpinnings of PTSD that lend themselves to the potential healing that occurs as a result of horse-human relationships have led to a multitude of innovative equine therapeutic programs and facilities. One group that is often helped is returning war veterans with PTSD; the other is a large and varied population of troubled teens.

Currently both residential wilderness programs and therapeutic boarding schools for Youth at Risk are successfully using horses in their rehabilitation programs and achieving dramatic positive results with high school dropouts, substance abusers, children raised by alcoholic or abusive parents, and other emotionally challenged young men and women.

For returning war veterans with PTSD, the most recent and innovative development in the field of equine therapy is a cutting-edge program called Horses for Heroes. An in-depth examination of today's equine therapy programs for Youth at Risk and war veterans with PTSD can be found in Chapters 4 and 6.

Healing the emotional pain of so many wounded men, women, and children has been extremely challenging. Compounding the challenge is the often reported widespread ineffectiveness of traditional treatments that use talk therapy and/or prescription drugs.

Many of today's drugs used to relieve emotional pain can numb and mask its source, which is often the original traumatic experience itself. This can complicate the process of identifying and feeling the original traumatic occurrence, both of which are crucial to the healing process. It's not enough to know intellectually that something bad happened to you. To initiate the emotional healing of a trauma, one must be able to safely reexperience the feelings experienced at the time the trauma originally occurred. Or as it is often said, "You can't heal what you can't feel."

Regrettably, not only do some prescription drugs inhibit emotional recovery but their debilitating side effects can often impair the normal, everyday functioning of the patient or become a life-threatening chemical addiction.

Though horses have long been primary in my life, I might never have continued to investigate their unusual yet ingenious ability to heal the emotional wounds of people were it not for a prior lifelong interest in human psychology. As far back as I can remember, I had a deep and persistent desire to know why I and other people thought and felt the way we did.

It seemed logical to me that there were worthwhile benefits to be gained from honest self-awareness. If a person had a psychological blind spot, it could render them unaware of behaviors such as arrogance, anger, or impatience. Being hypersensitive and self-conscious at that time, I certainly didn't want others to experience me being like that.

I have since learned that psychological blind spots, which can result in various types of negative or unattractive behavior, most often have their origin in some emotionally painful childhood experience. Not being aware of how one appears to others can have a negative impact on both personal and professional relationships. To overcome psychological blind spots, a person needs to have some type of self-awareness breakthrough. Years ago I thought this was possible only with some form of psychotherapy.

In the late 1980s, in an effort to heal some of my own childhood wounds, I entered psychotherapy. I found it both enormously helpful and fascinating. While in therapy, and in an effort to learn more about the dynamics of talk therapy, I also worked for a number of years as a volunteer group-therapy facilitator in a chemical-dependency rehabilitation outpatient program for a major New York City hospital.

It was while facilitating group-therapy discussions that I was introduced to a self-awareness technique that was simple yet profoundly accurate. One evening after a session ended I remarked to my co-facilitator, David, that I thought a certain member of the group had sounded quite pompous. David smiled, looked at me, and said, "Tim, if you spot it, you got it."

He went on to tell me that every time I see something in someone else that either annoys me, causes some emotional reaction, or pushes one of my buttons, I am seeing something that either I also do, used to do, or will do at some time in the future. He said this simple axiom was both an easy and an insightful way to become less self-centered, more compassionate, and less judgmental of others.

Today, after many years of personal observation, I have found that this technique has not only completely proved itself but continues to be a hundred percent accurate whenever I catch myself "spotting" something in another person.

It is also the same self-awareness technique that occurs in equine therapy and has become an invaluable tool for me in helping people establish better relationships with their horses.

Even when a rider asks for help, constructive criticism can be hard for them to hear without feeling defensive. Often it is easier to point out to a person something that is showing up in their horse that will remind them of themselves, even if it may be unattractive.

When a person says, "My horse won't stop and it's not listening to me," I ask them to show me what they did right before the horse resisted their request.

If they show me that the way they asked their horse to stop was by pulling hard on the reins, I suggest that their horse may have resisted and continued walking as its way of trying to communicate "You don't need to pull so hard." When I point this out to riders, most of them quickly realize that it was they who in fact had not been listening to their horse. "If you spot it, you got it" also works with horses.

As my own therapy continued, I began to recognize some positive and negative patterns that, in the past, had led me to a number of personal and professional choices. Some discoveries were useful, while others just confirmed what I had already known. For example, I had always known I was an extrovert, or a "people person." I did not like being alone and felt the most peace and comfort being with others. (What I didn't know until years later was that I shared this trait with horses.) I therefore concluded that anyone who liked to be with horses was like me, also a "people person," and did not like being alone.

Surprisingly, when I began to work with other "horse people," I discovered that this was not always the case. In fact, a great many of the humans I encountered in the "horse world"—owners, trainers, cowboys, barn workers, and so on—often seemed to be both introverted and a lot more comfortable with horses than with people. In fact, many of them often admitted to preferring horses to people.

Upon reflection I could see a certain amount of logic to their preference. Knowing the potential for hurt feelings, not to mention the amount of effort necessary to maintain a comfortable relationship with other humans, I could understand how for many people it was much easier to coexist with the "four-legged" as opposed to the "two-legged."

Horses, unlike people, don't talk back, complain, ask for anything, expect anything, judge, criticize, or act passive-aggressively. And all it takes is the slightest nicker from a horse or the feeling of warm breath on the back of one's neck for a person to feel appreciated, if not loved.

The more time I spent with horses and humans, the more I was able to see some of their remarkable similarities. Even more fascinating was the unexpected gift of personal insight and self-awareness a person could receive from a horse by simply creating a relationship of shared communication and understanding, and all of this had nothing to do with horseback riding.

What I found equally noteworthy was that many people who said they knew about horses, as well as those who admitted that they knew nothing, were often masters at creating and giving fabricated useless meaning to many equine behaviors. Until they began to learn and understand the true nature of this remarkable animal, people didn't see the horse the way it was; they saw it the way they were.

Countless times people would actually reveal themselves by telling me with great conviction things like "My horse is so bashful" or "I think my horse is arrogant." There is no greater misjudgment or misunderstanding of an animal than that which is created by humans anthropomorphizing horses.

There are, however, some people who truly understand the nature of horses, what's important and meaningful to the animal, and how to read their actions; these people are also familiar with the underlying scientific basis of a horse's behavior. Many of them are found among the ranks of high-level horse trainers, equine therapists, and people who have learned and practiced what is today referred to as natural horsemanship.

They are the ones who know that a horse is a mirror of one's own personality, attitudes, and intentions. They comprehend that one's reflection from an equine mirror is not only a means to improve one's relationship with a horse, it is also a cutting-edge way to improve one's character. They understand that some of the natural qualities of the horse are acceptance, tolerance, patience, forgiveness, and compassion and that to emulate these equine attributes is to grow or expand those most cherished, often unrealized, yet much sought after qualities of one's humanity.

It is also possible for those without this knowledge, as well as those who may have never even been with a horse, to have this experience. One does not need to have been kicked out of high school or to be suffering from PTSD.

Today, with the guidance of a professional equine specialist, a horse with its natural mirroring ability can help initiate therapeutic psychological epiphanies for anyone in need of emotional healing.

If a person behaves with kindness, the most likely response from another will be positive. If a person behaves in a controlling, forceful manner, the most likely response from another will be annoyance or resistance. In other words, if one wants to be positively accepted by another, one usually needs to behave in a positive manner.

The same is true with horses. A person, with or without the assistance of an equine therapist, can see himself or herself reflected back from the behavior of a horse. A horse will consistently mirror back the exact feelings, attitudes, and intentions of a human who initiates even the slightest interaction. This can instantly be observed by how the horse responds to the person.

A good example of mirroring one's intentions that I often see occurs when a person goes to brush a horse's forelock, the part of the mane that hangs forward, down onto the horse's face. They walk toward the horse holding the brush out in front them. The moment they get close enough to brush, the horse walks away. When I ask them what just happened, they often say, "I thought the horse's mane might be getting in his eyes. I went to brush him, but he walked away."

I say to them, "Horses are mirrors of our intentions. If they think our intention is something that will feel good or be comfortable, they will stay. If they think our intention will not feel good or will feel uncomfortable, they will leave. A horse usually feels uncomfortable when we do something *to* him and comfortable when we do something *for* him. When you went to brush his mane, were you going to do that *to* him or *for* him?"

At this point, as the person contemplates my question, I say, "If it was your idea to brush the horse, then you were doing something *to* him. If you want to know if a horse wants to be brushed, you might walk over to him but not hold the brush out in front of you. Then stand next to him, allow him to smell the brush, and wait to see if he stays with you. If he stays, start to brush him. If he continues to stay with you, then he's letting you know he wanted to be brushed. Then you are doing something *for* him."

Humans and horses are mirrors that reflect each other's intentions. And just like people, horses much prefer when another does something *for* them and not *to* them. It's similar to when I was a boy and my mother would brush my hair off my forehead with her fingers. She said she was doing it because it looked better and she didn't want it to get into my eyes. She was doing something *to* me (for herself) and not *for* me (because I hadn't asked her for it). I knew it, I felt it, and I didn't like it.

Mirroring is also one of the primary building blocks of one's feelings of self-worth and begins in the early stages of human infancy. If an infant consistently sees love, happiness, approval, and positive affirmation reflected back to him when he looks into his mother's eyes, he will most likely grow up with a strong self-image of confidence and self-worth. If he sees anxiety, disappointment, or disapproval, he will most likely grow up with painful feelings of low self-esteem, inadequacy, and shame.

Self-affirming mirroring is one of the most important yet most often neglected necessities of healthy parenting. A low-level and continual feeling of shame or the sense that one is inherently flawed or inadequate often results in anxiety, depression, and the repetition of self-defeating behaviors in adulthood. Though many people suffer from these feelings, most are unaware that the cause of these painful emotions began in infancy from the lack of healthy, positive parental mirroring.

My first awareness of mirroring began years ago, from the simple act of unsuccessfully attempting to look at the back of my head. I realized it was physically impossible to see the back of my head. The only way I could do it was with a mirror; in fact, I would need two of them.

Next I remember thinking, "What if there are parts of my personality I am also unable to see? What if sometimes I come across as self-centered and therefore alienate people? How would

I know that? And [like trying to see the back of my head] wouldn't I also need some type of mirror—an instrument that could help me see it?"

I realized that since my personality always showed up in relationships with other people, they could be my mirrors. If someone said something to me like "Don't be so controlling" or "You're very kind" or "You're quite demanding" or "You seem preoccupied," they were verbally mirroring back to me some of my behaviors—ones that, until that moment, I had often been oblivious of. In fact, I might have been coming across in some off-putting way of which I was completely unaware.

Therefore, if I could allow myself to withstand hearing what might sound judgmental or critical, I might be able to acknowledge, see, and possibly eliminate some unwanted shortcomings in my personality. This could lead to acquiring new and more appealing qualities and, subsequently, having better relationships with others, both personally and professionally.

Who I truly am is most accurately stated in the conversations that others have about me when I'm not there. No matter what I think, if three or more other people say I'm being selfish, I'm probably selfish.

One might ask, Why go to all this trouble? I would answer that self-awareness tells me what's real and true in my life. It gives me a more accurate understanding of how I come across to others, and that helps me feel less anxious and more at peace.

Self-awareness compels me to be rigorously honest with myself and others, and that, in turn, enables me to be happier and more comfortable in my own skin, something that in my past had often been painfully elusive.

Although mirroring is a term that emanates from human psychology, further biological research has revealed it to be present in horses and other animals. Equine therapy is basically interspecies mirroring. All the mirroring effects that take place between horses and humans happen as nonverbal communication.

One of the most intriguing pieces of neuroscientific research to support this comes from the discovery and knowledge of what has been identified as "mirror neurons."

Mirror neurons reside in the brain of both humans and animals (including horses). The reason they are called mirror neurons is because they are activated both when the subject takes an action and when the subject observes the same action performed by another. Thus, the mirror neurons of the observer internally mirror the behavior of another being, and the observer experiences the act as though it were his own behavior.

Many researchers in the field of neuroscience believe that one function of mirror neurons is to create the capacity for emotions such as empathy and compassion. If this is true, it would add scientific credence to the existence of the powerful nonverbal communication and connections between horses and humans.

According to this scientific theory, horses are able to identify with both other horses and humans, and vice versa. Because horses think in pictures and communicate in nonverbal body language, their mirror neurons are naturally able to read the unconscious body language of humans, which reflects a person's true feelings, regardless of what they say or do.

Therefore, in addition to their hypervigilance and herd dynamic social skills, having and utilizing the same mirror neurons as humans has further enabled the horse to become a cutting-edge tool in the field of human self-actualization and healing.

Their ability to identify, give acceptance to, and feel compassion for all humans, especially those with conditions such as emotional repression and PTSD, has enabled and continues to enable horses to heal our emotional wounds.

4

HORSES DON'T GET DIVORCED . . . TODAY'S YOUTH AT RISK

John Wilson was one of my best friends. I had known him, his wife, Sandy, and their two sons for many years. John and Sandy had met in high school. They got married, had two boys, Kyle and Mark, and lived in a comfortable home in a middle-class suburban neighborhood outside New York City. John worked in finance, and Sandy was a librarian.

After nine years of marriage, when Kyle was seven and Mark five, John and Sandy divorced. As divorces go, theirs was relatively amicable, and after about two years both parents were in new committed relationships.

Kyle and Mark made the painful adjustment to joint custody, commuting weekly between the two homes where their parents lived with their new partners. As time went on, Mark developed a mild stutter and Kyle was increasingly withdrawn in class according to his teachers. Many of the kids at Kyle's school also had divorced parents and were often in trouble at school or at home. As he got older, Kyle found himself hanging out with some of them.

The first time Kyle smoked marijuana, he was twelve. His parents didn't find out until much later, but they did notice that he frequently was irritable and quick to anger. One day he came home with bruises all over his face. He told his father he had been in a fight. His mom had him see a therapist once a week, but Kyle said he hated going, and after three months he stopped. This happened multiple times with different therapists.

By the time Kyle started high school, he was smoking marijuana weekly, regularly getting into fights, and picking on his younger brother, sometimes physically. One night his father got a call from the police. Kyle had been arrested for trying to steal money from one of his classmates.

His father and mother went to the village police station and picked him up; no charges were pressed, but they were stunned. After two months of agonizing soul-searching and exploring therapeutic options, they brought Kyle to In Balance Ranch Academy, a therapeutic boarding school outside of Tucson, Arizona, to begin a one-year marijuana-addiction rehabilitation program. (For more information about In Balance Ranch Academy, see the Appendix.)

In Balance Ranch Academy is a member of the National Association of Therapeutic Schools and Programs (NATSAP), whose members include therapeutic schools, residential treatment programs, wilderness programs, outdoor therapeutic programs, young adult programs, and home-based residential programs for troubled adolescents. NATSAP was formed in 1999 and today has over 150 member organizations with centers in more than thirty states. (For more information about NATSAP, see the Appendix.)

Like all its members, In Balance Ranch Academy uses a number of different therapeutic models to heal and rehabilitate at-risk youths. However, it is often the equine therapy program that provides the most effective breakthroughs in the restoration of the emotional health and self-worth of troubled teens.

When Kyle and his parents arrived at In Balance, they each had individual intake sessions with Dr. Will Parker, the therapist who would be in charge of Kyle's recovery program. Kyle was also asked to write an essay about himself.

Dr. Parker asked Kyle to talk about his parents. Kyle said, "My dad gets angry and screams at me a lot. Then he tries to cover it up by being funny, and I hate that. I guess I love him but I really don't like him. My parents got divorced when I was seven. It's always bothered me. It still does, but I didn't talk about it for the first couple of years. I don't remember what it was like to have two parents. I've been bored a lot. Dad promised that when he moved out he would live no more than five minutes away. Then he moved in with his girlfriend, so now he's forty minutes away."

Dr. Parker asked Kyle to tell him about his previous therapy. Kyle said, "I told my mom I don't mind therapy. I've been to six of them, but I don't like it. I don't think it's helpful or does anything. I talk because I have to be there. It's kind of a waste." When Dr. Parker spoke with Kyle's mom, she said that since the divorce, Kyle had been distant and angry with her. He was often dishonest, and she had found him stealing money from her. Kyle had told her that he hated going to his father's on the weekends and felt very uncomfortable around his girlfriend. He'd also said that although he liked some of his therapists, they hadn't helped much. Sandy said she thought Kyle had been dishonest with all of them.

Kyle's dad told Dr. Parker that he felt their relationship started to change when Kyle began using marijuana. A lot of the time he was very distant. He said he'd tried to set boundaries for Kyle when he visited on weekends, but he didn't really know what happened when he was at his mother's. John remarked, "I know his mom has taken him to therapy, but I don't think it's helped. I think Kyle's basically gamed the system. It's probably been a waste of money."

From the intake interviews plus Kyle's essay, Dr. Parker compiled a profile with the recovery challenges he believed Kyle would face at In Balance. Although his report was quite extensive, there were specific observations that convinced Dr. Parker to begin Kyle's recovery with equine therapy.

He felt that the divorce of Kyle's parents had contributed a great deal to his emotional difficulties and the struggles he was having in relating to his family and other people. Kyle compared himself unfavorably with other kids, often felt inadequate, and consequently suffered from low self-esteem and poor self-awareness. His interpersonal guardedness had repeatedly made it difficult for him to establish a genuine relationship with a therapist. And finally, Dr. Parker believed that Kyle's pattern of presenting a positive façade to others would most likely make an honest and open therapeutic interaction with another person extremely difficult.

Kyle was assigned to work with an equine therapist named Chris. In their first session, Chris asked Kyle to take a soft rope and step through a gate, into a small corral that held six horses. Next he asked him to walk toward the horses, choose one, gently put the rope around its neck, and lead it back to the gate. Kyle walked toward a small black horse named Cassidy. He got to within about three feet from it when the horse suddenly walked away and across the corral.

Kyle followed the horse to the other side or the ring, and the same thing happened. He turned around and looked at the other five horses and began walking toward a large draft horse named Billy. The same thing happened. For the next ten minutes, Kyle tried to catch a horse, any horse. He tried all six. They all left him.

What Kyle didn't know was that these horses, like all horses, always respond to another being, whether human or horse, by communicating in body language. If they feel comfortable with the body language of another, they will remain where they are. If not, they will walk away. Something about Kyle—his attitude, his intentions, something that made the horses uncomfortable—was showing up in his body language, and the horses were letting him know. Kyle was angry, and the horses could sense it.

Kyle came out of the corral and sat down on the ground next to Chris. Chris asked him what had happened. Kyle said, "I never liked horses. They're stupid." Chris asked Kyle what it felt like when every horse kept walking away from him. Kyle thought for a moment, then said, "It's like gym at school. Nobody wants me on their team." Chris asked Kyle how he was feeling. Without thinking Kyle said, "I think this is freakin' stupid."

"Are you angry?"

"Yeah, I'm angry."

"Are you angry at the horses?"

"Yeah."

"Who else?"

Kyle stared at the ground for about ten seconds and then said, "My father."

Chris said, "Does he know you're angry at him?"

"I don't know."

"Have you told him you're angry with him?"

"No."

"Do you want to tell him?"

"I don't know."

"Do you want to tell the horses you're angry at them?"

Kyle looked up from the ground and out toward the horses standing quietly in the corral. He slowly moved his eyes from one horse to another, looking hard at each one. When he got to the last one, his tight lips curved slightly up into a faint smile. As he continued to stare at the last of the six horses, he said, "I'm not angry at the horses . . . I'm angry at my father."

Chris said, "Why don't we go get out of the sun, sit under that tree, and talk about it."

Kyle and Chris got up off the ground and started to head over to a wooden picnic table under a large desert ironwood. As they walked next to the fence, one of the horses ambled over and stuck his head over the railing. Kyle stopped, slowly lifted his hand, and gently stroked the horse's face. The horse dropped his head and began to gently nuzzle Kyle on his head. Kyle quietly began to cry.

Though Kyle Wilson had been emotionally devastated by his parents' divorce, he'd never talked about it or told anyone how he felt. Human emotions can often be complicated and challenging, and for many people, they can be difficult to identify, name, or even feel. If you don't know what you're feeling, what it's called, or why you're feeling it, having healthy relationships with others becomes problematic. All emotions have a component of physical energy. There are basically three outlets for this energy. It can be *expressed, acted out,* or *acted in.*

To grow into a healthy, functioning adult member of society, a child must learn by example to feel, identify by name, and express simple to complex emotions. By the time they reach high school, teenagers who have not been taught to identify and express their feelings are left with only two alternatives to handle the powerful energy that is created by human emotions.

They can act out their feelings or they can act them in. Certain acted-out emotions can manifest themselves in violence, crime, and unwanted pregnancy. Acted-in emotions can result in depression, addiction, drug abuse, and suicide.

Kyle felt angry with his parents, but for any number of reasons he had not been able to *express* that or tell them. Instead he had been *acting out* his anger by fighting, picking on his younger brother, and getting into trouble at school and at home. He had also been *acting in* his anger at himself, which produced feelings of depression and low self-esteem. He endured but self-medicated his feelings by smoking marijuana.

Expressing anger in an appropriate or healthy way can be difficult for many people. In Kyle's case, he may have been unable to say he was angry because he was afraid of his father's anger, or he may never have learned how to express or talk about his feelings. For these or any other reasons, Kyle's inability to acknowledge or express his feelings to his parents or a therapist made it impossible for him to begin the process of healing his emotional pain. But the feelings and the negative behavior it was causing were immediately seen in Kyle's body language and were reacted to when he attempted to interact with a horse.

Not just one but all six horses could see that Kyle was angry, and therefore they wanted nothing to do with him. When his therapist Chris pointed this out, Kyle could finally perceive his unexpressed anger. The horses also helped him see the negative effects it was having on himself and others in his life.

Unlike a parent, a teacher, or even a therapist, the horses didn't judge, criticize, or tell Kyle that he was right or wrong, good or bad. They simply mirrored Kyle's anger back to him by walking away, letting him know that it made them uncomfortable to stay with him. Anger is predatory behavior that makes horses feel threatened and thus causes them to leave where they are.

Kyle was at In Balance for eleven months. A year after he returned, I asked his dad, John, how he had adjusted to being home and if In Balance and its equine therapy program had been effective and helped Kyle. John said, "Before Kyle went to In Balance, we couldn't talk to him. He was failing academically, using drugs, dealing drugs, and had been expelled from school for violent behavior. Today he's doing really well in school. He is a gifted athlete playing three school sports, and he's also started to love the outdoors. One of his favorite activities is to leave his cell phone and iPad at home and go on walks or hikes in the woods with his friends. He also recently started a personalized-baseball-cap business, and he sells them on weekends at local street fairs."

I was glad to hear that. But then John continued: "However, I think the greatest thing he got from being at In Balance and especially from the horses has been his ability to connect with himself and others. He is so much more vulnerable. He can actually get to tears of frustration when he talks to his mother and me. Instead of the old angry outbursts, we can now have helpful and loving conversations about his struggles. I think the whole experience gave him a sense of purpose. I think the horses helped Kyle begin to discover who he is."

Shortly after John shared all of this with me, he called and asked me if I would like to meet him, Kyle, and Mark for dinner at their favorite Italian restaurant. When I arrived, they looked like a different family from the one I remembered seeing two years earlier. Of course Kyle and Mark had both gotten bigger, but everyone seemed so happy. The boys were fooling around with each other, and John gave me the most wonderful smile when he saw me. I asked Kyle what he thought about horses. He said, "I used to think they were kinda big and dumb, but they're not. They're really smart and perceptive. Sometimes I think they know what's going on before a person does."

After dinner and just before we said good-bye, I asked Kyle if he knew anyone else I could speak with who had also been in the equine program at In Balance. Kyle said, "You gotta speak to Sam. I thought I was pretty messed up. I'm amazed he's still alive." I said good night and walked to my car. Again I thought about how horses could truly help humans feel better about themselves and bring healing where sometimes another human could not. A month later, I spoke with Sam. Kyle was right; Sam had quite a story.

Sam Butler was born and grew up in Windsor, Ontario, Canada. His father owned and ran a restaurant; his mom worked for an insurance company. They got divorced when he was seven, so every week Sam traveled back and forth to live with both parents. He was the youngest of four boys and in trouble almost from the beginning, getting kicked out of third grade for refusing to do his homework. He started using cocaine at twelve, dropped out of the eighth grade, and was sent by his parents to a military academy for troubled teens in the United States.

As a thirteen-year-old freshman at the academy, Sam found himself in a class with a number of nineteen- and twenty-year-olds who had been left behind. He had never liked violence, and whenever the older boys beat him, he never fought back. He said he used cocaine for the pain from his injuries and secretly sold cigarettes in order to pay for the drug.

Sam was five foot ten and weighed 150 pounds. One night he was forced by some of his classmates to fight a kid named Joseph, who was six foot two and weighed 300 pounds. Sam told me, "Something happened that night. I felt trapped. I still don't know why, but I snapped; it was like I was a different person. I ran at Joseph and hit him hard in the face. I hit him with a lamp and a chair, knocked him to the floor and strangled him until he passed out. After that I fought a lot. I broke my wrists and my hands, but I never lost a fight."

Sam stopped using coke during his second year there. He said he had gotten a girl in town pregnant and "didn't want to be a fifteen-year-old dad strung out on drugs." He was really excited about having a kid, but the girl miscarried and lost the baby. He said, "I relapsed and started using again. I remember thinking, 'Don't love people, they're going to die.'"

Sam's parents brought him back home and told him he had to see a therapist. He refused to go. They put him in a Windsor prep school. Sam hated it. He started dealing drugs and traveling between Windsor and Detroit, which are separated by the Detroit River and connected by the Ambassador Bridge. He carried knives, was often violent, and once almost got killed by a Russian gang over a drug deal gone bad.

Sam said, "It was bad, I was out of control. I was high all the time and surrounded by violence. I hated my parents. I hated living in two places. One night I came home and swung at my dad. He grabbed me and held me down on the floor. I felt I couldn't move; I felt trapped. It was the same feeling I had in military school when I fought Joseph. I head-butted my dad and broke his nose and one of his teeth. He pushed me away. I fell down the stairs and got knocked out, with a concussion. My dad's girlfriend called 911; they came, strapped me down, and took me to the emergency room. When I came to and realized I was strapped down and couldn't move, I went crazy. They had to tranq me.

"When I got out of the hospital, I kinda freaked. I started drinking and drugging around the clock. One day I woke up and said, Life sucks, I need to die. There was a twelve-story parking garage a few blocks from my house. I waited till about five P.M., walked over to the building, and took the elevator to the twelfth-floor roof. I went over to the edge, jumped up, and sat on a four-foot-high wall with my feet hanging over the side."

Sam paused, then went on: "I don't know what happened. I don't know what you call it. I was just sitting there thinking, 'I need to jump,' and I looked up and saw the most beautiful sunset and view of Windsor. A voice in my head said, 'What are you doing? There's so much.' I got off the wall and went home.

"For the next few months, not much changed. I told my parents I was going to visit a friend of mine in Chicago, and my dad said he'd drive me. It was a long drive, so we stopped on the way at a hotel in Detroit. That's where I got 'gooned' and taken to the In Balance Ranch Academy." Sam explained what he meant: "If you live in Canada and don't want to voluntarily go away to a therapeutic boarding school, they can't make you or forcibly take you, the way they can in the U.S. I guess my parents had been planning to send me there and were waiting for some way to get me into the States, so I could then be legally 'escorted.' People call it getting 'gooned' because these two huge guys [goons] show up in your hotel room and literally take you that second on a plane to the boarding school in Arizona."

When Sam arrived at In Balance, he was sixteen and put into a group with eight other boys, aged thirteen to seventeen. His initial psychological intake report stated that he could potentially be diagnosed as a sociopath. The group was constantly involved in different activities, had three counselors, and met with two therapists three times a week. After a month, one of the therapists said that if Sam's anger and violent outbursts, which often led to fights, didn't improve, he might need to be transferred to a "lockdown" (a therapeutic boarding school more like a prison, with facilities for confinement).

After six weeks Sam had his first equine therapy session. His therapist for the session, Keri, asked him to walk into a corral of six horses, choose one, and walk him back to her. Although Sam had never ridden or been around horses, he took a halter and rope and calmly walked into the corral as if it was something he had done his whole life. He looked around at the small herd, walked over to a sorrel quarter horse mare named Cricket, and gently petted her neck.

Sam had trouble putting on the halter, so he asked one of the counselors to show him how and then brought the horse back to Keri. She asked him to brush Cricket and take her for a walk. When the session ended, Keri asked Sam how he felt being with horses. Sam gave a little smile and said it was okay.

At his next session, Sam chose Cricket again, brushed her, and took her for a walk. Keri asked Sam to lead Cricket to the other end of the corral and then walk with her in a space between the corral's wood-rail fence and a three-foot-tall blue plastic barrel that stood about four feet from the fence. Sam led Cricket and was halfway through the space between the barrel and fence when Cricket stopped and wouldn't walk any farther.

Sam turned around and quietly stood for a moment, looking at Cricket. Her head was up in the air, pulling back on the rope, the muscles in her neck looked tight, and he could see the whites of her eyes. Sam walked back, stood next to Cricket for a few minutes, gently stroked her neck, then turned and began to walk forward again. Cricket followed him through the space, and they walked back to Keri.

Keri asked Sam why he thought Cricket had stopped at the barrel. Sam said, "I don't know, but she looked a little unsure, y'know, a little scared. I just figured I'd pet her and let her know everything was okay."

Keri said, "You're right, Cricket was a little apprehensive. As a prey animal on the lookout for predators, all horses need to know that they can run anywhere, in any direction, in order to feel confident and safe. If any of their paths of escape are blocked, they become a little anxious or fearful. By asking Cricket to go between the fence and the barrel, you were asking her to go into a place that would eliminate two paths of escape: one to the right, blocked by the fence, the other to the left, blocked by the barrel."

Sam was looking at Keri and listening intently to what she was saying. When she finished, he stared at Cricket and said, "Wow, I know just what that feels like. I hate feeling trapped. If I can't move, I go crazy."

As his stay continued, Sam asked if he could spend more time in the equine therapy program. One afternoon Sam returned to the corral after riding all around the ranch. He got off Cricket and sat down on the ground next to Keri. He said, "Y'know, she's afraid of just about everything. We were riding and she spooked at one of the mailboxes. What a stupid thing to be afraid of."

Keri said, "All horses are hypervigilant. They're always on the lookout for predators. When they come upon something they don't recognize, they will often spook and think about running. If they realize it's not a bear or a mountain lion, they'll relax and continue on. It may seem stupid to us, but it makes perfect sense to a horse. If Cricket doesn't get ready to run and the mailbox is really a strange-looking predator, she could get eaten. Sam, can you think of anything that frightens you that maybe you don't need to be afraid of?"

Sam thought for a moment, looked up at Cricket, then back at Keri. He said, "I'm always afraid of what people think of me, y'know, like their opinions of me. Maybe that's stupid. Cricket is so much like me. I guess if she doesn't need to be afraid of a mailbox, I don't need to be afraid of what someone is thinking about me. Horses aren't stupid, they're just really cautious—they don't trust so good."

Sam stayed at In Balance for twenty months. During that time he worked on healing his feelings of rage and low self-worth. He also accepted the fact that before he'd arrived at the ranch, he had become addicted to drugs and alcohol, and so he started attending AA meetings, which were held at the ranch daily. When he finished his stay, he was sent to a halfway house in a small country town in New England. A halfway house, or sober house, is a place where someone from a residential treatment facility can live as they begin the process of reintegration with family and society, while still receiving counseling and support.

The last time I spoke with Sam, he had been at the New

England house for three months. I asked him how he was doing and about his experience with the equine therapy program. He said, "It's like I have a totally different relationship with my mom and dad. I know they love me and want to help me. I didn't know anything about horses when I got there. Now I love them. I don't know if anyone could have taught me what and why I was doing and how I was messing up my life. Cricket taught me to be okay with myself."

During my visit to the Wild Horse Inmate Program at the supermax prison in Colorado, I met with one of the prison counselors who had worked at the facility for thirty-three years. I asked him if he thought there was one compelling factor or common denominator in the background of inmates.

He smiled and looked at me as if he was surprised I didn't already know and said, "I believe the single most common factor in bringing one to prison is the lack of love and discipline from a two-parent family." I have never forgotten his answer.

Since that time, I have found his assessment validated multiple times, especially in a number of recent studies. According to one examination, by Cynthia Harper of the University of Pennsylvania and Sara S. McLanahan of Princeton University (cited in research from the organization Americans for Divorce Reform, which reports on both cultural and legislative efforts to reduce divorce), young men who grow up in homes without fathers are twice as likely to end up in jail as those who come from traditional two-parent families.

When I watch how a mare raises her foal, I sometimes think about the importance of healthy parenting—or, often, the lack of it—in human child development. Horses learn how to be a horse from their parents. As soon as a foal is born, its mother begins to purposely model everything the baby must do to survive, create relationships, and function physically, mentally, emotionally, and socially with other horses in order to grow up to live a full and healthy life as a horse.

The mother accomplishes this with a balance of love and discipline. Whether the foal is male or female, at one point, as it gets older, it learns from its father either how to be a stallion or how to relate to one. Horses don't get divorced, go to prison, kill each other, kill other species, lie or steal from each other, call each other insulting names, or hurt each other's feelings. In their natural world, they live together in equine family structures called herds, and for most of their lives they usually help, look out for, and get along with one another.

Humans, it would seem, also need healthy parenting. However, what has to be learned from one's parents takes far more time and is much more complicated. Not only does a young man or woman need to develop physically, mentally, and emotionally, their emotional development must allow for their unique human characteristics of complex feelings, ego, self-awareness, self-worth, imagination, and sexuality.

The success, contentment, and well-being of every human are all directly tied to the quality of their relationships with themselves and others. To have successful relationships, humans, just like horses, must learn and have modeled for them qualities that will create and establish mutual love, trust, and respect, such as acceptance, tolerance, patience, kindness, understanding, forgiveness, honesty, fairness, truthfulness, respect, and compassion.

Most humans need at least eighteen years of healthy parenting to learn and acquire these abilities. These qualities are not taught in schools or universities, they cannot be purchased, and they are usually not learned from books. They are learned and have always been learned from parents, whether biological, foster, surrogate, or adopted. If a child becomes an adult and lacks some of these qualities, she will often find having and maintaining contentment in her interpersonal relationships to be difficult.

Horses are naturally hardwired with these qualities so that they can live harmoniously in a herd, which increases their chances of survival. In other words, the survival of every horse is dependent on his or her ability to get along with other horses and stay together.

As a result, horses, in addition to having the ability to heal a person's emotional wounds, can also become a resource capable of modeling highly desirable interpersonal relationship qualities that enable men, women, and children to have more meaningful and satisfying relationships with themselves and others.

Recent U.S. government statistics report that more than eight thousand students drop out of high school every day. As a result, every year some three million of America's young men and women slip through the cracks of society, many finding themselves in a life of drug addiction, crime, or unwanted pregnancy.

The United Nations has defined Youth at Risk as "young people whose background places them 'at risk' of future offending or victimization due to environmental, social and family conditions that hinder their personal development and successful integration into the economy and society."

The U.N. states that the condition most often found in the background of these young men and women is divorce. According to the Annie E. Casey Foundation, which has been working on behalf of disadvantaged children for more than thirty years, in 2011 there were 24,718,000 children being raised in single-parent families in the United States.

A large number of these single-parent families are raising healthy, wonderful, and successful children. But the percentage of Youth at Risk produced by the effects of divorce and broken family systems continues to be significant enough to warrant additional resources of recovery for these wounded young men and women.

There is no such thing as a painless divorce, and the most damaging long-term effects are always those inflicted on and felt by a couple's children. Divorce can be destructively complicated for everyone involved. It can turn parents against each other and against their children. New partners or spouses can often find it difficult to be accepted by either the children or the other parent.

Where there is joint custody, it can invariably create painful visitation decisions. Children of divorce who are most at risk of emotional and even physical abuse are those whose parents are untreated alcoholics or drug addicts. Once the court has recommended joint parental custody and until one can show proof of a harmful environment, a parent must turn over their child to the home of the other parent even with the unsettling knowledge that there is always potential for some form of emotional or physical abuse.

Though a number of different issues can lead to the creation of a Youth at Risk, it is rare that a wounded young man or women comes from a stable two-parent home that provided consistent healthy parenting.

Furthermore, psychologists have continually provided mountains of research demonstrating time and again that it is love, both given and modeled, in the act of healthy parenting that becomes the template for all of a child's future relationships.

Children who grow up missing one or both parents experience some degree of self-developmental loss. And even though many survive and go on to live successful lives, large numbers are left to function lacking some of the emotional, social, moral, or ethical skills necessary to create healthy interpersonal peer and adult relationships with either themselves or others. The impact of this is both personal, often resulting in a series of painful love relationships, and professional, with unfulfilled career expectations.

What can begin as a parent confronting their child's repeated unexcused school absences can often expand into the emotionally devastating reality of their son's or daughter's problem with drugs, alcohol, or the police. The cost of these broken lives is not only felt by the young men and women and their families, it is passed on to everyone in the loss of billions of tax dollars and our society's quality of life.

One of today's most troubling realities for Youth at Risk has been the painful realization that the traditional solutions of counseling, talk therapy, sex education, and the continuing declaration of the "war on drugs" have all frequently had limited success.

By contrast, the recent and unique method that uses horses to interact with troubled teens has been able to elicit profound self-awareness breakthroughs for large numbers of troubled young men and women. These psychological epiphanies provide previously unattainable conscious starting points that can then lead into a successful emotional healing process.

Today a significant number of therapists and therapeutic communities have discovered equine therapy as a valuable method that can initiate powerful psychological healing for at-risk youths in unusually short periods of time. It is these breakthroughs in self-awareness that enable a teen with unexpressed emotional pain to recognize and finally verbalize his feelings. This is the imperative first step in the emotional recovery process.

When horses are brought into the lives of these young men and women, something positive, lasting, and transformative occurs. Through a simple yet meaningful interaction with a horse, teenagers can often gain profound insights into their own lives, attitudes, and relationships.

Horses don't get divorced. Their need for self-preservation creates socially harmonious herds. Equine herd dynamics utilize, demonstrate, and model the same human qualities found in functional families and necessary in forming all healthy relationships.

For humans of any age, horses are unrelenting mirrors reflecting one's true nature, belief systems, and life coping skills—all with razor-sharp accuracy. By observing a person's body language, they can communicate using their body language exactly what that person is thinking and feeling . . . and they always tell the truth.

Being with a horse compels one to acknowledge who they really are, and not who they'd prefer to be for others. It is only by seeing and accepting one's true self that a person can begin to heal their emotional wounds.

If you don't know that you, your attitude, or your behavior is the problem, then you need someone or something to show that to you. To change, you must see it, hear it, and accept it with a hundred percent certainty without feeling judged, criticized, or shamed. Amazingly, this occurs when one interacts with a horse.

Today this unique natural ability of the horse has made equine therapy the fastest-growing and most effective technique in the emotional rehabilitation of Youth at Risk.

Horses don't care who you are, what you've done, or what you believe. They care only about how you behave with them. This enables them to give unconditional acceptance to a troubled teen who is revealing his or her true self. This acceptance creates a feeling of self-worth, which can often be hard to obtain with the typical rehabilitation methods of traditional psychotherapy and/ or prescription drugs.

Horses are mirrors of human emotions. They help people become more aware of their true feelings. At the most crucial time in a young person's development, they can enable a teen to gain a more authentic sense of him- or herself.

A horse will know instantly if a teenager is angry, bored, or afraid, regardless of any attempt on the teen's part to behave differently. When asked to interact with a horse, a teen may try to use any of a number of techniques involving pretense or a false self, to gain acknowledgment. With a horse, this is immediately rendered ineffective, and the troubled teen is forced to face and deal with his or her own dysfunctional coping strategies.

In turn, the horse's behavior tells a person exactly what emotional state it is picking up from that person. Horses reveal all of this information through their body language. For troubled teenagers, establishing a relationship of mutual trust and respect with a horse is entirely unlike establishing one with a human authority figure.

Horses have no expectations, prejudices, or malevolent intentions. This unique difference can create remarkable personal insights and breakthroughs that traditional therapy often can't. Developing a trusting relationship with a horse inspires young men and women to transfer this new skill to their human relationships.

Another profound difference that shows up when one is interacting with a horse, as opposed to another person, is the fact that horses have no egos, pretense, or ulterior motives for how they act. What you see is what you get. Although they have thoughts and feelings, they do not, as far as we know, have the gift of left-brain conscious self-awareness. I don't believe there's a horse that ever woke up and wondered, Am I a good enough horse?

Horses are incapable of feeling one way and behaving another. If they're afraid, you know it; if they're willful, you know it. Much of their behavior emanates from the intuitive right side of their brains. Humans, on the other hand, usually interact from the intellectual, reasoning left side of their brains.

This left-brain approach to life makes us susceptible to the self-judgment of our own behavior. This, in turn, becomes the basis for our many pretenses—or, to use a term coined by the eminent British psychoanalyst D. W. Winnicott, our "false self."

Humans learn early that some expressed feelings are more socially acceptable than others. Certain feelings, such as insecurity, can make one more vulnerable to the emotional pain that can result from the judgment of others.

Therefore, humans, with the reasoning ability of the left side of their brains, can chose to hide these feelings from others by acting as if they don't exist. This can set a person up for a false belief system, such as "boys don't cry" or "girls should be more compliant." Underneath many a big-shot adult man is often a painfully insecure little boy.

Horses, on the other hand, interact with both other horses and humans from the intuitive, emotion-based right side of their brains, using body language as their primary means of communication. How they feel is how they appear and behave.

So human emotions that can be hidden or disguised from another person can always be seen or felt by a horse. Any true feeling a person is hiding will always be revealed to a horse by that person's body language.

Humans fear many things and are often afraid to show or express these fears to others. Horses, on the other hand, have only one fear for their entire lives: being eaten. Unlike us, they are never concerned with what others think of them. More important, horses do not judge us; they only judge our behavior.

They don't see us as right or wrong, good or bad, sick or well. If a horse feels safe, it will accept us unconditionally. It is our actions they deem to be acceptable or unacceptable—friendly or unfriendly.

For many people, having a positive relationship with a horse can be the first time they have ever experienced a small yet genuine sense of unconditional acceptance or love. It is a brief yet remarkable moment between two species.

Damaged feelings of self-esteem, self-worth, or self-love impair a person's ability to have a happy and rewarding life. The unique capability of a horse to provide loving acceptance without seeking anything in return has become one of the most successful methods to help humans learn or relearn to love themselves.

Equine therapy has become one of the most beneficial and cost-effective programs for today's Youth at Risk. To think that millions of emotionally wounded teenagers can get a second chance at a healthy and meaningful life is heartwarming. The idea that this can be achieved from a breakthrough in self-awareness that occurred from simply interacting with a horse is extraordinary.

5

A TRAIL LESS TRAVELED—MY JOURNEY WITH HORSES

It's one thing to interact with a horse and experience the healing from their unconditional acceptance, love, and nonjudgmental acknowledgment. It's also enlightening to see them mirror back your personality and to gain enormous meaningful insights, self-awareness, and positive personal growth.

However, to sit on a horse's back, create a joint working relationship, perform a multitude of complex tasks, and physically control another species of animal (such as an eight-hundred-pound cow moving at high speed) is not only enlightening; it's electrifying.

This one-of-a-kind experience is still possible today with the ranch horse of the American cowboy. Long before I discovered the power of horses to heal our emotional wounds, I worked as a cowboy. This is where I first fell in love with horses.

By 1990, Joseph Black & Sons beef cattle ranch had been operating out of Owyhee County, in southwestern Idaho, for more than 150 years. The family was composed of Joseph Black and his wife, Margaret, their nine children, countless grandchildren, and a whole lot of uncles, aunts, and cousins. Continuing in the family tradition of beef cattle ranching, sons Jay and Chris, along with their families, had each set up their own cow-and-calf operation.

The ranch lay in the middle of nine million acres between the borders of Oregon and Nevada. Only a few thousand people lived in the entire area, which was home to a diverse population of wildlife. It had the nation's largest herds of California bighorn sheep and the world's largest cross section of nesting raptors. The land was also host to a number of rare and endangered plants found nowhere else in the world. Between the private and the leased public land, the ranch area managed by the Blacks was over 160,000 acres.

Jay Black's section was referred to as the Desert: thousands of dry lowland acres covered sparsely with sagebrush and cheatgrass, plus a few man-made watering holes. Chris Black's range was also thousands of acres and was known as Camas Creek. Most of it was high country: green grass, natural streams, pine trees, and hills. Both were worlds of spectacular beauty, void of all things human.

Jay and his family lived in the main homestead, on about a hundred acres they called the Muleshoe. The shape of a muleshoe (like a more narrow horseshoe) was also the brand they put on their cattle. They had a two-story stone house originally built in the mid-1800s; it was surrounded by corrals of horses and fields of roaming cattle.

Jay was a big man: six foot four, 240 pounds, with short black hair and a mustache; he was loud, gruff, good-natured, and impatient. Jay's wife, Penny, had a pretty face and was a foot shorter. They had been high school sweethearts, gotten married, and had two boys, Mark and Scott. Penny made sure all the men minded their manners, and she managed the running of the house; but no matter what she said or did, there were always mountains of clothes lying everywhere. I had never seen so much laundry washed and dried on a daily basis.

The whole family team-roped together. Team roping, in addition to being a rodeo event, is a sport families participate in, with teams made up of husbands, wives, kids, and grandparents. It's an extremely popular cash-prize affair held in arenas throughout the West. Teams of two riders compete to be the fastest at roping a running calf from head to toe.

One rider is called a "header" and ropes the calf's horns; the other rider is called the "heeler" and ropes the calf's two hind legs. The calves are in no way hurt and have a fair shot at winning by outmaneuvering the riders. All in all, cows, horses, cowboys, and families seem to have a good time.

At the Muleshoe, behind the Blacks' house there was a professional 200-by-150-foot roping arena with a mechanically operated cow-holding chute so the family could practice their team roping. There was also a trampoline and an electric mechanical bucking horse so the kids could work on their rodeo skills. Everyone had their own horse; some had two. All the Blacks, regardless of age, were seasoned horsemen and horsewomen.

Cowboys are amazing men. They ride, rope, shoe horses, and brand livestock. They administer veterinary medical procedures to baby and adult cows—that's called "doctorin'." They cook, sew, do electrical and plumbing repairs, and are not only competent auto mechanics but can pretty much fix any piece of ranch or farm equipment there is.

Cowboys usually eat twice a day: a real big breakfast around five-thirty A.M. and an even bigger dinner around four-thirty P.M. They don't eat lunch, they do eat desserts, they eat a lot, and they never get fat. Most don't drink alcohol, don't smoke, and can always be counted on to tell the truth. When they're finished working, they invite you to join them for some fun: "to sit around, drink Cokes, and tell lies."

In 1993, as a friend of the Black family, I was invited to help out at the ranch. It was here that I had my first experience working cattle, which is essentially sharing an idea with another species—a horse—in order to achieve a common goal by controlling a third species—a cow. It was my first time working with cattle, so Jay gave me his best ranch horse, Frosty, and sent me to work with his brother, Chris, and a hired hand named Joel Herrmann. Chris Black and his wife, Dixie, and their children, Joseph, Justin, and Bridget, lived just a few miles down the road from Jay and his family.

Chris was a soft-spoken, gentler version of his older brother, Jay. Joel, however, was a unique fellow. He stood six foot six, weighed 250 pounds, had a big blond handlebar mustache, and had been "cowboyin'," as he put it, with the Blacks for about three years. He and his dog, Luna, lived year-round in a small covered sheepherder's wagon out in an isolated part of Jay's spread, the Desert.

Joel's little covered wagon had the same basic design as most sheepherder's wagons. In a space about eight feet by five, there was a bed, stove, table, bench, and cabinet; the only light came from a Dutch door with one window. But what struck me most about Joel, even more than his primitive mobile home, was that he was forty years old and had never been out of Idaho.

One day as we were out riding we came upon about three hundred head of steers (castrated bulls) and cows. I watched as Chris and Joel took turns riding into the herd, quietly cutting out a steer and then pushing him about 150 feet down the fence line. The goal was to end up with two groups of cattle separated by a couple of hundred feet: a herd of cows and a herd of steers, the latter to be shipped off and sold for beef.

Since most of the cows were mothers of the steers, they did not want to be separated. Every now and then, when Joel or Chris got a steer halfway down the fence line, the animal would fake left, turn right, and then charge back toward the original herd and his mother. It was the cowboy's responsibility to ride hard and fast, go after the steer, turn him around, and ride him back to where he came from. After a while, Chris called over to me: "Hey, Tim, do a few."

During the past few days at the ranch I had attempted a number of new and unfamiliar jobs as a cowboy. Each time I had ridden a different horse, and I always felt safe, without ever giving the experience much thought. However, this task required some extreme athletic maneuvering performed at a high rate of speed.

I looked out at the herd and then down at Frosty to check my confidence level, and although it made no rational sense, I still felt safe. I was relieved, but it took another moment before I understood why. I realized that I completely trusted my horse. I knew he had done this before, and even though I was green, he knew what to do. It wasn't logical, but I actually felt like he would look out for me.

Cowboys do a lot of different things with cows: roping, branding, inoculating, castrating, doctoring, mothering, weaning, moving, and sorting. The key to sorting—separating cows into different groups—is being good at cutting, which means separating one cow out from the rest of the herd. From the first time I tried cutting, I fell in love with it. It's like playing one-on-one basketball. It's fast, exciting, graceful, and psychologically challenging. The cow tries to fake you and your horse out and then go around you. You and your horse try to fake out the cow and stop him. It's fun; it produces an adrenaline rush and is one of the most exhilarating experiences one can have sitting on a horse.

Horses that have a gift for cutting are special. They know what to do, where to go, when to go, when to stop, when to back off, and when to wait. They can sense your every intention. They immediately know the cow you've chosen to go after at the exact same moment you pick it. Many years later, I learned that what I was experiencing was the horse's reaction to what is scientifically referred to as a "proprioceptive change."

A proprioceptive change is the smallest imperceptible physical change that occurs in one's body right before a larger, perceptible physical change occurs. My intention creates a thought, and my thought creates this invisible physical change in my body: for example, an almost imperceptible tightening of my leg muscles or a slight shift in my weight as I turn my head (which weighs about ten pounds) to look at the cow to my left.

Although I am totally unaware of this change in my body, my horse, one of the most physically sensitive and fastest-reacting animals on the planet, can immediately feel this shift and therefore my intention. People say that if you're riding and you're afraid, your horse knows it; this is true, because he can actually feel it. Maintaining total mental focus and feeling physically re-laxed is mandatory for success in riding, just as it is in any ath-letic endeavor.

To be successful at cutting, a cowboy needs to sit relaxed, hold on, allow his horse to do his job, and stay out of his way. While working at the ranch, I discovered firsthand why cutting was such a big-money equine event and why cutting horses were the most expensive of all the high-dollar Western breeds.

The most talented horses usually come from a long line of champions and possess a one-of-a-kind hereditary athletic gift. To sit on such a horse as it reacts with lightning reflexes, to let go and move together as one . . . there's no feeling like that.

From the moment I mentally picked my steer, Frosty began to move in a way that felt as if he was silently acknowledging my choice. If he could talk, he would have said, "That one? Okay. Let's go, gotcha covered." Together we moved forward, left, right, then forward again.

We had the steer running down the fence for about eighty feet when the four-hundred-pound animal gave us a head fake, turned, and blasted back toward the herd. I turned Frosty around, and we took off after him.

Cows are fast, but even though they can run close to thirty miles per hour, they can't outrun a horse. The American quarter horse was specifically bred for power, speed, temperament, ath-leticism, and outrunning cows. They're like Corvettes. They're called quarter horses because they can beat anything in a quarter-mile sprint—usually run on a straightaway—including a Thor-oughbred racehorse.

I was flying down the fence line when I heard a voice in my head scream, "What about gopher holes?!" I hadn't thought about them when Frosty and I had been walking, but now as we were running I suddenly remembered that the ground was covered with them. If my horse stepped in one, we'd both go down hard. He could break his leg. I might never get up. As fast as I heard the first voice, I heard a second voice answer back: "Frosty's done this before. He knows how to do this. Trust him." Frosty and I kept running.

There's a point when you've gotten right opposite a cow's shoulder and he knows you've got him beat. He immediately stops dead, turns, and simply heads back to where he came from. When this actually happened with my cow I felt elated, as if I had won some event. But it was more than that.

I had attempted something dangerous and exciting. I had never done it before, and I had succeeded. But it wasn't just me who had done it. *We* had done it, Frosty and I. I'd believed that he could do it, and so I had counted on him. For some reason, I'd known that I'd be safe; I'd felt that I could trust him with my life. I'd been right.

My cow headed off toward the other steers, and as I started riding back to Chris and Joel, I was struck by a feeling of awe and wonder. I had achieved something together with a horse that neither of us could have done alone. I had partnered with an animal that didn't speak and was born hardwired to fear and escape from man, and yet we'd shared a moment together, helping each other, just like two old friends.

The next morning I headed out of camp with Chris, Joel, Jay's two sons, and another cowboy named Okie McDowell. We rode for what seemed like about four hours. Chris said we were going to set up a "rodear" and do some "sortin'." A rodear is a circle of cowboys on horseback; they surround a herd of cattle in order to sort them into smaller groups. It was much like what we had done the day before, except this time there would be no fences to help control the cows.

After the circle is set up, one cowboy slowly rides into the herd and, one at a time, drives out ("cuts") all the steers, heifers, or calves. Depending on the size of the herd, if you're not doing the cutting, you can end up just sitting on your horse for hours, making sure all the other cows stay put. In other words, most of the time you're doing nothing.

Sitting on my horse for the next two hours turned out to be anything but nothing. When we first arrived at the herd, it was sunny and about ninety degrees. As time went on, it grew cloudy and started to rain. More clouds continued to roll in, and soon it not only became very dark but the temperature dropped into the fifties. Just before we finished, the sky opened up with hailstones the size of walnuts.

As we started riding back to camp, the hailstones turned back to rain. I could hear thunder begin to rumble, and way out in the darkened sky I saw lightning. Okie rode up alongside me. As casually as he might remind me to roll up my car windows he said, "Hey, Tim, if that lightnin' gets a lot closer, get off your horse, lie down, roll up into a little ball, and hold on to your horse's reins. Just lie quiet till it passes." Then he rode off to round up a stray.

The lightning never got closer, I didn't get off my horse or roll up into a ball, and after about four more hours in the saddle we were all back at camp, drinkin' Cokes and tellin' lies. I asked Okie about what had happened. He explained that lightning usually hits the tallest object first (which would have been me on top of my horse, with our bodies touching each other). Horseshoes, like lightning rods, are made of metal. If your big old horse is shod and you get off and make yourself scarce, he may not make it but you'll still have a chance of taking that long walk home. I thought, "Unbelievable. Back home, I would have just ducked into a doorway."

As a kid, I had loved cowboy movies and television shows but had never given much thought to why cowboys dressed the way they did. Now I knew: it was all because of their horses. Western hats, such as the ten-gallon hat, were designed with big crowns specifically to allow a cowboy to take care of his horse.

Horses, like humans, can go only so far without water before a ride in an endless wide-open space turns fatal. If a man and his horse are out in the hot sun with no water, the horse will eventually perish while he can always drink from his canteen. If he's wearing his hat, however, he can also let his horse drink by pouring the water from his canteen into the bucketlike crown of his big ten-gallon Stetson.

Cowboy boots have no laces, and their big heels keep one's feet from accidentally sliding through the stirrups and getting "hung up." Should a boot nevertheless manage to slide through the stirrup, the moment the cowboy attempts to pull his foot back and out through the stirrup, the boot, which is not tied onto his foot with laces, will immediately fall off on the other side.

Getting hung up means a rider, wearing a boot that laces up, has fallen or been thrown off his horse; his laced-up boot slid through his stirrup and didn't come off his foot. His booted foot is now stuck in the stirrup, he's hanging off on one side, and his horse has taken off at a run, trying desperately to unhook himself from the helpless, dangling rider. No matter how it ends, the rider's head gets dragged over and into every rock for miles, and it's usually not very pretty.

Wrangler jeans are cut different than Levi's so that they're more comfortable in the saddle. Cowboys wear Wranglers. They always pack a slicker for rain, even when it's sunny. Before they ride, cowboys familiarize their horse with their rain slicker on the ground, instead of introducing this strange object by attempting to put it on while sitting on his back. Horses can spook when they see unfamiliar things. This is not only being considerate to your horse but one of a number of precautions a rider needs to learn so as not to get bucked off.

And finally, cowboys always carry a knife. In a wreck (a bad accident with a horse), cowboys can end up becoming unintentionally attached to their horse by their equipment. To prevent serious injuries to both horse and rider, they need to be able to quickly cut through ropes, saddle leathers, or anything else in order to free themselves, their horse, or some other object—such as a sixteen-hundred-pound bull. There are many reasons a knife can save a cowboy's life, and none of them have to do with using it as a weapon.

I found learning about cowboys fascinating. What I learned from horses, however, was transformative. To truly understand and appreciate another being, one must attempt to live, if only briefly, in their world. Like most humans—especially one who was raised in a city, as I was—I had always believed that our species was superior to all others. As humans we could control, own, love, kill, or eat all of the other creatures on the earth.

As a species we had evolved with unique intellectual abilities, enabling us to invent, create, and produce amazing technology, art, and material wonders. We had brains capable of self-awareness, contemplation, and spirituality. We could travel into worlds far beyond the one we lived in. There was never any question as to our supremacy.

However, being with a horse in his natural world, surrounded by endless terrain and removed from all the utilitarian inventions of human civilization, caused me to rethink and question the absolute certainty of humankind's superiority.

The more I have learned about the incredible and often superior characteristics of the horse, as well as other nonhuman species, the more I have grown to consider human superiority a potentially flawed belief based on an attitude of arrogance born from the human ego. Humankind as we know it has been on the planet for about two hundred thousand years. Our primary source of survival has come from our superior intelligence and its ability to create a world embodied with unimaginable sources of food, shelter, and weapons.

These creations have saved and protected us from a vast array of natural elements, violent forces of nature, and other animal species that are bigger and faster and have sharper teeth and flesh-cutting claws. Without our man-made civilization, repeated encounters with any of these could have easily caused our extinction.

The irony of human intelligence as our primary source of survival is that it has also created certain beliefs, attitudes, weapons, and sources of environmental destruction, all of which have the potential for eradicating the entire human race. The horse and its hardwired nature of getting along with others has survived on the earth for fifty-five million years. Will our "superior human intelligence" be capable of doing the same for us?

I might never have even considered these questions or given any thought to the fragile nature of the human animal were it not for a long ride home on a horse named Bugs. It began as a simple journey filled with peaceful contemplations of Idaho's spectacular wilderness. It ended with a profound realization of my own physical vulnerability that has left me forever humbled and in awe of the improbable existence and longevity of the horse.

I met Bugs one summer while working with Jeremy Mink, a twenty-four-year-old cowboy and another one of the Black family's hired hands. At five foot six, Jeremy was about a foot shorter than Joel but had the same sort of handlebar mustache; his traveled far down both sides of his mouth. He wore a black hat with a level crown and a flat five-inch brim; he looked out at the world through Coke-bottle-thick eyeglasses and always tied a white polka-dot bandanna around his neck. The Blacks had hired him to manage their cattle in a harsh and peculiar area of the ranch known as Dickshooter (actually named after a man named Dick Shooter).

In one sense, Dickshooter resembled the other cowboy camps I had worked at: its remote, rustic living quarters had been set down like some hideout from another century, a solitary speck on millions of acres of the American West. But it also had its own unique elements.

Much of the land was covered with endless fragments of prehistoric volcanic black rock, giving the entire area an eerie moonscape appearance. I was amazed that the ranch horses had totally adapted to this surface; though it slowed them down a bit, they walked sure-footedly.

Home at Dickshooter was an antiquated two-man camping trailer, white paint peeling off its metal exterior. Inside were two wooden bunks, a Formica-topped foldaway dining table, a Dutch oven, a mini-fridge, and a hot plate—these last two ran off a propane tank. All of this fit neatly into a space about nine feet by seven feet. Jeremy loved his job, and he loved Dickshooter. He rarely left. He had his own horses, dogs, cooking gear, and opinions. He had read so much about so much that he knew more about more things than anyone I had ever known, and he could cook.

Across from the trailer was a one-story rectangular building made from slabs of the same volcanic rock that covered the land. It had been constructed sometime in the late 1800s and was now mostly empty except for horse grain and saddles. Dickshooter had a dozen of the Blacks' ranch horses, all turned out and running free.

Every morning like clockwork they'd trot back to camp for breakfast, into a large, round corral made from decades-old cedar trees. I'd watch as some would bite and kick their herd mates, attempting to reestablish their "who eats first" pecking order. It always reminded me of growing up with my three brothers. It wasn't so much about going last; it was the fear that there would be nothing left.

You had to travel fifty miles over inhospitable terrain to get to Dickshooter. You began by driving a pickup truck thirty miles along a dirt road, to an isolated and abandoned turn-of-the-century log homestead called Old Yellow House. From there the only way to Jeremy and his camp was to go the remaining twenty miles on an all-terrain vehicle or a horse.

When I arrived at Old Yellow House, I was met by Chris Black and his Kawasaki Brute Force four-wheel-drive ATV. I threw my gear in the back of the ATV, sat down next to Chris, and the two of us drove the jarring last twenty miles out to Dickshooter. Because of the uneven volcanic rock, the ATV frequently got stuck or stalled, so the trip ended up taking us over three hours.

We finally made it there just in time for some cowboy-camp

home cooking. Dinner included Jeremy's homemade Dutch oven sourdough biscuits, which I could see he was quite proud of. When it came time for Chris to head back, he said, "Tim, I know you need to leave two weeks from next Thursday, but I won't be able to come back and get you. Just take Bugs and ride him back to Old Yellow House. When you get there, turn him out in the corral, hang his saddle in the shed, and make sure he's got water."

I was pretty green and new to ranch work. I had never ridden twenty miles alone in unfamiliar country. I said, "Okay, Chris, thanks," but I was thinking, "Are you serious? It's over twenty miles back to Old Yellow House. How do I go? Don't I need a map? What if I get lost or something happens? I have no way of calling for help! There is nothing and nobody between Dickshooter and Old Yellow House." This was way before cell phones and GPS.

At first I thought it was my macho pride that stopped me from asking any of these questions. But after Chris left, I realized it was more. I had come to genuinely trust and respect Chris. I had watched how he fathered his kids and treated his livestock. Every time I had come to work for him, he'd always made sure I had one of his best horses. He never asked me to do anything new that could turn out to be something I couldn't handle.

Chris, it seemed, knew more about what I could handle and had more confidence in me than I did. Chris had, in fact, become my leader as long as I was on the ranch. Just as I have now discovered how horses choose their leader, I realize I was using the same criteria with Chris.

The horse is a prey animal. His survival depends on being hypervigilant to attacks from predators. When a horse finds another horse that is wiser, more experienced, reliable, and trustworthy, he chooses that horse for his alpha, or leader. He knows that if he follows that horse, he'll be safer and have a better chance of survival.

I remember watching Chris's ranch horses one evening as they grazed out behind the main house where Chris lived with his family. Chris came home on a motorcycle, and when the horses heard what would have naturally been the scary sound of a loud motor, instead of lifting up their heads in the direction of the sound, they all glanced in the direction of the horse that was the herd leader.

The leader, who had heard Chris's motorcycle many times before, knew that it was not a threat, paid no attention to it, and continued grazing. The herd knew that if their leader did not lift his head in the direction of the sound that meant he felt safe, was not afraid of the noise and therefore they, too, were safe. Although I knew they could see the leader in their peripheral vision, they never lifted their heads and continued to eat.

And so it was that I had now come to trust and respect Chris, his decisions, and his requests. After many visits he had proved himself completely reliable, whether he was asking me to rope a steer for the first time or ride back alone from cowboy camp. Just like a horse that entrusts his survival to the leader of his herd, I had come to trust Chris with my life.

The day I was to leave camp, Jeremy woke me up at three A.M. with hotcakes, biscuits, and bacon. After we had eaten, we walked outside, into the darkness, and over to the corral. Jeremy got a halter and lead rope, went in, and came out with a muscular sixteen-hand bay quarter horse gelding with kind eyes. He handed me the rope and said, "This here is Bugs. He's Chris's number one. Saddle 'im up and come get me before ya take off." Then he walked back to the trailer. I stood in a pool of moon shadows looking at Bugs, him looking at me. I had never saddled a horse at night. I had never ridden a horse in total darkness.

It was time to go. Jeremy came over and said, "I know it's hard to see, but it's better to leave now than ride when it gets really hot. It'll be light in a few hours." He turned, walked back to the trailer, and Bugs and I started our ride to Old Yellow House.

I was cold. With the help of the moonlight, I could almost see about eight feet in front of Bugs. Most of all, it was dark, vast, and completely soundless. I never forgot what went through my mind: What if this horse spooks, I get thrown, and he takes off? What if we meet a mountain lion? What if I can't find my way back and I don't have food or water?

I was not only overwhelmed by my vulnerability, I was in awe of Bugs. He didn't need me, but I desperately needed him. I remember how these thoughts led me to a much greater understanding and appreciation of the horse-human relationship.

Most domestic horses like Bugs have jobs: racing, jumping, dressage, reining, ranching, doing police work, performing in circuses, acting in movies, playing polo, providing therapy, pulling carriages, participating in rodeos, or simply being backyard companions. Each job has a specific purpose. The horses that are considered great and become famous in the human world do so with jobs where they compete and win at some human-devised event. The horse wins; the person gets the cash and prizes.

To be the best and win an event, a horse, just like a human, must not only be a superior athlete, he must possess enormous heart and desire. Sometimes it is only this invisible quality of heart and desire that provides the extra one-hundredth of a second needed to create a Kentucky Derby winner.

Do horses know when they come in first and win a race? I don't know, but I believe some of them do. How do these horses feel about winning? Again, I don't know, but whatever they feel, I believe it's different from what humans feel when they win something. What's important and meaningful to most humans tends to be praise ("You and your horse were outstanding"), recognition ("We are awarding you and your horse a first-place blue ribbon"), and materialism ("Here's $100,000 for you and your horse").

All of this, which is of primary importance to humans, is meaningless to horses. But even though horses are not influenced or motivated by the cash and prizes of winning, they, like other animals, are capable of having a sense of purpose, and all domestic horses quickly learn the purpose of whatever job they are being asked to perform by their humans. I believe that if a horse is capable of having a sense of purpose, then, just like a human, it can also differentiate between the different levels of importance or meaningfulness of purpose when performing its different jobs.

A jumper horse whose job is to train, compete, and jump year after year, solely for the enjoyment of his human, develops a different disposition and attitude than a therapeutic horse that helps rehabilitate the leg muscles of a child rider with cerebral palsy, and both of these horses see things differently than a police horse that is asked by his human to help protect or control large crowds of people.

In addition, the sense of purpose that a rider feels about her chosen activity is also conveyed to and experienced by her horse. More than anything else, it is this joint sense of purpose between human and horse that creates the level of quality in their relationship.

The relationship between a cowboy and his horse is like no

other. It is based on a mutual multitasking work ethic that most often includes controlling another animal: a cow. The cowboy and his horse share a purpose, a goal, and a silent sense of partnership. The nature of this partnership generates a palpable bond of mutual love, trust, and respect. This is what has created the unparalleled magnificence of the American ranch horse. This was Bugs. This was who was leading me home.

Riding in darkness across endless miles of nothingness was almost incomprehensible to me. Just before light appeared on the horizon, I heard the distant wailing of coyotes. I looked hard into the predawn grayness but could make out nothing. Seeing the sunrise had always given me a feeling of joy and gratitude but never as much as at this moment.

I didn't know how far I'd ridden, but now that I could see I felt like I was going somewhere. As the sun took its place in the sky I watched herds of antelope bounding high in the air, as if the ground they kept hitting were an invisible trampoline. The sun got higher, the air got hotter, and the antelope disappeared.

Riding alone in the unknown for more than twenty miles created a shift in my sense of time. I didn't know where I was, and I wasn't always sure if I was going the right way. Just like a horse, I was totally living in the moment. I knew I hadn't made a wrong turn; there were no turns.

We had been riding for a couple of hours in the sun, and it was hot. Bugs and I were both sweating pretty good. I got off and loosened his saddle and blanket. Then I stuck my hands underneath his blanket and started scratching Bugs's sweaty-hot skin.

For a while, I held the saddle and blanket up off Bugs's back, as high as I could, letting whatever breeze there was blow over his wet skin. I poured some of my canteen water into my hat and let

Bugs lick it up before I took my drink. When we were ready to go on again, I made sure his saddle was securely on and started walking, leading Bugs behind me, giving him a rest from my weight.

After we had traveled for quite a while I stopped, walked back to Bugs, and gently petted his neck. He looked so at peace and confident. I felt like we could go anywhere together and he'd be there for me. I rechecked his saddle, grabbed the reins together with a piece of his mane, and put my foot in the stirrup. And then, as I was about to get on, I stopped and looked at Bugs.

Like no horse I had ever ridden, he proceeded to spread his two front feet slightly apart, preparing himself for the extra weight I would be asking him to take. When he finished establishing his balance, he stood perfectly still, as if to say, "Okay, Tim, I'm ready now, you can get on me."

I got back on, and we continued our ride under what was now an unforgiving Idaho sun. We'd walk some, then trot some. Horses can go only so far at a canter or lope (as cowboys call it) before they tire, but they can trot for most of the day. I didn't know it then, but most riders back East find it easier to either walk or canter.

Riding a horse that's trotting requires that the rider continually stand up and sit down in the saddle, in rhythm with the horse's gait. This technique is called posting, and it prevents the rider from bouncing hard in the saddle. For many people, posting can quickly become tiring. Not for cowboys. In order to cover a lot of ground, save their horses from exhaustion, and get the most out of their workday, cowboys post and trot. Unlike most of the riding we see in Western movies, cowboys post and trot endlessly. They are masters at posting and trotting.

Bugs and I went on for another couple of hours before I saw

Old Yellow House. I stopped and gently stroked Bugs's neck. I looked at the empty, ghostlike house, surrounded by overgrown tall grass, sitting beneath a brilliantly blue, cloudless afternoon sky. I imagined it was one hundred years ago and wondered who might have walked out to greet me.

I hung my saddle in an old wooden shed, then put Bugs into the corral, made sure he had fresh, clean water, and closed the gate. For one last time before I left, I looked at Bugs, quietly standing in the hot sun, letting a small breeze blow through his mane. The perfect horse: noble, dignified, brave, powerful, thoughtful, kind, and filled with grace. I suddenly realized I had actually trusted this horse with my life.

Every time anyone anywhere climbs on the back of one of these amazing, incomparable creatures, they, too, whether they realize it or not, are doing the same thing. In the course of human history, no other animal has been entrusted with this power.

Today, with our understanding of a horse's emotional intelligence and its unique survival skills of hypervigilance and herd dynamics, humans are not only able to create a physical relationship built on mutual trust, we can also trust horses with our hearts. We can lay bare our deepest wounds, sorrows, and fears to a being capable of mirroring back, without judgment, the love and acceptance of our true selves.

As I watched Bugs roll in the dirt to scratch the dried sweat on his back, I knew I had experienced a level of self-reliance that doesn't exist in modern city living. Surprisingly, I'd discovered that I liked solitude. I'd further realized how profoundly necessary it is for the human soul to stay connected to all things alive and natural: everything on the planet that has not been processed by the human mind.

I can now look back and realize that I have a completely different understanding of all living creatures. By learning how to understand and communicate with horses, I have discovered that they are no better or worse than humans beings. We are just two different species of animal with different languages and abilities, each of which, up until now, has allowed us both to evolve and survive on the same planet.

Most people bring animals into their human world without giving much thought to how unnatural and challenging it can be for the animal. Life, not to mention survival, looked a lot different to me when I entered the natural environment of the horse.

The situation of sitting in the middle of nowhere, surrounded by thousands of acres of country untouched by humans, without food, weapons, or shelter, and having only the mind and body I'd been born with was baffling, mysterious, and humbling. Whether I was to compare myself with a horse, a bear, or a mountain lion, in their world I discovered that my human superiority had been an illusion. They are stronger, faster, and more perceptive. They hear better, smell better, see better, and are capable of living and surviving where I am not. This knowledge has become precious to me.

I believe that connecting with another species or to some part of what is still natural in our world is the truest way to both join and feel a part of our shared global humanity, as well as to unite with all life. Anyone who has a meaningful relationship with an animal of another species knows this. I found this connection with horses.

Horses changed me from the inside out; they changed my relationships with people. They made me a better person, a better parent, a better husband, and a better friend. They taught me that when I wasn't getting what I wanted, I was the one who needed to change, either what I was doing or who I was being. Horses allowed me to touch, feel, and reconnect with what was natural and real in me, in others, and in the world. Horses became my greatest teachers, for, as I was to learn, a horse is never wrong.

If someone forces me to do something, I will always resent and resist it. If I force my horse to do something he, too, will resent and resist it. When I feel forced, I get angry, argue, or quit. When my horse feels forced, he gets angry, bucks, or takes off. Horses respond positively to communication, kindness, and understanding. They want to be treated with dignity. So do I. So does everyone.

I watched the way cowboys treated their horses. They didn't just ride them like bicycles or motorcycles. They had relationships with them. The cowboys and the horses had a job to do, and they did it together. They helped each other. They looked out for each other. They were partners. They treated each other with love, trust, respect, and dignity.

Because of horses, I came to love, respect, and appreciate our country's greatest horsemen: the Native Americans. Indians believe that the human is just another species living on the earth. I have often heard them refer to our planet as a shared resource for both the two-legged and the four-legged. They believe we are all equally loved by and connected to each other. Learning how Native Americans live and how they treat everyone, including animals, has given me the gift of something I didn't know I needed but have come to deeply cherish: humility.

One day I listed all the character traits I saw horses exhibit with one another: acceptance, tolerance, patience, understanding, kindness, generosity, trustworthiness, justice, respect, truthfulness, compassion, and forgiveness. These were all the qualities my parents, my teachers, the Boy Scouts, and the Bible had told me I needed to possess in order to be a good person.

I have learned more from horses than from any book, class, or person on how to be a better human being. Horses are love in its finest form, and because of horses all my human relationships became better than they had ever been. If this could happen for me, it could happen for anyone.

6

THE WALKING WOUNDED—HORSES
FOR HEROES

Blood and pieces of flesh were everywhere, impossible to avoid, so she walked right through them. Her job was repairing radios in medevac helicopters that brought back the dead and wounded. She had witnessed the unthinkable for months. Each time, she felt herself mentally pushing back against the horror that fought to enter her mind.

She forced it out long enough so she could do her job, but the images always returned: eyes hanging from blood-oozing sockets, severed arms resting on the chests of men who prayed they could be reattached, while their buddies held their good arms and kept screaming, "Stay with me, you're going to be okay!"

She was a military communications specialist E5 (sergeant). She knew every piece of digital and electronic radio equipment. She could repair any radio faster than anyone on her team, whether it was in the front panel of a medevac chopper in Fallujah or in a forward operating base bunker in Ramadi.

Sergeant Francis Kirkson, United States Marine Corps, part Austrian, part Polish, part Norwegian. She was exactly five feet tall, weighed an even one hundred pounds, and had been born into a large family in Rochester, Minnesota. At home her friends called her Frannie. After joining the Marines and completing four years of training, she was Sergeant Kirkson. But by then no one wanted to be her friend. No one wanted to be her "battle buddy." Women weren't supposed to be marines.

Frannie got her first rifle when she was nine. Her father sent her out to kill squirrels and rabbits for dinner. She loved playing soldier. When she was twenty, she joined up. They shipped her to Parris Island, South Carolina, to learn how to kill people. She told her family she was proud to be accepted into what she called "America's best fighting force."

She worked hard to be the best soldier she could be. In basic training she did everything the men did, even forcing herself to shoulder a 250-pound marine trainee in a fireman's carry and haul him more than fifty yards. It didn't matter that she marched twenty miles the next day with multiple stress fractures in her back and legs. The proudest moment of her life was graduation, when she was handed her Marine Eagle, Globe, and Anchor. She said, "I truly felt I could help make a better world."

In May 2006, after training at bases in the United States, Japan, and Kuwait, she arrived in Baghdad, the epicenter of America's Operation Iraqi Freedom. She wanted to be there. She wanted to do her job with honor and dignity. She thought making friends in a war zone would be easier. It wasn't. It was worse. Her fellow soldiers were abusive.

There were few women in the Marines, and the men didn't like them. This they relentlessly conveyed using the most degrading profanity imaginable. Fran said there was no one she could talk to, no one who would help. If she told her male superior, he'd call her a "problem soldier" and send her back to the States, so she said nothing. She just wanted to do her job. She wanted to feel good about herself.

Off duty she'd go running as often as she could, alone, five miles at a time, thinking it would help. She'd run on a dirt road next to the base. Once, on a run, she thought she heard kids playing with firecrackers, but then she heard the screaming. There was a wall, so she couldn't see anything, but she knew it was gunfire. She had heard it before: bullets being fired, crying, shrieking. It never mattered who was shooting or who was being shot or even if she could see it. It always felt like someone was slicing through her brain with a buzz saw.

Her mind wanted her to stop, it wanted her to cry, but her will would not allow it, so she kept running. She said, "Running was all I had that was mine. I needed to keep it." The whole time she was in Iraq, she never cried. She said, "No one has ever seen me cry, even when I was a little girl. I always cried alone and on my own time."

Sergeant Kirkson was in Iraq for only eight months, but when she came home she wasn't the same person. She began working as a preschool teacher. She thought being with young children would be healing and bring her peace. It didn't.

It didn't matter that Fran had never needed to fire her weapon. She had still needed to step over men and women bleeding from unthinkable wounds and repair their radios. Sleeping meant night terrors. Horrific images of war would cause her to bolt upright, her eyes wide with fear. In an altered state, she'd immediately search her bedroom for an M16 that was never there.

The next day she'd head out for a run on her favorite country road, but her vision would go blurry, her body would start to shake, and she'd have to stop. She could drive, but any time she saw roadkill, her mind would change it into a body bag. She would start to hyperventilate and have to pull over. Finally, one day, alone in her car, on a quiet road in a small Minnesota town, she broke down and sobbed.

The military sent her to a VA hospital in West Haven, Connecticut. She filed a mental illness claim, hoping medication would help her function better. Her claim was denied. She began to abuse alcohol and became obsessive-compulsive about her daily activities, terrified to miss or alter any of them.

She did everything to excess: work, exercise, dieting, physical therapy. She hoped it would build walls in her mind to help keep out the anxiety, the flashbacks and night terrors. Gradually she lost her connections with her family and friends. Anyone's physical touch was intolerable; her ability to trust anyone or anything had entirely ceased.

She continued to send in claims to the VA, asking for help. After two years of wading through swamps of government bureaucracy, she was approved for psychotherapy.

It took over a year before she began to trust her therapist. She'd arrive for her evening session, exhausted by the obsessive-compulsive existence that had become the only thing that allowed her to function. After five minutes she'd break down, crying hysterically. While she was in that hyperanxious state, it was impossible for the therapist to help her process her contaminated thoughts and emotions. It seemed that any relief from talk therapy was out of reach.

Her therapist finally put her on medication. The pills allowed her to sit with her therapist for an hour without becoming hysterical at the thought of exposing what she had experienced. When her session ended, she would leave with all her nightmares still stuffed deep inside.

Her obsessive-compulsive days got worse. If she couldn't get to the gym, she'd panic and feel out of control. She became obsessed with food: eating, not eating, calories, carbs, portions, weight. Mental obsession became her only defense against horrific thoughts. Her therapist told her she had become anorexic and she would have to see a specialist.

Sergeant Kirkson called people at the VA hospital. They said they didn't treat eating disorders. She drove to an eating disorder recovery center in South Windsor, Connecticut. At the end of a four-hour evaluation, the doctor told her that although she did in fact suffer from anorexia nervosa, it was not her primary illness.

He said that she was exhibiting severe post-traumatic stress disorder and that until she received help for it, he couldn't begin to work with her on her eating disorder. He recommended a four-week program at the Renfrew Center, in Old Greenwich, Connecticut, a facility that could address both her PTSD and her anorexia.

In July 2008, Sergeant Kirkson's younger sister Tori drove her to Old Greenwich. Fran knew that here she would begin the most frightening battle of the war. As they got closer to Renfrew, Fran began hysterically screaming, "Please don't make me stay here. I promise I'll change."

By the time they arrived, Fran was exhausted. Now there was just a painful sadness in her eyes. She looked at her sister and said, "Go home, Tori, I'll be okay. I'll do it." Tori left to go back home. Fran began her trip into the invisible horror that lived inside her.

Sometime during her second week, Fran began to understand what had happened to her. She started to realize the depth and magnitude of what it meant to be traumatized. Her month of treatment felt like a year. She said it was the hardest thing she had ever done.

What had happened to her in the past had really happened. The nightmares came from people and things that were real. She finally had to admit and accept the truth about everything that screamed from deep within her. Her doctors told her that when she left, the next part would also be hard.

She would have to allow herself to feel, and she would have to try to avoid escaping from those feelings by using substances (drugs, alcohol, food) or engaging in compulsive behaviors. Stay awake and reexperience her nightmares, they said. Let herself feel the horrific feelings embedded in her traumatized brain. It was more than hard, she would find; it was unbearable.

When it came time for Fran to transfer to outpatient recovery, her doctors said she would need a therapist experienced in treating PTSD. The closest one was in New London, Connecticut. Fran moved there and began meeting with that therapist twice a week.

After almost two years of outpatient therapy, she still continued to shake whenever one of any number of benign sights or sounds triggered her PTSD. For Fran, trying to live a simple, ordinary life had become intolerable. Her therapist would later tell her that her recovery was beginning to seem hopeless when something unexpected happened: Fran Kirkson came face-to-face with a horse.

It happened by accident. On one of her weekly five-mile runs, Fran encountered two women on horseback coming toward her down the road. The riders had come from a nearby horse farm prophetically named High Hopes. Fran knew nothing about horses but had always loved the way they looked. She stopped running, slowly approached one of the riders, asked if she could touch her horse, and ever so gently put her hand on the horse's neck.

Months later, she would tell her therapist that being close to the horse, smelling him, hearing him breathe, and feeling his soft yet powerful neck brought her a feeling of connectedness she had never known and couldn't explain. She said it was the first time she ever remembered feeling "okay in my own skin."

Fran Kirkson shared her story with me during our first meeting at the High Hopes horse farm, in southern Connecticut, in January 2011, shortly after her twenty-ninth birthday. A month earlier she had enrolled in its new therapeutic equine program, called Horses for Heroes, which had been created in 2007 by NARHA, the North American Riding for the Handicapped Association. (In 2011, NARHA became PATH International, the Professional Association of Therapeutic Horsemanship International. For more information about PATH International and Horses for Heroes, see the Appendix.)

Horses for Heroes began as a therapeutic riding program for the physically disabled to specifically help the thousands of veterans who had served in combat from World War II to Iraq and Afghanistan. Its original focus was to use horseback riding as physical therapy for those who had lost either the use of their limbs or the limbs themselves. Today Horses for Heroes maintains facilities in many locations in the United States and is managed and available through PATH International.

As time went on, it became apparent to the therapists at Horses for Heroes that the horse-human connection was also having a dramatic impact in healing the emotional wounds of many of the soldiers. Not only was it helping them overcome depression and anxiety but, to everyone's surprise, it was having a profound therapeutic effect on soldiers who suffered from PTSD.

I had been to prisons and had witnessed the amazing transformations of inmates. I'd seen former violent gang members become decent young men who, through the process of gentling terrified wild mustangs, were able to feel compassion for the first time in their lives.

I had spoken with a therapist who'd told me how he'd seen an autistic child who had never spoken a word say "Hi, Mommy," the first time he sat on the back of a kindly old retired ranch horse.

I had seen high school dropouts—teenage men and women robbed of their self-esteem—participate in equine therapy programs to regain a sense of self-worth and respect for themselves and others. Many returned to school and a hopeful future. All learned to trust people again.

All of these transformations had been initiated simply by teaching a human how to form a positive relationship with a horse. But the idea of using a horse to break through the rapacious symptoms of PTSD long enough to enable the beginning of an effective healing process for an emotionally wounded war veteran was something no medical expert had imagined.

The natural ability of a horse to accept, without judgment, anyone, including a soldier who had seen or done horrific things

and, by so doing, express compassion and benevolent acknowledgment was another extraordinary gift that horses were capable
of giving to humans.

I had driven to High Hopes horse farm to meet Sergeant Kirkson on a clear, cold January morning. It had snowed hard the day
before, and under the glare of the sun the open fields looked as if
they had been painted a brilliant white.

Fran and I sat on a bench inside an old tack room filled with
English- and Western-style saddles. On one of the barn walls
hung a row of worn-out, cracked leather bridles. Under each one,
a horse's name—Oreo, Cheyenne, and others—had been written
in black ink. Outside the window we could see horses running in
the snow, like children playing tag, jumping, kicking, alive, and
filled with joy.

Fran told me that after she had met the two women riders she
had gone to the farm and asked if she could work there as a volunteer. When the director of the farm learned of Fran's background, she asked her if she'd like to join their Horses for Heroes
program.

As Fran told me her story, her face softened with a warm smile
and a faraway look. She said, "That was the day my life changed.
It was the first time since I had come back from Iraq that I felt
excited about something, anything. I didn't know why; all I knew
was I was going to be with horses and there was something about
being with a horse that felt good."

I went outside with Fran. We walked to an old gray wooden
barn, where she led me down a long center corridor with stalls on
either side. Halfway down she stopped in front of a stall with a
small brass plaque that had RAINBOW written on it in bold let-
ters. She slid open the stall door and stepped inside. A dark brown

horse lifted up her head and looked at Fran, who whispered to me, "Here she is."

I watched as Fran moved in close, lowered her head, and gently blew some of her own breath into the horse's nostrils. She looked back at me, smiled, and said, "That's how horses say hello."

Fran said that when she first began playing with Rainbow, she was immediately drawn to the horse's personality; she described Rainbow as "spunky, stubborn, and a free spirit." When she'd watch the horse stand in the paddock, looking so majestic, then suddenly roll in the dirt to get rid of flies, she'd laugh and say, "That's my girl—not afraid to get dirty and doesn't like to be told she can't do something."

I had known Fran only a short while, but I had a sense of her. As she told me about Rainbow, I don't think she was aware of it but she was literally describing herself. Humans are often attracted to other humans who possess many of their own personality characteristics and preferences. Like all animals, we seek to be comfortable and are therefore drawn to what is familiar. Even if hidden in a person's unconscious, this trait is so powerful it defies logic and can prevail even when what is familiar may be harmful.

A classic example is a young girl who grows up in a physically abusive home, gets away from it once she's an adult, and unwittingly starts a relationship with a physically abusive man. She becomes a battered woman and eventually leaves her abusive relationship, only to find and form a new one with another abusive man. The new man, though violent, initially covers up his negative qualities with charm and pretense. However, the unconscious human attraction to what is familiar has inevitably drawn the woman into yet another painfully abusive relationship.

But what can be hidden or disguised from a person can nevertheless always be seen or felt by a horse. No matter what we may do to cover up our emotions when we're with another person, a horse instantly knows exactly what we are feeling. More important, horses do not judge us; they only judge our actions. Horses accept us unconditionally. It is our behavior they deem to be acceptable or unacceptable, friendly or unfriendly. For Fran, connecting with Rainbow was quite possibly the first time in her life she had been or had felt unconditionally accepted.

Gaining the acceptance and friendship of a horse requires effort. Other animal companions, such as dogs, can bestow huge amounts of love and affection on humans they have literally just met. This occurs because most dogs, unlike horses, are naturally hardwired to seek out human attention and praise, and they quickly learn that both can be easily obtained from humans by exhibiting behaviors such as licking and tail wagging.

Unlike horses, whose acceptance and affection must generally be earned, a dog's energetic acknowledgment and friendship will often be given without any human solicitation. The freely given unconditional love of a dog has made major contributions in the emotional healing of a number of ailments in both adults and children, and their very companionship can often enhance one's feeling of well-being. Frequently this has occurred with the elderly, as well as those confined to hospitals.

But establishing and earning the trust and acceptance of a horse is different from gaining the trust of a dog. Dogs and humans are both predators. As a predator species, dogs do not have the same level of fear of humans that horses do. As a prey species, horses are born afraid that humans may eat them. Therefore, they require a much deeper level of connection and trust to overcome this genetically hardwired fear and create a relationship with a human that contains mutual acceptance and emotional comfort.

Often six months of traditional talk therapy can be needed to connect an adult's painful repetitive behavior with some blocked-out traumatic childhood experience. Remarkably, the same connection has often been uncovered in one therapeutic encounter with a horse.

Horses are social animals. They prefer to be in herds. In a herd of two, if one member is a human, she must prove herself to be friendly and trustworthy for the horse to remain part of the herd.

As previously mentioned, in any relationship, whether horse or human, one way to be truly loving is to find out what the other loves and unconditionally give that to them. When a person is able to establish a relationship with a horse by offering unconditional love, trust, and respect, as opposed to praise, ribbons, treats, or trophies, it is only then that the horse will relate to that person with the same three characteristics. For many people, this can be the first time they have ever experienced a small yet genuine feeling of what ideally constitutes unconditional love.

Although I was deeply moved, I was not surprised when Fran began to recount the short history of her relationship with Rainbow. "When we first met each other," Fran said, "she was pretty standoffish. When I tried to touch her, she'd move away. I remember thinking she was like me. I hated to be touched. So I figured I'd slow down and back off a little. I would hold out my hand and wait till she would move a little closer to me."

Fran was patient. "One day, after about two weeks, I put out my hand and she touched it with her nose. Then she dropped her head low and let me gently rub her face and give her a kiss. I think it was the first time in my life I ever felt love, like her to me and me to her. I felt safe with her. I felt I mattered. I know this sounds weird, but when I looked in her eyes I felt like she knew who I was."

Still, Fran knew that she had a lot to deal with. She said, "I remember thinking that Rainbow liked and accepted me even though in Iraq I had seen and done some terrible things. Once we were driving in a Humvee to fix the radio in a Black Hawk chopper that had gone down outside of Fallujah and we drove right past this woman and didn't even stop. She was screaming and holding up a baby. One of the baby's arms had been torn off, and she was gushing blood. I kept yelling at Robert, the driver, to stop and help them, but he said it wasn't part of our mission and we had to keep going. I knew there was nothing I could have done, but it felt horrible. I hated myself. I remember thinking of this while I was standing with Rainbow. I stayed with her for over an hour. I couldn't stop crying."

Fran said it was time for Rainbow to be turned out for her daily exercise. She led the horse out of her stall, and we all walked down a gravel path toward the bright white snow-covered fields. At the gate, Fran turned Rainbow loose to join her herd mates: a noble, gentle family, all standing perfectly still, facing the sun, soaking up its warmth.

Fran walked me down a frozen dirt road to my truck. Just before we said good-bye, she told me this: "The hardest part of war isn't being there, it's the coming home. You're not the same person. When I came home, I felt like everyone wanted something from me—my friends, my family. They wanted me to spend time with them; they wanted me to be happy. They wanted me to help them feel okay about me. They meant well, but they didn't understand. I just wanted to be alone—that's all I could handle."

I could tell talking about this wasn't easy for Fran, but she went on: "War kills your sense of trust. I didn't know if somebody wanted to be with me to make me feel good or to make themselves feel good. Rainbow didn't know me from before the war. All she knew was what she saw when we met. She didn't want anything from me, didn't expect anything. I didn't have to talk about my feelings; I could just feel them, and she was okay with it. She opened me up. When I realized she had started to trust me, it was the first time since I had come home from the war that I felt like me, like I had gotten my old self back." Fran smiled at me with tears in her eyes, shook my hand, and walked away.

Two years after meeting with Fran at High Hopes farm, I called and asked if she would share how Horses for Heroes had contributed to her PTSD recovery.

She said she was glad I'd called and that she had much to tell me. She said, "Being with horses at High Hopes helped me learn that I was able to make a connection with another living being. I learned that environments where I feel safe and secure do exist. When my depression heightened and suicidal ideation would creep in, I would just tell myself, *Only a few more days until I get to ride or do some barn chores.* If I could just make it until then, I knew I would feel better."

Fran went on to explain that since we had last talked, she had worked with a number of other horses in addition to Rainbow. She said, "Last month I rode a five-year-old American gypsy pony that was very challenging and made me work very hard. Remarkably, I had patience with him and never got frustrated when riding. I looked at him with love and acceptance."

Fran paused for a moment and then said, "My goal is to look at myself with that same kindness and acceptance. Working with horses has helped me tremendously with my PTSD. I have gone from being on seven different medications for depression, anxiety, sleeping, blood pressure, and flashbacks to just one medication at a very low dose. Just last month I finally slept the entire night for the first time in years!"

Fran told me that the year before, she had moved to Colorado to be near her sister. After arriving, she began volunteering at an equine program for veterans called Hearts and Horses. She loved doing it and was actually working on becoming a registered therapeutic instructor with PATH International. She said there were a number of war veterans in the equine program at Hearts and Horses and that they might also be willing to speak with me about their PTSD recovery.

Even though it had been a long time since we had spoken, I could hear a difference in Fran's voice. When we'd first met, two years earlier, her voice had been shaky and she'd sounded cautious. Now she sounded relaxed and self-assured. The last thing she said was "It's been a long journey. I'm not there yet, but I have faith I will get there. I guess all I can say is that because of horses I have found peace."

I thought about what had happened to Fran: her childhood, her war history, and her crippling PTSD. I thought about the horse Rainbow, who had broken through to her heart and helped her reconnect to herself, others, and all that was good in her life. It was truly extraordinary. At Fran's invitation, I was introduced to some of the war veterans in the Hearts and Horses equine program.

A month later, U.S. Marine Sergeant Cody Martin told me how he, too, had been unable to recover from his PTSD after years of prescription medication and traditional talk therapy. He said he was astounded that the healing he so painfully needed had come from a horse.

Cody had been born in Wichita, Kansas, and was the youngest of two brothers and three sisters. He said he was "the runt" and was always getting into fights at school because of his size. His parents got divorced when he was nine, and he went to live with his godparents. His father and his grandfather had both been in the military, and so while Cody was still in high school he enlisted in the Marines. After graduation, he was sent to Camp Lejeune, in Jacksonville, North Carolina.

Cody told me that after the terrorist attacks of September 11, 2001, he always loved it when he and his buddies had to fly commercial. He said, "It was such a good feeling to be out in public because they knew we"—the marines—"were supposed to take care of everybody." After artillery training and becoming proficient in operating an M198 howitzer, he was shipped out to the Persian Gulf on a Navy LPD (landing platform dock).

When the war with Iraq began, his ship anchored off the border between Iraq and Kuwait, in the Persian Gulf. His M198 howitzer fired rounds that traveled eighteen miles to destroy people, places, and things that no one could see. He remembered thinking, "If this was all I had to do, it wasn't so bad." He loved the adrenaline high he was constantly on, and he loved that he was part of what America was calling its "Shock and Awe" campaign.

When his first tour of duty ended, Cody returned to Camp

Lejeune and trained to get a military license that would qualify him to drive an MTVR (medium tactical vehicle replacement), also known as a seven-ton truck. When he completed his training, he volunteered to return to the war for another one-year tour. He said, "It was the right thing to do." However, this time his assignment was in-country, and it was very different. He wasn't offshore, unable to see what he was shooting at; he was driving on roads where people were shooting at him.

His job was transporting supplies from Kuwait to Fallujah. Two AAVs—amphibious assault vehicles—were his only protection. One drove in front of his truck, the other directly behind. He said he remembered it was early on a Sunday because he had just come from morning prayers. He and his two AAV escorts drove off the base to bring supplies out to FOB (forward operating base) Cheyenne. It was a ten-mile drive from Fallujah to FOB Cheyenne through small villages, with local merchants and families waking up, leaving their homes, and walking down the road to start the day.

The hypervigilance was always the same. His mind raced, his heart pounded, and his whole body was infused with adrenaline. He could see the Iraqi people through his windshield. They looked so gentle, so right at home. But in his head he kept hearing the voice of his base commander shouting at him and his buddies: "Never stop your vehicle! Never stop it for anything or anybody. They look like innocent women and children, but some are not. They will hurt you, they will kill you. Whatever they say, do not believe them, do not trust them."

Cody's truck kept moving forward as the sun rose, and the heat collecting in the vehicle made it feel like an oven. As he drove into the next village, he spotted a little red car parked on the side of the road. A man got out, opened the trunk, pulled out some wires, and twisted them in his hands. The next second, the car exploded. Cody hit the gas, but through the smoke he could see the man's decapitated head lying on the road.

The marines were told that all local people had been instructed multiple times by the American military to immediately get off the road whenever any U.S. vehicles drove by. Some did, some didn't. For a moment, Cody thought how back home he would simply stop to let someone cross the street in front of his car. Now anyone he saw looked like a suicide bomber; anything he saw looked like it could be an IED, an improvised explosive device.

After the explosion, Cody drove fast and never stopped. He said he didn't know how many bodies he hit—men, women, kids, animals. When all the vehicles got to FOB Cheyenne, it was hideous. There were guts, body parts, and blood from the people he hit covering the front of his truck. He said some of the guys laughed and took pictures of it. Cody felt nothing. He told me, "Marines are trained not to ever show feelings."

Six months later, Cody came home. He said he hated himself for so many things he had done, but the one thing that haunted him the most was running over animals—"the dogs . . . the puppies." He said, "I know it sounds a little twisted, but it's just that animals are so innocent. They're like children who don't have a mom or a dad to protect them. Now that I'm back home, if a dog looks at me and I look at him, I feel like he doesn't trust me. I know that's dumb, because they don't even know me. Maybe it's not them but me. I don't trust anyone."

Right before Cody was deployed to Iraq, he got married. When he came home, his relationship with his wife, Debbie, was in tatters. He said he fell apart emotionally: "I started crying, shaking, and hyperventilating. I knew I would never trust anybody again."

Cody got a job with the Wichita Police Department. "It was really bad," he said. "Driving was a huge trigger. I kept seeing IEDs on the side of the road, so I'd change lanes and floor it. After two weeks, they let me go. I went into a kind of shock. I told Debbie I felt suicidal. She said I should get counseling. I told her I didn't want anyone to know. If anybody found out, they'd never hire me. I also didn't want to tell anyone what I had done and seen, especially a therapist or someone who hadn't been in the military."

In every job interview, when Cody was asked if he had PTSD, he always told the truth. He was out of work for two years. He said that to save his marriage, he finally agreed to see a therapist. He was immediately put on prescription medication. "It was the same stuff they gave out after Vietnam," he said. "It took me to nowhere. It zeroed my mind out."

Eventually Cody got a good job at AT&T, and for a while things seemed to be getting better. But he hated how the drugs made him feel, and he slowly began to wean himself off all of them. A year later, he still had problems with anger and anxiety.

He and his wife continued having marriage difficulties. A week after a two-week trial separation, Cody had an uncontrollable panic attack. The Veterans Affairs hospital sent an ambulance, which took him to the VA hospital's psychiatric ward.

"They gave me drugs to calm me down," he recalled. "By the third day I felt better, but I couldn't believe where I was. There were serious drug addicts strung out on heroin, guys who kept cutting themselves, people who were seriously nuts, so I left." About a month later, Cody's wife told him that one of her friends had said that he might be able to get help from a new special veterans' organization. That afternoon Cody called the Wounded Warrior Project (WWP). Years had now passed since he had come home from the war.

The Wounded Warrior Project is a nonprofit veterans' service organization that offers a variety of programs, services, and events for wounded veterans of all military actions that followed the events of September 11, 2001. As of August 2013, WWP has helped more than thirty-five thousand men and women find some program of help and recovery with more added every year. The WWP website states, "There are no dues here—those were paid by wearing the uniform and on the battlefield." The organization's motto is: "The greatest casualty is being forgotten." (For more information about the Wounded Warrior Project see the entry "Horses for Heroes" in the Appendix.)

Cody spoke with the people at WWP. He told them of his years of PTSD agony, what he had done to try to find relief, and how nothing had helped. WWP sent him a packet of information on equine therapy and a pamphlet from Hearts and Horses. Cody had never been on a horse, didn't know anything about the animal, but, he said, "I had nothing to lose."

Cody was given a horse named Dusty to partner with. He said, "They had me start on the ground and learn how to lead him around. He seemed anxious when I was with him. Sometimes when we'd finish walking, I'd just stand and look at his eyes. They seemed so soft. I felt like he was thinking, 'This guy isn't so bad.'

All I really wanted to do was breathe with him, y'know, hold him around his neck so I could feel him breathing and then do it with him, together."

It wasn't always smooth going, though. Cody recalled, "One time I asked Claire, one of the therapists, why she thought Dusty always seemed anxious. He'd often pin his ears back or be nippy; it seemed like he didn't trust me. She asked me if I was anxious, and I said, 'Are you kidding? How about all the time.' Claire said maybe I was making Dusty anxious. That made me feel horrible. I remembered all the dogs I had killed with my truck. I started to cry. I thought, 'God, I don't want to do that. He's so good, he never hurt anything.'"

Claire made a suggestion. "She said if I would keep breathing together with Dusty and try to relax more, it might help him to feel safer and more trusting. I did everything Claire said. It took me about a month, but it was amazing. I couldn't believe how much more gentle and quiet he became. But what was really unbelievable was that everyone who knew me said I was very different, y'know, more laid-back.

"Drugs don't help you trust another person. I use to have to take drugs to go to the movies with my wife. Now I take nothing, and this year Debbie and I went to Costa Rica. Can you believe because of a horse I can go to another country and not fall apart?"

Cody told me, "I've been riding and hanging out with Dusty for about a year. I feel a sense of accomplishment—my health is definitely not in the clear, but it's in my rearview. What's really incredible is my trust. When I came home, I couldn't trust anybody or anything. Dusty got some of it back for me. It's like he brought me home."

Thousands of men and women like Fran and Cody have self-lessly traveled to Iraq and Afghanistan, where they confronted death and horror on a daily basis. They survived unimaginable acts of war only to come home to a life of emotional trauma, broken relationships, paralyzing depression, and hopelessness. Prescription drugs and traditional talk therapy have repeatedly failed to break through to the psychic wounds of post-traumatic stress disorder.

In 2013, both the Wounded Warrior Project and a study from George Washington University estimated that there were between 300,000 and 400,000 veterans in the United States suffering from PTSD. The suicide rate for these young men and women averaged one per day, or 20 percent of all U.S. suicides. These findings also reported that the cost of treating war veterans with traditional talk therapy and prescription drugs has grown, with spending to date of more than $2 billion of taxpayer funds. In 2011, the *New York Times* reported that widely prescribed drugs for treating veterans with PTSD were not only ineffective but caused serious side effects.

Equine therapy from programs like Horses for Heroes has been around for only a few years, but it has quickly and dramatically demonstrated an unmistakable ability to help in the healing of our country's returning combat veterans. Its methods are often faster, cheaper, and more effective than many of the more traditional procedures and medications. Thousands of lives could be helped, maybe even saved, if only there was more awareness of and support and resources for programs like the Wounded Warrior Project and Horses for Heroes.

"There is nothing on the inside of a man that the outside of a horse can't cure." For years, variations on this well-known quote have been attributed to any number of wise men, including Winston Churchill, Theodore Roosevelt, and Ronald Reagan. But no matter the source, these words could not be truer or more hopeful than they are for the thousands of our country's male and female combat veterans who live in agony with PTSD. For them, horses have become their heroes.

7

HORSES, HUMANS, TRAUMA, AND PTSD

Both horses and humans are vulnerable to trauma. Both can experience traumatic events. However, a number of today's trauma experts believe that only humans are susceptible to what is specifically referred to as post-traumatic stress disorder, or PTSD. For a wild horse traveling through the mountains of Montana, being attacked by a mountain lion is a traumatic event. But if the horse escapes and continues on with his life, he will not experience the human equivalent of PTSD and its debilitating symptoms; nor will he usually have any fear of returning to either those same mountains or any similar terrain in his natural environment.

Not only is the reason for this dissimilarity (which I will discuss later) fascinating, it is also remarkable that a horse, emotionally and biologically incapable of contracting PTSD, is yet able to provide meaningful healing for a human who painfully suffers from it.

What is diagnosed as PTSD in today's military is not new. As the organization Disabled World points out, PTSD has probably been in existence for as long as humanity has endured traumatic events. However, the disorder has been recognized formally as a diagnosis only since 1980.

Disabled World provides a brief history of PTSD: "During the American Civil War PTSD was referred to as 'Soldier's Heart,' in combat veterans. During World War I it was referred to as 'Combat Fatigue.' By the time World War II occurred, the disorder was being referred to as a 'gross stress reaction.' The Vietnam War found PTSD being called 'Post-Vietnam Syndrome.' Other names for PTSD have included 'Battle Fatigue' and 'Shell Shock.'"

In 2013, the American Psychiatric Association published the fifth edition of the *Diagnostic and Statistical Manual of Mental Disorders* and included the following diagnostic criteria for PTSD:

> A person has been exposed to a traumatic event in which both of the following have been present: the person has experienced, witnessed, or been confronted with an event or events that involve actual or threatened death or serious injury, or a threat to the physical integrity of oneself or others. The person's response involved intense fear, helplessness, or horror. Note: in children, it may be expressed instead by disorganized or agitated behavior.
>
> It is marked by clear biological changes as well as psychological symptoms. Identifying PTSD is often complicated by the fact that it frequently occurs in conjunction with related disorders such as depression, substance abuse, problems of memory and cognition, and other problems of physical and mental health. The disorder is also associated with impairment of the person's ability to function in social or family life,

including occupational instability, marital problems and divorces, family discord, and difficulties in parenting.

Today, the painful suffering and problematical healing of PTSD are most often addressed in conjunction with our military's young men and women. Having been subjected to the unimaginable horrors of war, thousands return home only to begin an equally agonizing struggle to return to a normal life. But war is not the only traumatic breeding ground for PTSD. There are many life situations that are experienced as traumatic; these, too, can and do cause PTSD in people of any age.

For some time there has been a significant parallel between the symptoms of PTSD found in war veterans and those found in men and women who grew up in alcoholic, dysfunctional, or abusive families. Interestingly, both the terms ACOA (adult children of alcoholics) and PTSD originated in 1980.

In her books Dr. Tian Dayton, an expert in treating ACOAs and trauma survivors, describes adult children of alcoholics as children walking around in the bodies of grown-ups. She states that a child growing up in a family who is subjected to any form of physical, mental, or emotional abuse is highly susceptible to PTSD and suffers the same effects whether the abuse is directed at the child or witnessed by them as their parents direct it at each other.

The symptoms of PTSD can be experienced throughout childhood and/or far into adulthood. Although there are many, the most common are hypervigilance, free-floating unidentifiable anxiety, black-and-white thinking, hyperreactivity, unresolved anger and sadness, depression, dysfunctional relationships, feelings of shame or inadequacy, mood-altering compulsive behaviors, alcoholism, and drug addiction.

One of the most painful effects of PTSD that can originate from a wounded childhood is the contamination of one's ability to give and receive love and emotional intimacy as an adult. To be able to form healthy love relationships as adults, children must not only receive all the elements of unconditional love from their parents, they must observe them being modeled in their parents' relationship.

A child's parents are his primary source for receiving unconditional love, affirmation, safety, acceptance, self-worth, and identity. In an abusive family, not only is a child denied most, if not all, of these elements, he experiences this emotional loss from the very people who are supposed to provide them. Often this will produce an unconscious feeling of betrayal and, when he reaches adulthood, lead to extreme difficulty in his ability to trust anyone or anything. Without feeling loved for who they are, children inevitably internalize these painful feelings and blame themselves. This damages their feelings of self-worth and self-love and therefore prevents them from forming a healthy sense of themselves.

Because a child is incapable of defending himself against adults (fight) or running away to feel safe (flight), he remains physically and emotionally trapped in an abusive and sometimes dangerous situation. Without the understanding, maturity, and healing that comes from expressing one's feelings, all the thoughts and emotions of the child's frightening and painful experiences remain trapped or frozen inside him.

As he grows up, any time he encounters either a situation or another person's behavior that is similar enough to remind him consciously or unconsciously of one of his painful childhood experiences, he will involuntarily react (with an overreaction) to it as if it were the one that happened to him in childhood. This is an effect of PTSD, and this reaction is similar to what occurs when a combat veteran hears a car engine backfire, thinks it is a roadside bomb, and dives underneath a parked car for protection.

In order to survive emotionally and function in a painful or dysfunctional family, a child will usually activate one or more of their ego-defense mechanisms. These devices of emotional protection—such as denial, rationalization, disassociation, and idealization—operate out of the intellectual left side of the human brain. They enable the child to both emotionally endure and to survive by blocking out the painful feelings of the abuse, which are experienced in the emotional right side of the brain.

Although any of these defense mechanisms, as well as others, can enable children to survive emotionally, cope, and function, they can often remain with the child into adulthood, becoming both unnecessary and dysfunctional coping methods. This greatly reduces a man's or woman's ability to experience, identify, and express their true feelings.

Painful childhood feelings that remain unconscious and are never expressed stay buried indefinitely and never heal. They are one of the most pervasive problems in many adult relationships and are frequently found in couples struggling with intimacy.

Adults who are emotionally healthy and able to appropriately express how they feel *respond* to their partner as an emotionally healthy adult. Adults who are emotionally wounded from childhood and don't know what they are feeling or why they are feeling it, *overreact* to their partner as if they are still a child reacting to a parent.

If a man comes home extremely angry because he didn't get a bonus at work, his wife may emotionally withdraw and put up a wall in order to disassociate from her husband's anger. This could also be an unconscious reaction to her alcoholic father coming home and yelling at her mother when she was a child. This, in turn, could cause her husband to feel ignored and uncared for and now prompt him to redirect his anger at his job onto her.

Whether the original wound is caused by a raging father or a roadside bomb, the reaction to these traumatic events is endured and survived with the help of the human's thinking left-brain ego-defense mechanisms, while at the same time the feelings remain frozen, buried, and unconscious in that person's emotional right brain. Until they can be acknowledged, resolved, and healed, they will forever be painfully reexperienced any time the person is emotionally triggered by a sensory stimulus that is similar to the original traumatic event. This is PTSD.

As we are now witnessing, a significant number of humans afflicted with PTSD from populations as diverse as at-risk youths and adult war veterans are experiencing emotional healing breakthroughs initiated by interacting with a horse in what is referred to as equine therapy. But why?

One potential scientific reason horses are able to initiate the healing of PTSD is examined in the groundbreaking trauma research in Dr. Peter A. Levine's book *Waking the Tiger: Healing Trauma*. As Dr. Levine points out, both humans and animals are vulnerable to trauma caused by any real or perceived life-threatening event. However, he states that PTSD is exclusively a human condition, one not found in any other animal species; nor does it exist elsewhere in nature. The effects of PTSD are enormously difficult to heal and in many cases have proved impossible to completely overcome.

The hardwired response to any life-threatening event, one that causes trauma for all animal species, including humans, produces three options: flight, fight, or freeze. Most humans are familiar only with fight or flight and are unaware of the freeze response. However, all three are critical survival mechanisms. If the victim of a traumatic event is unable to either fight or run, the thwarted physical energy and surge of brain chemicals created by either of those responses are, for a brief period, somatically frozen, and thus create the freeze response.

If a horse is caught, overpowered by a pack of wolves, and is unable to flee or fight, he will collapse and freeze. His brain will then release chemicals that shut down his bodily systems, rendering him numb and partially unconscious to the pain of being torn apart. A predator capturing a prey animal that is suddenly frozen and lifeless may believe him to be sick. Rather than risk their own survival by eating the bad meat of a sick animal, the wolves may leave, giving the horse the opportunity to escape. The freeze response would have thus enabled the horse to survive.

When the horse comes out of the freeze response, and before he can run to safety, he will commence an involuntary shaking. It is this shaking response that discharges the physical energy that was frozen, converting it back into the energy needed to flee. The ability to discharge the frozen energy from the death trauma is what prevents animals from having PTSD. As long as a horse can either use his adrenaline-fueled energy for fight or flight or discharge it with some form of somatic release, such as physically shaking, he can experience emotionally traumatic situations, survive, and recover without acquiring PTSD.

A traumatic experience can also occur for a horse in a domestic situation outside of his natural environment, such as from a trainer whipping and physically forcing him into a horse trailer. However, his superior size, speed, and strength give the horse the ability to use his adrenaline-fueled energy to either escape from the trailer or fight his human predator.

Being able to use and thus discharge this energy prevents the horse from acquiring the disabling symptoms of PTSD. He does not need to freeze; nor does he emotionally shut down and feel powerless, as would a child growing up in an abusive home.

The horse may continue to have an emotionally traumatic re-action around the trainer, some other humans, or other horse trailers, but he will otherwise be able to function normally without such human PTSD symptoms as depression, panic attacks, or suicidal ideation.

This situation is totally different from that of a soldier in war who is exposed to countless life-threatening bomb explosions in situations where he is pinned down and unable to utilize his adrenaline-fueled energy to fight or run.

With no avenue for discharge, the adrenaline-fueled traumatic energy of both the soldier and the child becomes somatically and indefinitely frozen, only to be triggered later ("post-") by any stimulus that in some way replicates the original event.

After a soldier returns home, the harmless sound of a child's balloon popping can instantly cause her to drop to the ground, hold her head for protection and safety, and yell "incoming." When the child from an abusive home becomes an adult, the breakup of a romantic relationship can cause abnormal and devastating feelings of loss triggered by his original traumatic childhood experience of emotional abandonment. In both cases, this is PTSD and it is accompanied by a plethora of painful, life-damaging symptoms.

———

If animals were susceptible to the damaging effects of PTSD, it would negatively impact their ability to survive and reproduce. Eventually, a species whose members frequently experienced PTSD would become extinct. The freeze response, just like fight or flight, is one of nature's brilliant creations that protects and fosters the survival of the species.

It seems the reason only humans experience PTSD stems from our inability to navigate the freeze response. This is true whether we are physically in danger or experiencing some disturbing horrific event. We emotionally shut down, numb out, and mentally disassociate in order to survive the trauma.

When a person "goes into his head," even after the traumatic event has passed, he is unable to discharge both the frozen physical energy and the excess brain chemicals created by the trauma. Our trauma emotions are internalized instead of physically discharged, so we never fully recover. Unlike animals, we mentally override our traumatic feelings, which blocks the somatic release of the physical and emotional energy that would have provided trauma resolution and healing.

As a result, humans are left with a "thwarted freeze response," which, Dr. Levine believes, is the basis for PTSD. PTSD is caused not by the traumatic event itself but by the reaction in our brain's neocortex to the event. We don't experience the trauma, mentally and emotionally process what happened, then cathartically feel the painful feelings and move on to heal and recover. Instead, we mentally and emotionally shut down, endure, and tolerate the traumatic event and continue our lives emotionally disabled and dysfunctional.

Dr. Levine is not suggesting that if we were able to physically shake at the end of a traumatic event we could avoid the onset of

PTSD, but he does believe that treating and healing PTSD must begin with therapy that originates with some form of somatic release technique.

Traumatic events such as war, psychological abuse, or rape cause emotional damage and can change one's brain chemistry, often making it extremely difficult to cope with life. Conversely, behaviors such as exercise, eating, and sex, as well as substances such as drugs and alcohol, can also change one's brain chemistry. Consequently, many people use these things as a way to self-medicate painful feelings and make it easier to function.

Ironically, in many cases these substances and behaviors change one's brain chemistry to medicate the painful emotions that were caused by the previously altered brain chemistry, which occurred as a result of the original trauma.

With PTSD, long after the original trauma has passed, it can still be mentally or emotionally triggered by seemingly benign everyday events. These are called stimulus generalizations, and they cause us to reexperience the original trauma, both chemically and emotionally. Trauma is a physiological as well as a psychic event. In addition to its mental and emotional effects, PTSD results in a number of symptomatic physiological responses, including hypervigilance, increased heart rate, hyperventilation, sweating, and physical numbness.

Based on the work of Dr. Levine, it would seem that if one is to completely heal from PTSD, he or she must also physically discharge the frozen energy that was originally created by the traumatic episode. Prescription drugs do not heal PTSD; they mask the emotional pain, allowing a person to minimally function. Healing with traditional talk therapy is limited because most often it doesn't incorporate or allow for the physical discharge of the frozen traumatic energy.

A major difficulty inherent in these customary methods of healing is the need for the trauma victim, whether a war veteran or a troubled teenager, to socially interact with a therapist while still under the unresolved effects of PTSD.

For a patient to effectively heal, some type of somatic resolution of the original trauma must take place, preferably before the patient is asked to emotionally tolerate the basic social interaction of simply talking with another person. Ideally the patient will do something that allows him or her to release some of both the physical and the emotional energy that was frozen at the time of the original traumatic event. Remarkably, interacting with a horse can accomplish this.

Establishing a positive relationship with a horse requires the awareness and recognition of a mutual trust between horse and human. Being able to experience these feelings of trust, which are initially established by interacting nonverbally with the horse, enables the patient to then interact and verbally create trust with the therapist.

The nonverbal, right-brain communication that is necessary for interacting with a horse enables a human with PTSD to momentarily stop engaging in his or her left-brain thinking. The person's physical movement and somatic interacting with the horse can then help initiate the physical discharge of a small amount of his or her painful yet frozen feelings.

The emotional healing that begins with the nonjudgmental acceptance of a horse enables patients to feel safe enough to be themselves. This helps bridge the barrier of PTSD isolation and facilitates the social reintegration of talk therapy with another human. A horse can therefore become a crucial and even life-saving component in the beginning stages of PTSD recovery.

This is what happened to Marine Sergeant Francis Kirkson when she began her relationship with a horse at the High Hopes therapeutic riding facility, four years after she returned from the war in Iraq. Rainbow enabled Fran to finally feel some of her frozen emotions long enough for her to safely open up to her therapist and begin her PTSD healing.

This is also similar to what happened with Kyle Wilson and a small group of horses at In Balance Ranch Academy, a therapeutic boarding school. Divorce is achingly painful for all children. Some are able to recover enough to grow up and function without the need of an intensive therapeutic treatment center. For others, the traumatic effects of divorce can manifest into forms of self-destructive behaviors that render traditional talk therapy ineffective. At this point, some adults are unable to effectively parent their children without the additional help of a treatment facility that can offer alternative options, such as the equine therapy program at In Balance Ranch Academy.

Kyle's inability to verbally express and heal his painful feelings caused him to try to medicate his repressed emotions by acting them out in a number of self-defeating ways. This was similar to the self-destructive coping behaviors of Sergeant Kirkson, who used alcohol, food, and compulsive exercise in an attempt to medicate the frozen traumatic emotions of her war-induced PTSD.

The fact that not only a troubled teenager and an Iraqi war veteran but many other men and women suffering from the life-threatening symptoms of PTSD are able to experience significant emotional breakthroughs in healing by interacting with horses is remarkable. Increasing the resources and support for such programs, from the government as well as private sources, can help millions more people recover from the devastating effects of PTSD.

PTSD triggers a loss of self and emotional regression, and takes one mentally out of the present moment. Horses, on the other hand, are physically, mentally, and emotionally present every second of every moment of their entire lives. Horses communicate both acknowledgment and acceptance of others, whether to horse or human, with nonverbal, right-brain behavior. The thinking, logic, reasoning, self-judgment, and criticisms of a human's left brain are unnecessary and useless.

When a human with PTSD physically interacts with a horse, it becomes possible for them to receive and to feel the emotionally therapeutic effects of unconditional acceptance. Communicating in the touch, feel, and body language of the horse can initiate the beginning of a somatic release, which can enable the physical discharge of the person's frozen traumatic energy. This allows them to go on and verbally express their painful buried feelings to a therapist and truly begin to recover and heal. This is yet another unique and extraordinary element that gives horses the power to heal our emotional wounds.

8

"I WISH PEOPLE HAD EARS LIKE HORSES"

It was eight o'clock on a Monday morning and time to help four-year-old Rachel get dressed for the day. Her mother, Lynn, brought in some clean clothes and entered Rachel's room. Rachel was already standing up on her bed, looking out her window and quietly humming. With her long, light brown hair and dark brown eyes, wearing a soft flannel nightshirt covered in puppy dogs, Rachel looked adorable.

As Lynn went to help Rachel step off the bed, Rachel grabbed her mother's right hand, pulled it to her mouth, and bit down hard. Lynn screamed, recoiled in pain, looked at the bite marks in her hand, and glared at Rachel. Rachel continued to hum and look out the window. Lynn moved in toward Rachel again, but this time she approached her from the back. She put both arms around Rachel and held her in a firm hug, preventing Rachel from biting or using her hands. She held Rachel tight and slowly rocked her back and forth, repeating, "I love you, Rachel, it's time to get dressed."

After about ten minutes, Rachel stopped humming and turned to look at her mother. Lynn let go of Rachel, faced her, and held both of her arms straight up in the air, like a football referee declaring a field goal. Rachel instantly raised her arms in the air, copying her mom, and in a firm voice that mimicked Lynn's she said, "You get dressed." Lynn pulled Rachel's nightshirt over her head and replaced it with a bright yellow T-shirt. She helped Rachel sit back down on the bed and began to put Rachel's legs into a pair of soft cotton pants. The moment the pants touched one leg, Rachel started screaming and kicking both feet.

The first kick hit Lynn hard in the face, and blood dripped down from her nose onto the bed. She stood up, took a piece of a used tissue from her pocket, and pushed it into her right nostril. She walked behind Rachel and again put her arms around her, hugging firmly while repeatedly saying, "Put pants on Rachel's legs." After about ten minutes, Rachel stopped kicking and screaming, and Lynn quickly pulled up and buttoned her pants.

She took Rachel's hand and walked her into the living room, to an area under a bright, sunny window. She helped Rachel sit down next to a pile of toys, which included Lego pieces, plastic musical instruments, crayons, drawing papers, puzzles, and a number of stuffed animals. Rachel immediately grabbed a top and started to spin it in her hands.

Lynn walked to the other side of the living room, into the kitchen, where she could continually watch Rachel over a three-foot-wide opening in the wall that separated the two rooms. As

Rachel played, Lynn started making breakfast while continuing to put digital pressure on her bloody nose.

This was a typical morning for Lynn and Rachel. This process or something similar happened four or five days every week. It had been like this for more than two years, and this pattern might continue without any improvement for many years to come. There was no cure for what was causing it. There was no medicine that could prevent it. Nobody knew where it came from. It was called autism.

Autism is referred to as a "disorder" rather than a "disease" because it is a collection of behaviors that vary widely. It is not a single illness, with consistent signs and symptoms, though some of the most common are difficulty communicating and interacting with others, problems making eye contact and reading facial expressions, and severe language deficits, characterized by problems with the use of language for social purposes.

One difficult symptomatic behavior parents of autistic children cope with is called "stimming," which is short for "self-stimulatory behavior." Stimming can include physical repetitive behavior, such as the flapping of arms, rocking, and spinning, as well as the repetition of words or phrases. It is thought that autistic children use stimming as a method of self-soothing, to regulate uncomfortable or overloaded sensory input. The behavior of some children with autism can sometimes be violent, including biting and head banging, causing injury to themselves or others.

The inability of autistic children to interact socially with others creates an enormously painful challenge for their parents. For parents who spend years going to any lengths to love, nurture, and care for a child who is incapable of returning that love or showing any affection, having a child with autism can be emotionally devastating.

Lynn Robbins and her husband, Neil, had been married for twenty-nine years and lived in the little town of Johnson, Vermont. They had raised two well-adjusted sons, who had both succeeded in college and were now happily living with their own families, one in Maine and the other in Illinois. Now in her fifties, Lynn volunteered and became an emergency foster care parent for a child-care facility in Burlington, Vermont. Emergency foster parents are specialists at taking children on almost no notice and providing them with shelter, food, clothing, and other immediate necessities.

Foster children range in age from infants to teenagers and arrive at their foster home with issues that can include psychological damage from physical and/or emotional abuse, any number of traumatic or mental disorders, and the need for parental care that often requires 24–7 supervision. The average stay with foster parents is between two and three years, at which time the children are reunified with their biological parents, relatives, or a state-approved primary caregiver.

One day Lynn received a call from the emergency foster care center asking if she could begin caring for a two-year-old child named Rachel. Lynn went immediately to the center and was given some of Rachel's background. The center's pediatrician said Rachel might be suffering from RAD, or reactive attachment disorder. Reactive attachment disorder develops because the child's basic needs for comfort, affection, and nurturing haven't been met, and loving, caring attachments with others are never established. A child with RAD has typically been neglected, abused, or orphaned. Rachel's mother had died from a drug overdose shortly after giving birth to her; there was no record of the father and no known relatives. Children with RAD cannot tolerate being hugged or touched and are frequently upset, screaming and/or crying.

Though everything she heard sounded overwhelming, Lynn was committed to helping and brought Rachel home. Lynn read everything she could about RAD, and even though it seemed daunting, some of what she read led her to believe that it might be possible to bring a better quality of life to Rachel.

One year later, Lynn adopted Rachel. She said, "I never planned on adopting a child. I thought helping out in an emergency situation for a few months or even a few years was something I could do once or, at the most, twice. After having Rachel in our home for a year, the thought of giving her back, knowing she would most likely end up in some type of state institution, felt unacceptable."

Shortly after the adoption, Lynn brought Rachel to a specialist, who found that what had originally been thought to be symptoms of reactive attachment disorder were actually those of autism, which shares many of the same behaviors.

"When we adopted her, I knew it would be demanding," Lynn told me. "I had done a lot of research on reactive attachment disorder, and there were many examples of things I could do, along with certain therapies that could lead to some healing and recovery for Rachel. When I found out it was autism, I was terrified that I wouldn't be able to cope. There's no cure for autism." And so Lynn began the sometimes agonizing, self-doubting, debt-producing, "I don't know if I can do this anymore" life of loving and raising a child with autism.

I first met Lynn on a beautiful summer day at the Lovin' Cup

Café in Johnson, Vermont. She told me that after Rachel was diagnosed, she became obsessed with treating her autism but had no idea how pervasive and heart-wrenching it would be. For the first few years, Rachel cried almost continuously and couldn't tolerate the slightest hug or touch. Lynn said, "When Rachel was four, we started with both occupational and physical therapy. Looking back, I don't think either made any real difference. Half the time, before the therapists could even start an exercise, they would have to get her to stop punching and kicking them."

Lynn said when Rachel was seven, she took her to three different child therapists for what she called "traditional talk therapy." Rachel hated it and, after a while, refused to go. Most of the time Rachel, was simply unable to sit still. Although there are no drugs that can cure autism, Rachel was periodically put on medications—including haloperidol, thioridazine and fluphenazine (all antipsychotics) and carbamazepine (an anticonvulsant and mood stabilizer)—in the hope that one of them might improve some of her everyday functions. Lynn said, "It was like there was something inside her that kept making her move which she couldn't turn off."

At one point, Rachel's physical therapist suggested that Lynn might consider having Rachel try equine therapy at the Champlain Adaptive Mounted Program. CHAMP, as it's known, is intended for children and adults with special needs and is offered at Good Hope Farm, in South Hero, Vermont. Lynn said, "I really didn't know anything about equine therapy. I thought it was just kids riding horses. I didn't see how or why it would help, but by then I was willing to try anything." (For more information about CHAMP, see the Appendix.)

The first time Rachel arrived at the farm, her equine counselor,

Sherri, had to wait about an hour for her to settle down and stop stimming. Eventually Sherri led Rachel over to a large gray horse named Alfie, who was standing alone in a round corral. Sherri told Rachel that Alfie was going to be her horse and that she could go into the corral, meet him, and say hello. Rachel followed Sherri into the corral and over to Alfie. She stopped about two feet in front of Alfie and looked up at his soft, dark eyes gazing down at her. Nobody moved; nobody spoke.

After about a minute, Rachel lifted her hand toward Alfie's nose. Alfie dropped his head and sniffed Rachel's fingers. Rachel quickly pulled her hand away, turned, and walked toward the gate. Alfie followed her. When she got to the gate, she turned back and was amazed to see Alfie standing right behind her. Sherri walked over, looked at Rachel, and said, "Alfie likes you." Rachel's mouth opened in an overwhelming smile. As Lynn told me this, she became emotional and said, "I had never seen Rachel smile like that before in her whole life."

Horses are naturally curious. Their curiosity is often motivated by the possibility of finding something that might feel good, taste good, or be fun to play with. Once they know they are safe from predators or anything that exhibits predatory behavior, their apprehension or fear of any person, place, or object turns into curiosity. Rachel was nonthreatening and had offered her hand to Alfie; he had investigated and smelled it, and then she had simply walked away. Alfie had become curious and followed Rachel.

Alfie followed Rachel as she continued to walk slowly around the corral. Each time she stopped walking, she'd turn, look back at Alfie, and see that he was looking at her. The last time Rachel stopped and turned to look at Alfie, Sherri mentioned to Rachel that she could always tell when Alfie or any other horse was interested in her by simply watching their ears. When a horse is interested in something or someone, he simultaneously directs his attention with his eyes and his ears to whatever that person or object is doing. Sometimes a horse can use each eye to look in two different directions at the same time. When this happens, his ears will also be turned in two different directions. Their ears always point in the same direction as their eyes.

Still looking at Alfie, Rachel walked three steps to the left. Though his head barely moved, Alfie's ears rotated toward Rachel. A look of wonder came over her face. The experience was like that of a blind person who could see for the first time or a deaf person who could suddenly hear; something dramatic and profound had happened to this autistic child. She could tell that Alfie was interested in her and that it didn't matter to him that she was autistic.

Sherri walked over to Rachel and Alfie and again said, "Alfie likes you. He's paying attention to you." Rachel said nothing, kept looking at Alfie, but her eyes and her smile were bright. Sherri asked Rachel if she knew what Alfie was thinking. Rachel turned toward Sherri and said, "He's listening to me." Sherri asked, "Do you know when people are listening to you?" Rachel lightly shook her head no.

Rachel, like many children with autism, had difficulty interacting socially with people. Children with autism lack the ability to read and understand facial expressions and body language and are thus often unable to interpret what a person is feeling or thinking. An autistic child may be unresponsive when a person says, "Come to me," because for them there is no differentiation between an inviting face with a smile and a menacing face with a frown.

Rachel also had difficulty regulating her own behavior and her speech. She was constantly doing or saying something with seemingly uncontrollable repetition. But after she and her mom left the barn and arrived home, Lynn noticed that something was different. For the first time in a long while, Lynn said, or possibly ever, Rachel seemed "comfortable in her own skin." For over an hour she sat quietly, playing with a stuffed animal. Lynn said, "I don't know what just happened, but whatever it was got through to Rachel."

Rachel continued to go to Good Hope Farm and work with Alfie and Sherri. Her progress was slow but significant. When Rachel first started spending time with Alfie, she was often unable to regulate her own behavior. What would start with her walking around the corral with Alfie could occasionally become Rachel walking over to the fence and hitting the wooden rails with her fists. A year later, not only had her ability to control her behavior improved but she would often stand quietly for up to ten minutes, holding Alfie's neck and breathing with him.

Sherri noticed that Rachel had learned to see subtle differences in Alfie's eyes, ears, and body language and could tell when he didn't want to play with her. Even more remarkable was when Rachel started to make eye contact and connect with Sherri. Sometimes she would say little things to Sherri, such as "I like your shirt." One day when Rachel was leaving, after saying good-bye to Alfie, she walked over to Sherri, put her arms around the therapist's waist, and hugged her.

Horses reveal their thoughts and feelings with their body language and behavior. They do not ask, demand, or expect anything from us. They want to feel safe, comfortable, and get along. When Rachel experienced this with Alfie, it was unlike any interaction with another person she had known. Lynn said that Alfie showed Rachel that she could trust him, and if she could trust him, one day she might learn to trust people. As Rachel continued at Good Hope, she started interacting with other girls and their horses.

Rachel was eleven the last time I spoke with her mother. This time we sat at a picnic table outside the barn at Good Hope and were joined by Sherri as well as Dr. Patricia Wilcox, a New York psychiatrist who oversees the equine therapy of many Good Hope participants, including Rachel.

Lynn reported that Rachel had made significant improvements and was now attending a special-needs school three days a week. In addition to Alfie, Rachel was also playing with other horses. Lynn said, "Rachel loves to see how different horses react to her by watching their ears. This has made a huge difference in how she self-regulates when she's with people. It's quite amazing, but horses have helped Rachel begin to trust people. Last week, when we were driving home from the barn, Rachel said, 'Mom, I wish people had ears like horses.' I said, 'Why?' and she said, 'Then I would know what they were thinking and feeling.'"

Lynn went on to relate how Rachel had started riding and had even ridden in the local town parade. She said, "It was quite remarkable. She rode Alfie, smiling and waving, in between a marching band and a pumpkin float. I felt like I was watching my heart on four legs. Believe me, Rachel still has her bad days. She still needs to take some of her medications, and I know she will always be autistic. But when she's riding a horse, you can see a completely different look in her eyes. It's like she's saying: 'I'm Rachel and I'm okay!'"

Lynn pointed something else out: "Rachel knows she's not like other kids, but when she's on a horse she knows it's something special that some other kids don't have, and this helps her feel better about herself and more like she fits in."

Sherri had to leave, and so I thanked her again, told her to say hi to Rachel for me, and we shared a big hug. I remained sitting at the table, talking with Dr. Wilcox as other children walked by, leading their horses back to the barn. Dr. Wilcox was in her sixties and had been working with Good Hope for the past seven years. She told me about an autistic five-year-old boy named Peter who had recently started equine therapy. His father had told her that although Peter had made sounds, he had never spoken any words. One of the therapists had him begin riding a horse named Thunder two times a week. The third week he was riding inside the barn, he looked at his father and said, "Look at me!"

Dr. Wilcox told me that even though the scientific community had not, to her knowledge, done any formal studies that might explain the dynamics of equine therapy and why it has been an effective treatment for healing certain conditions, she knows from her work and her personal experience that horses can enable a person to touch and heal a painful place that another human is often unable to reach.

We talked about how equine therapy was becoming a significant and reliable clinical tool in the healing of so many different human ailments. She said, "In some ways, children with autism are much like horses. We don't really know what's going on inside them, what they're thinking or feeling. Rachel was correct when she said it would be easier if we all had horse ears."

As I stood up to say good-bye, Dr. Wilcox asked me to wait for a moment. I sat down again, and when I looked at Dr. Wilcox, I saw a different expression on her face. It was a softer look, more open, vulnerable, less medical or professional. She said, "Tim, I'd like to tell you something that happened to me last year. I was diagnosed with stage three breast cancer. I had chemo, radiation, and a double mastectomy. I seem to be okay right now, but it will take quite a while till I'm in the clear. When my husband picked me up from the hospital to drive me home, I was wearing a pros-thesis. I remember he was about to turn onto the interstate and I told him to stop and take me to the barn. He said, 'What are you talking about!' I said, *Just take me to the barn*. He brought me here, and I told him I'd call when I was ready to go home."

Dr. Wilcox glanced at the barn, then went on: "There's a horse here named Charlie. When I finish my work, I usually spend time with him. He's about twenty-four and partially blind in his left eye. Sometimes I just sit with him in his stall, sometimes I take him for some grass. We seem to have a connection. After my hus-band dropped me off, I went into Charlie's stall and sat on his empty water bucket. He looked at me for a minute like he always does, then walked over, dropped his head, and exhaled his warm breath onto my face. I started to cry—I couldn't help it.

"I sat with him like that for a while, just stroking the side of his face with my hand. I stood up, and without even thinking, I took off the prosthesis. Charlie smelled it and just stood looking at me, licking and chewing with his mouth. I remember think-ing, 'If he doesn't care if I wear it, I don't care if I wear it.' I've never worn it since. I know what these horses are doing for some of these kids. I hope you'll also tell people this story."

Autism is now considered the fastest-growing developmental

disability in the United States. Some of the most enlightening discoveries about the healing effects horses can have on people with autism are revealed in a book entitled *Animals in Translation,* by Dr. Temple Grandin, a professor in the Department of Animal Sciences at Colorado State University.

Dr. Grandin's findings in the field of animal-human relationships are not only remarkable, they're transformative. Some of her most compelling research is found in the similarities between horses and people with autism. It is based on Dr. Grandin's first-hand knowledge, as she herself is autistic.

In *Animals in Translation,* Dr. Grandin reports that there is often a special connection or identification that occurs when an autistic person begins to interact with a horse. She points to a possible basis for this, stating that both horses and autistic people think in pictures, not words or verbal language.

In the brains of both humans and horses, the right side deals with pictures and nonverbal communication. I believe it is the brain's nonverbal right side that creates an emotional identification between horses and autistic humans and that this connection is unintentionally expressed yet mutually recognized in their respective body languages. Whether it's a horse or a human, we are both powerfully attracted to that which is most familiar.

Since the publication of *Animals in Translation* there have been a number of reported cases where this connection has motivated some autistic children to spontaneously exhibit certain verbal and nonverbal behaviors that had previously never been seen or heard.

In a 2009 *New York Times* article, Dr. Grandin stated, "I have had a number of parents tell me that when their child was in a therapeutic riding program, their child spoke their first words.

It's rhythm and balance. These activities are really good for the autistic brain."

Another fascinating fact, according to Dr. Grandin, is that people with autism don't have an unconscious mind. Unlike other people, they can't push things out of their conscious minds or use primary ego defenses such as projection, rationalization, repression, or denial when confronted with something that causes them mental or emotional discomfort. They express exactly what they are thinking and feeling. So do horses.

Unlike most adult humans, children, autistic people, and horses do not have mixed emotions in their relationships. In all their social interactions, horses and humans with autism only see, hear, and smell the truth. However, humans without autism can and often will manipulate the truth for their own mental and emotional comfort. How often does a man or a woman with a broken heart bump into an ex-lover and act happy in order to hide their painful feelings of rejection?

Dr. Grandin goes on to report that horses and autistic people are extremely similar in how they see their respective worlds. She refers to them both as being "hyperspecific." This means they see *differences* between things in their environment much more than they see *similarities.*

Dr. Grandin states that fear is the main emotion in both autistic people and in prey animals, such as the horse. Some of the things that scare horses also scare children with autism. From her research, it appears this fear-based response in both is based on the need for survival or to feel safe. This would also make for both a positive attraction and a sense of connection between people with autism and horses, by creating a feeling of mutual safety.

An autistic person will instantly see the difference in a room if a lamp has been moved to a different place. This can immediately cause a pronounced reaction. A non-autistic person might not only be completely unaware that the lamp has been moved but also have no idea why the autistic person is suddenly behaving so differently. A horse, just like an autistic person, has this same sort of hyperspecific view of its environment.

Being hyperspecific is an element of a horse's hardwired hypervigilance. In keeping with all its other evolutionary traits, a horse's ability to instantly see differences in its environment is based on its need for survival.

As a prey species, in order to stay alive, a horse must continually be on alert to the presence of predators. The slightest change in its environment might indicate the potentially lethal presence of one of its natural enemies, such as a mountain lion or wolf.

In discovering the connections and similarities between horses and people with autism, I believe Dr. Grandin has also uncovered one of the reasons horses can initiate the often difficult-to-achieve healing for humans suffering from PTSD. A unique fear-based hypervigilant identification and connection with a horse could also instantly create a therapeutic feeling of compassion and safety for a person with PTSD, whether that person is a war veteran or someone who grew up in an alcoholic or abusive family.

Dr. Grandin's work has given us remarkable knowledge of and insights into understanding autism. She has brilliantly revealed the profound similarities between animals—in particular, horses—and people with autism. Although autism is not considered an emotional disorder, it is the emotions and some of their associated behaviors of many children with autism that begin to improve and heal as they learn to form a relationship with a horse.

A significant number of the parents of autistic children are reporting on the emotional growth and healing that is occurring from their children's participation in equine therapy programs. For these children, when it comes to communication, horses are easier to understand because, like many of the children, they are also nonverbal.

One of the most thoughtful, comprehensive, yet often heartbreaking overviews of autism appears as a chapter in Andrew Solomon's brilliant *Far from the Tree*. To read his account is to travel back and forth between fascination, shock, and despair. More than once, out of professed love or hate, a parent has taken the life of their autistic child. At one point Solomon quotes a mother explaining to the police what had driven her to try to kill her autistic son. As if attempting to express a modicum of logic and reason for her actions, she states, "I waited eleven years to hear him say, 'I love you, Mom.'"

Horses don't see a child with autism. They see a child. Autistic children know this, and it feels good to them. A huge amount of an autistic child's life is spent surrounded by loving parents and other adults who are all trying to change them. They believe their autistic children will be happier if they can learn to be more like "normal" children.

Although in many cases this might prove to be true, might not the autistic child, at the time, experience this effort as implying that there's something wrong with the way he is? If an autistic child's behavior is problematic and unacceptable for his mother, might not the child feel that *he* is unacceptable? I believe that when an autistic child feels the unconditional acceptance from a horse, a small part of their soul is healed.

In this book I have attempted to focus specifically on the ability of horses to heal emotional wounds. Autism is not considered an emotional illness; rather, the fifth edition of the *Diagnostic and Statistical Manual of Mental Disorders* (DSM-5) classifies what it calls "autism spectrum disorder" as a neurodevelopmental disorder. Nevertheless, the emotional wounds that can occur for those who suffer from the condition can be extremely painful.

In order for anyone, autistic or otherwise, to grow, heal, and have positive relationships with others, they must first have a positive relationship with themselves. Horses have the ability to make humans feel good about themselves. As with so many other men, women, and children, horses have enabled some of those with autism to become more confident, more trusting, and to feel, even if only for a moment, love for themselves and others.

9

WHAT DRAWS HUMANS TO BE WITH HORSES?

I believe that what draws most humans to be with horses is a *feeling*. Just seeing or being with a horse has the ability to make people feel good. What is surprising is that creating a relationship with a horse can also make people feel good about themselves. I believe this is true whether one is wounded or healthy.

Horses enable humans to touch an unconscious inner emotional need. When this need finds its expression in an equine relationship, it can provide a unique and dependable feeling of contentment and self-affirmation that is emotionally gratifying yet often difficult for people to characterize or explain.

At the core of all relationships—whether between or among humans or horses—is the principle that one is always attracted to what is familiar. Horses and every other nonhuman animal, whether lions, elephants, or dolphins, can instantly recognize their own species. This simple physiological fact has enabled many nonhuman animals to coexist with other members of their own species for millions of years.

I believe that the single most important factor in the historical failure of the human animal to globally and peacefully coexist with other members of its own species has been the inability of people to see, feel, and acknowledge our shared identical humanness instead of focusing on our professed differences.

People have historically compared how they feel on the inside to what others look like on the outside. This comparison is almost always inaccurate and often results in one person feeling either superior or inferior to another person. Frequently, a person compares his or her invisible yet vulnerable flaws and insecurities with another person's visible, best possible, most engaging image, which has often been years in the making.

It's not until some spiritual, joyous, transformative, tragic, or life-threatening event occurs that people of different races, religions, nationalities, sizes, or shapes suddenly realize that, yes, we are all the same. Sadly, our heartfelt collective global humanity becomes instantly recognizable, with families of different races and religions coalescing as we share the love for and loss of the victims of a mass school killing. Self-affirmation, pride, and euphoria are shared equally by two people of different races, religions, or cultural backgrounds who fall in love and get married. And there is probably no greater example of people discovering their shared humanity than the overwhelming identification one experiences upon becoming a member of Alcoholics Anonymous and realizing that anyone can be an alcoholic.

Doctors, taxi drivers, movie stars, professional athletes, priests, politicians, plumbers, university presidents, mothers, fathers, people of every race, religion, and nationality go to AA meetings. They share their most personal fears and secrets, are embraced with unconditional love and acceptance, and dramatically discover that, just like everyone there, they are all very much the same, no matter what they do or look like on the outside.

It is only by identifying one's emotional insides with the emotional insides of another that one can experience compassion. Without compassion for others, members of the human species, no matter where they were born, what they have, what they believe in, or what they look like, will never get along.

What makes an interspecies relationship between a horse and a human unique is the unexpected ability of both partners, though dramatically different in appearance, to identify and see themselves in the other. Because of the predominantly right-brain, nonverbal, instinctual nature of the horse, in order to have this relationship, a person (often encouraged to refrain from anthropomorphizing by an equine facilitator) is compelled to utilize his or her own nonverbal, intuitive right brain awareness and insights.

This thwarts the use of the person's intellectually analyzing, verbal left brain when forming opinions about the what and the why of the horse's physical behavior. Unlike the human's, the horse's emotional insides are almost completely represented and expressed on their outsides. The human is then able to see and identify with the inside, or the emotional nature, of the horse, and just as with emotionally identifying with another person, they can identify with the similar emotional attributes of the horse. Horses, just like people, can be playful, aloof, or fearful.

When a person sees another person or a horse physically or emotionally reacting to an everyday life situation in the same way they would react, they recognize a little piece of themselves. This inner identification with another—seeing oneself in either a horse or a human—usually brings an immediate feeling of positive affirmation.

When a person sees a horse, he or she might initially feel attracted but not consciously know why. A human's unconscious identification with something familiar in a horse can often be expressed in a statement of either positive or negative projection—for instance, "I like your horse; he's playful" or "That horse looks lonely."

The more I see myself in another, the more I feel a connection with something I already know: me. This identification causes me to feel a sense of sameness and reinforces the most common and universal human need: the desire to belong and feel safe.

If, however, I don't see anything familiar in another, I may initially feel apprehensive, insecure, or even fearful, at least until I have time to learn more about them.

The same is true for horses. As a prey animal, a horse is safer living in a herd with other horses. If a horse is alone, the instant he sees another horse, he feels safer. He recognizes something familiar. He has just increased his chances of surviving an attack from a predator by fifty percent.

When a horse or a human sees something familiar in another that is, in addition, extremely important or personal—for example, something associated with fear or trust—it intensifies the feelings of identification and often produces feelings of compassion. It is this interspecies connection to something truly personal that enables horses to initiate the healing of the emotional pain of humans and accounts for the remarkable effectiveness of equine therapy.

It occurs when a horse interacts with an emotionally wounded man or woman, whether a prison inmate, a child or adult raised in an alcoholic or abusive family, a person with autism, or someone who suffers from PTSD.

This is what happened to me when, at the age of forty-seven, I rode a horse for the first time, on the plains of an Idaho cattle ranch. The year was 1992, and the horse was named Spot. I experienced something wonderfully new yet soulfully familiar, and like so many other men and women, I felt a connection to something emotionally soothing that kept me coming back.

I grew up in New York City, in what today is referred to as a dysfunctional family. Both of my parents were emotionally unavailable and physically unaffectionate. Feelings were never identified, acknowledged, or expressed. My mother was constantly preoccupied with some community project. My father worked hard and was emotionally shut down, distant, and an alcoholic who left when I was seventeen.

When I was about twelve and well before he walked out, he and my mother would have horrible screaming fights, which eventually turned violent. For years, I tried everything to prevent their fighting and make them get along with each other. I became hypervigilant. To protect myself from their horrible, scary fighting, I would search for even the tiniest behavioral sign in their facial expressions and body language that might indicate an imminent explosion.

When I saw or felt even the slightest foreshadowing of a fight, I would do or say anything that might create a diversion. If they had already started yelling at each other, I would walk by their room, hoping that if one of them saw me, they would stop. If I sensed even the slightest tension, I would try to be funny and make one of them laugh. Eventually, I even found myself doing this in situations with people other than my parents.

Years later, as I learned about the nature of horses, I understood and immediately identified with their tools of survival:

both their acute social abilities, which allow them to get along with one another, and their hypervigilance to the slightest sensory indication of danger.

As I continued to learn the tools of horse training, I also noticed that the techniques I was drawn to were the gentler, more compassionate methods of natural horsemanship. It seemed that my desire to control horses through communication, as opposed to force, was in some way a link to the wounded relationship I had with my father and my rejection of his use of force, fear, and intimidation to control me and others.

On the one hand, I could see that being able to control a huge and powerful animal appealed to my masculinity and enabled me to be tough and strong, like my dad. On the other, I could also see and identify with the horse's fear and vulnerability the moment I tried to get my way by using force, fear, or intimidation.

And so I committed myself to learning the gentle training methods of natural horsemanship, which were based on understanding, communication, and compassion. At times I thought I was treating my horse the way I wished my father had treated me.

Years ago, I studied with and befriended some the world's most accomplished natural horsemanship experts. As they shared their personal journeys, I discovered that nearly all had suffered from wounded relationships with their fathers that were similar to mine. I learned that some had been raised in homes with violent, abusive, or absent fathers.

Growing up with an abusive father often creates a son who either replicates the abuse or strongly rejects it. I believe that not only did these men reject it but when they saw the abuse inherent in traditional horsemanship, they deeply desired a different way.

I learned that most of them had started out as old-school traditional horse trainers. Horses were "broken" as opposed to "started." A good horseman did whatever was necessary to "show the horse who's the boss." In time, every one of these master horsemen felt compelled to reject force and find another way of relating to horses, one that relied on understanding, communication, and compassion.

Even though they had different styles, all of these trainers had the same message: using respect, trust, understanding, compassion, and positive communication, not force, was the only way to create a truly positive working relationship, whether with a horse or a human.

Buck Brannaman was one of these horsemen. Today he's one of the most well-known, respected, and gifted teachers of natural horsemanship, as well as the author of a number of excellent books on horse-human relationships. In 2011, Buck and his teachings were featured in a powerful and moving documentary film entitled *Buck*.

In the film, he directly attributes his gentle methods of horse training to the traumatic childhood abuse he repeatedly suffered at the hands of his violent alcoholic father. In fact, his father's physical abuse became so horrific that it caused the authorities to remove Buck from his home when he was twelve and place him permanently in foster care.

Having visited with Buck, watched him work, and listened to what he had to say during one of his clinics and in his film, I deeply identified with his personal story. The painfully wounded relationship I had experienced with my father was similar in some ways to Buck's relationship with his father. I knew that this might have led me, and possibly Buck, to value and appreciate the sensitive, vulnerable nature of horses and seek out a way to relate to them without force.

In fact, Buck Brannaman once said, "There's only one thing I owe my dad: that I can understand how an animal feels when it's scared for its life." He also noted, "Whether you have horses, dogs, or kids, with that comes a great responsibility. You have to be able to teach them to get along in the world."

In many ways, horses are like children. They are playful, vulnerable, and dependent on their family, and they need the love and discipline of a leader. They can be easily hurt, frightened, or damaged by force, fear, or intimidation. When I think back to many of the most gifted and successful male natural horsemanship clinicians, I am reminded of this similarity between horses, children, and their fathers.

It seems that these men's desire to train or "parent" a horse with the supportive and compassionate methods of natural horsemanship quite possibly stemmed from a desire to be, for their childlike horse, the father they had each longed for but never had. Although it was initially unconscious, I now know that this was one of the most compelling components of what drew me so passionately to horses.

Creating a relationship with a horse requires natural equine communication—that requires body language, touch, and feel. And whether it's a man or a woman, a beginner or a professional, at some point everyone discovers that their ability to communicate in this nonverbal method is dependent on a proficiency in physical contact that ranges in degrees from gentle to firm.

And just as in parenting children, administering the right balance of firmness and gentleness with one's attitude (as opposed to equine physical contact), along with good timing, is most often the secret to creating a happy, confident, well-behaved, and thoughtful individual. For humans and horses alike, love without discipline equals disaster.

Becoming a well-liked, trusted, and respected leader in order to establish a positive working relationship with one's horse actually requires the same qualities that it takes to be a good parent to one's child. In the same way that we must understand, honor, and respect how a child sees the world, we must learn to see the world from the horse's point of view.

When a child tells us he doesn't want to go to bed because he's afraid of going into a dark room, it's not unlike a horse that's afraid to step into a horse trailer. A good parent, like a good horseperson, knows that there are no monsters in the bedroom. He or she also knows that there are no bears in the horse trailer, which to a horse looks like a metal cave on wheels.

Instead of becoming annoyed, impatient, or frustrated and showing the child or the horse that we think they're being stupid and silly, we must acknowledge their fears and understand that for them the "danger" is quite real. With a child, we can and must reassure him. We can do this by picking him up, holding him, walking into the room together, turning on the lights, and staying with him until he feels safe and lets us know it's okay if we leave. With a horse, we must not force him to go into the trailer. We must give him all the time he needs to inspect, investigate, go on and off the ramp, and become a hundred percent confident that he will be safe both getting into and staying in the trailer.

Using this method with a child not only positively resolves the immediate issue of going to bed, it creates a relationship that has our child looking to us as a source of comfort, safety, understanding, trustworthiness, and leadership. Are these not the same qualities we want from our horses, especially when we ride them?

Today, when I share what I have learned from horses, the most important message I try to pass on to others is the deep desire of a horse to receive the same healthy, loving leadership from its human as that which is desired by a child from its parents.

Years ago, I saw a small poster on a wall in my local library. It was entitled "Memo from a Child to His Parents," author unknown. At the time I thought it was a beautiful description of how to be a healthy, loving parent. I made a copy of it and have kept it for over thirty years. When I look at it now, I realize that all of the requests from a child to a parent are identical to what I believe a horse would ask of its human in order to accept him or her as its leader.

Memo from a Child to His Parents or
Memo from a Horse to His Owner

Please read this twice, once as if it were written by a child and once as if written by a horse.

1. Don't spoil me. I know quite well that I ought not to have all I ask for. I'm only testing you.

2. Don't be afraid to be firm with me. I prefer it—it makes me feel secure.

3. Don't let me form bad habits. I have to rely on you to detect them in the early stages.

4. Don't make me feel smaller than I am. It only makes me behave stupidly "big."

5. Don't correct me in front of people if you can help it. I'll take much more notice if you talk quietly with me in private.

6. Don't make me feel that my mistakes are sins. It upsets my sense of values.

7. Don't protect me from consequences. I need to learn the painful way sometimes.

8. Don't be too upset when I say, "I hate you." Sometimes it isn't you I hate but your power to thwart me.

9. Don't take too much notice of my small ailments. Sometimes they get me the attention I need.

10. Don't nag. If you do, I shall have to protect myself by appearing deaf.

11. Don't forget that I cannot explain myself as well as I should like. That is why I am not always accurate.

12. Don't put me off when I ask questions. If you do, you will find that I stop asking and seek my information elsewhere.

13. Don't be inconsistent. That completely confuses me and makes me lose faith in you.

14. Don't tell me my fears are silly. They are terribly real and you can do much to reassure me if you try to understand.

15. Don't ever suggest that you are perfect or infallible. It gives me too great a shock when I discover that you are neither.

16. Don't ever think that it is beneath your dignity to apologize to me. An honest apology makes me feel surprisingly warm towards you.

17. Don't forget I love experimenting. I couldn't get along without it, so please put up with it.

18. Don't forget how quickly I am growing up. It must be very difficult for you to keep pace with me, but please do try.

19. Don't forget that I don't thrive without lots of love and understanding, but I don't need to tell you, do I?

20. Please keep yourself fit and healthy. I need you.

There are approximately sixty million horses in the world. Of the more than ten million horses in the United States, more than two million are privately owned for either personal recreation or companionship. Many men and women are consciously and unconsciously drawn to the comfort and healing abilities of horses. However, just as many are drawn to horses for nothing more than their majestic, graceful, playful, noble, and lovable qualities.

There are also those with a desire to earn money from horse breeding or racing, those who enjoy riding in competitive sports, like the Olympics or Grand Prix dressage, and those who need partners in jobs that range from beef cattle ranch work to Central Park carriage rides. And finally, woven in and among the different reasons humans are drawn to horses is one that is not only understandable but also quite common.

Some men and women simply find it easier and more emotionally satisfying to have relationships with animals rather than with other people. Horses can offer both acceptance and companionship, and they don't talk back. They have no expectations, they do not judge or criticize, and if you don't hurt or frighten them, they will let you talk to them, pet them, and ride on their backs.

Humans initiate all horse-human relationships. Horses would be happy and do just fine if left on their own, without barns, racetracks, trail rides, or polo matches. The fact that they are still with us after two hundred thousand years, in spite of our predatory nature, is a testament to their ability to adapt and to get along with just about anyone in any situation.

Not everyone wishes to be with a horse. Horses are exceptionally large, fast, powerful, often unpredictable, and potentially dangerous. It is as common to see an eight-year-old girl kiss and hug the neck of a fourteen-hundred-pound Thoroughbred, as it is to hear a six-foot-three, 250-pound man admit that he is deathly afraid of horses and has no desire to be with one.

However, just as they do with those afflicted with life-challenging mental and emotional wounds, horses can provide anyone with the opportunity to experience valuable feelings of unconditional self-acceptance and positive self-esteem.

Both men and women usually feel good about themselves when they have a relationship with a horse, whether it's based on riding, playing with, or taking care of one. Horsemanship is a skill that can be taught, learned, and mastered, and just as with parenting a child, it requires caring, compassion, understanding, discipline, and time.

But there is yet another emotional connection to horses that can occur in some men and women that is both hardwired and unconscious. No matter what type of personality a human has, be it confident, strong-willed, timid, or insecure, interacting with a horse can unconsciously trigger primal characteristics of both a woman's femininity and a man's masculinity.

I believe that a horse's intimidating size, massive power, and reputation for being able to kick, bite, and inflict physical injury most often causes both men and women to unconsciously perceive a horse, regardless of its gender, as masculine. This, in turn, can trigger and initiate a gender-specific reaction for men and women, each of whom typically responds differently when interacting with a man.

Depending on the situation, when men meet other men, if they can communicate in a common language, this can potentially lead to mutual feelings of familiarity, friendship, and safety. However, if they are unable to communicate—for instance, because they don't speak the same language—most men will often unconsciously perceive another man as a potential threat or competitor.

When a man interacts with a horse without an understanding of the animal or the ability to communicate in a common language, it is initially quite difficult, if not impossible, to establish feelings of mutual familiarity, friendship, or safety. At this point, many men will not find horses compelling enough to pursue anything more than a cursory interaction.

On the other hand, because horses are most often perceived as masculine, if a man does not feel threatened, those with competitive natures may be motivated to learn how to master and control the horse for riding or some other competitive athletic equine event.

Finally, those men who perceive the potential physical threat of a horse as an unconscious challenge to their masculinity may wish to acquire the tools and knowledge necessary to control a horse so that they can feel physically superior. Many old-school traditional male horse trainers are often drawn to work with horses for this reason.

Since, like men, women often unconsciously perceive horses

as masculine, some of them are also drawn to horses and become old-school traditional horse trainers in order to feel physically superior. There are also women who enjoy controlling a horse as a means of sublimating their desire to be in control of a large and powerful man.

Unfortunately, with either gender, this can result in controlling a horse with force, fear, and intimidation. If either a man or a woman lacks self-awareness, it can also become a way of unconsciously acting out personal unresolved anger issues. No matter who the trainer is or what they call their method of training, this is always a form of unforgivable physical abuse.

Lastly, I believe that there are some women who are drawn to horses because they are unconsciously motivated by a hardwired maternal instinct. Though horses are indeed extremely large and powerful, they can also be emotionally like children: afraid of harmless things, noticeably vulnerable, and needing love, comfort, and safety.

Many women can intuitively see beyond the powerful masculine image and connect to their own desire to nurture, protect, and care for horses as though they were big vulnerable children. Women's natural maternal instincts may also provide one answer to an age-old question: "Why are young girls so strongly drawn to horses?"

According to a 2012 American Horse Publications Equine Industry Survey, when one excludes horse trainers, cowboys, and competitors in equine sports, over 90 percent of horse owners in this country are women. This percentage has been and continues to be identical to the number of women who attend my clinics, university classes, and private sessions. That also holds for the students of every other natural horsemanship clinician I know, and it makes no difference if the clinician is a man or a woman.

For years I've watched as some of the women I work with relate to their horse as if it were their child. The maternal instinct draws many women, both young and old, to love, ride, and own horses. It can also provide a deeply emotional and mutually rewarding relationship for both parties. However, treating a horse like a child (or sometimes like a big pet) is dangerous and often the cause of serious human injury.

Years ago, I was asked to work with a new horse owner named Jean. She kept her horse with about twenty others at a boarding facility in New England. Jean was a lovely young woman in her early thirties. She had ridden for a number of years and had just purchased her first horse. When I arrived, she gave me a big smile and said she couldn't wait to have me meet her "baby."

We walked into the barn, down an aisle of horses in box stalls, and stopped in front of a beautiful bay Thoroughbred gelding. I thought it was her new horse, but she said, "This is my friend Becky's horse. His name is Martin—isn't he gorgeous? He's three, and he just arrived yesterday." She began speaking to the horse in baby talk, saying, "What a beautiful boy you are." She put her mouth next to Martin's and moved in to kiss it.

Suddenly she screamed in horror, grabbed her face, and collapsed on the floor. In a nanosecond, Martin had reacted to Jean as if she were another horse who had just invaded his personal space without an invitation. He'd told Jean to move away the way any horse would: he'd bitten her.

But Jean was not another thousand-pound horse with a massive head and split-second reactions that communicated with body language. She was a 125-pound woman who had just lost a two-inch piece of flesh from her top lip. She was hysterical and bleeding heavily. I quickly helped her stand up and walk to the barn office for first aid. Twenty minutes later, an ambulance took her to the hospital.

For Jean, as with many other horse lovers, it was almost impossible to be close to a horse and not touch it. Many men and women want to rub, hug, or pet a horse just as they would a big teddy bear. Unfortunately, they don't know that horses naturally bite each other as a means of communicating their dominance. Horses continually play dominance games with each other to establish and reestablish a pecking order that has a leader, or alpha horse. This takes place whether it's in a herd of one hundred or a herd of two: the horse and its rider.

A thousand-pound horse when using physical dominance to establish a harmonious pecking order will bite, kick, bump, or swing its head in an attempt to physically make another horse uncomfortable enough to cause them to move away. The horse that causes the other horse to move away first is the winner of the dominance game and eventually becomes the leader. Being of basically equal size allows horses to physically interact this way and not get seriously hurt. Unfortunately, this is not the case with humans.

All good working relationships, horse or human, have preestablished physical and emotional boundaries that define the participants' personal space or comfort zone. The physical comfort zone for a human extends out about three feet, and for a horse it extends out about ten feet. Entering another's comfort zone and being accepted with total safety requires mutual acceptance, trust, and respect.

To ensure safety with a horse, a human must establish herself as the herd leader before allowing a horse to enter her personal space. If not, she will be treated like another horse of equal or lower ranking. Often a horse will attempt to move her with physically dominant behavior, such as biting, kicking, or pushing into her. The maternal instinct to unwittingly treat a horse like a child or a big pet can potentially lead a female horse lover who lacks sufficient equine knowledge to be hurt.

However, horse-related injuries that originate from a specific genetic response are not limited to women. In the same way that a woman's unconscious, hardwired female instincts can lead to equine-inflicted damage, a man with a desire to appear "macho" can also wind up with life-threatening horse-related injuries.

A few decades ago, the term "hypermasculinity" was coined to describe what is most often considered "macho." In the United States, it comprises three primary symptoms and beliefs: (1) callousness toward women is acceptable; (2) violence is manly; (3) danger is exciting. If a person believes that these are the qualities that define what it means to be a man, they are doomed to fail—with horses, with humans, and with themselves.

Regardless of what initially draws men or women to be with horses, interacting with one has the unique potential for increasing a person's self-awareness. One of the most profound changes is how horses can help us change the way we think by teaching us to think less. The unique cerebral ability of the left side of the human brain enables us to imagine, invent, and create a world of seeming superiority to that of every other creature on the planet. The idea that we might learn and personally incorporate something worthwhile from another species is most often easily dismissed.

The workings of our brain's left side provide us with conscious self-awareness, logic, and reasoning. This allows us to observe, examine, and immediately analyze every life situation we encounter. Utilizing our human reason and logic, we can ideally produce the most advantageous and rewarding decisions or choices, which will, in turn, theoretically benefit our personal welfare.

However, our left-brain abilities can also have the exact opposite effect. Sometimes they can lead us to a choice or decision that, upon reflection, could actually be considered of less benefit to our personal welfare. This can often occur from too much thinking or from overanalyzing. An example could be: "I spent a lot of time wondering about how to save money on our vacation. I kept thinking that if I waited until the day before we left on our trip to make a room reservation, I could get a lower rate at the hotel. Then I changed my mind and thought maybe if I call early I'll get a better rate. When I finally did call, there were no rooms; the place was completely sold out. Sometimes I think too much."

Although horses use the left side of their brains to think, solve problems, and make choices, their survival behavior is totally dependent on the hardwired sensory hypervigilance of the right side of their brains. When they are interacting with another horse or a human, some of their nonsurvival social behavior is also instinctual, emanates from the right side of their brains, and is expressed in their body language.

When a human interacts with a horse or attempts to create an equine relationship, they are unable to utilize the reason and logic of their left brain's verbal language to understand and communicate with the horse. They must learn to understand and respond from observing the horse's body language.

As a human spends more time with a horse, he or she becomes increasingly aware of its instinctual, right-brain, nonverbal behavior. For many, this can cause a significant awareness of not only their own right-brain human instincts but their own right-brain human intuition. This silent connection is the "felt sense" described by psychologist Eugene Gendlin in Chapter 3: "an internal knowing which is directly experienced but is not yet in words."

Every decision a horse makes is based on what is in its best interest for survival. Therefore, a horse is never wrong. Similarly, there are those who believe a person's intuition is never wrong. They believe that the right answer for every situation already intuitively exists and is always present in every human being. Typical examples of recognizing the infallibility of human intuition are often expressed with statements such as "I *knew* I should have done that" or "I *knew* I shouldn't have said that."

If asked, most people would probably report having had some experience with their intuition at some point in their life. Some would refer to it as "that still, small voice within" or "a sense of knowing" but not knowing how or why they know.

Malcolm Gladwell, in his best seller *Blink,* cites endless and fascinating examples of the power, the reliability, and, therefore, the need to trust one's intuition. He tells us that this inner knowing is now scientifically referred to in a new branch of study of human psychology as the "adaptive unconscious."

In another best seller, *A Whole New Mind: Why Right-Brainers Will Rule the Future,* author Daniel Pink asserts that it is the creativity, compassion, and intuitiveness that originates in the right side of the brain that will lead people to more successful and meaningful lives.

John Naisbitt, a futurist and the author of the groundbreaking book *Megatrends: Ten New Directions Transforming Our Lives,* has for more than thirty years been one of the world's foremost observers and analysts of global trends. In his opinion, "Intuition becomes increasingly valuable in the new information society precisely because there is so much data."

And, finally, Albert Einstein reminds us that "the intuitive mind is a sacred gift and the rational mind is a faithful servant. We have created a society that honors the servant and has forgotten the gift."

As we learn from other humans, so can we learn from the horse. We can "get out of our own heads," stop analyzing and overthinking. By accessing the right side of our brains, we allow our horse to help us trust and respond from our intuition. Being aware and taking actions from our intuition can help lead us to be who we truly are and who we were meant to be.

The more we learn about horses and how they live their lives, the more we, as humans, can identify with them. Humans are also greatly motivated by fear. If all horse fears can be reduced to one—the fear of being eaten—it could be argued that all human fears can be reduced to two: the fear of losing something we have and the fear of not getting what we want. It is said, "That which is most personal is most common." Perhaps what draws so many people to horses is the realization that they, too, on a deeply personal level and in so many ways, are very much like us.

10

AUSTIN

Tom and Dave, two old cowboys, were sitting by a campfire one night, drinking coffee and talking about life and love.

Tom asked, "Dave, how come you never got married?"

Dave said, "Well, to tell you the truth, I spent my youth looking for the perfect woman. In Denver I met a beautiful and intelligent woman with eyes like a crystal-blue lake, but she was a bit unkind. Then in Jackson Hole I met a woman who was a wonderful and generous soul, but we had no interests in common. For years I got to meet a lot of different women who seemed just right at first, but something was always missing. Then one day I met her. She was beautiful, intelligent, generous, and kind. We had everything in common. In fact, she was perfect."

"Gosh," said Tom, "what happened? Why didn't you marry her?"

Dave paused for a moment and took a sip of his coffee. Then he looked over at Tom and said, "Well, it's a sad thing. Seems she was looking for the perfect man."

The first time I heard this little story, I completely identified with cowboy Dave. However, it resonated with me not just in terms of finding the right woman; it was also exactly what happened to me when I went looking for a horse. To see how and why it took me so long and what I eventually learned from this experience, I need to go back about twenty years.

In addition to working on the Black family cattle ranch in Bruneau, Idaho, in the 1990s I spent much of my horse time at Deep Hollow Ranch, in Montauk, New York, near the eastern tip of Long Island. It was here that I began teaching natural horsemanship to local horse owners as well as taking tourists and ranch visitors for guided trail rides. Between the two ranches, I got to know and ride hundreds of different horses. Deep Hollow raised cutting horses and operated a flourishing year-round trail-riding business. It also had a fascinating history.

In the mid-1600s, when British and Dutch immigrants arrived from Europe, they settled in the area around New York Harbor. Long Island was quickly discovered as the area that possessed the richest and most fertile land for farming and raising livestock. In 1658, about three hundred head of cattle were driven from the village of New York to the far end of Long Island and into an area in the village of Montauk, which had been named for the local tribe of Montaukett Indians. The cattle ranch erected was the first of its kind in the new British colonies.

Although the ranch wouldn't be named Deep Hollow for many years, it was and is still today acknowledged as the oldest cattle ranch in America. Deep Hollow Ranch has also been the home to an amazingly diverse group of people throughout its history.

In 1898, President Teddy Roosevelt and his Rough Riders returned from the Spanish-American War and set up camp on the grounds where the ranch now stands. They were accompanied by more than twenty thousand American soldiers suffering from malaria, who were quarantined there. After the war, the ranch continued to raise cattle and horses. During this period, many Native American artifacts were unearthed, and in one section of land a large Indian burial ground was discovered.

In the 1950s, Montauk was affectionately referred to as a small fishing village made up of people who liked to drink. As time went on, it became known more often as a small drinking village made up of people who liked to fish.

Today, visitors who go out to the fashionable and world-famous Hamptons and continue on to take a trail ride at Deep Hollow Ranch might easily believe that they have somehow entered a time warp and found themselves riding a horse somewhere in the high low country of New Mexico.

Guiding groups on horseback through vast fields of tall grass and freshwater streams, I would often turn around on my horse to encounter riders whose faces were beaming with astonishment and joy. I would acknowledge the wonder in their eyes by smiling, nodding my head, and saying, "I know. Deep Hollow Ranch is the best-kept secret of the Hamptons."

Including public land owned by New York State, the ranch spans over three thousand acres. At that time, the trail rides consisted of going deep into these wooded acres and arriving on a magnificent sandy white beach overlooking the Atlantic Ocean and the coastlines of Rhode Island and Connecticut.

Deep Hollow kept about one hundred horses and was open all year, employing about fifteen trail guides during the busy summer season. Though I was almost fifty when I started and worked year-round as a teacher and volunteer guide, most of the trail guides were college-age kids. They came from all over the United States and even as far as Ireland for a fun summer job with tips.

In all, I worked at the ranch on and off for twelve years, guiding countless men, women, and children on hundreds of different horses over endless miles of narrow wooded trails and wide sandy beaches.

My time spent at Deep Hollow left me with the invaluable knowledge as well as the hands-on experience of learning how to handle unlimited types of horses, many with challenging equine personalities. It also provided me with years of significant insights into how the vast majority of humans tend to interact with horses.

Since most people do not have the knowledge or understanding of even simple introductory horse psychology, they invariably create a story when attempting to explain the behavior of their horse. The story is usually anthropomorphic in its rationale, and it seems nearly impossible for most people not to invent one, due to the hardwired necessity of the human brain to give meaning to everything in one's experience.

Probably the story most often expressed by a human when confronted with a horse that was refusing or resisting his or her request was: "I don't think my horse likes me." For a typical rider, this was completely logical and made total sense. Like most humans, including many horse owners themselves, they lacked the knowledge of equine body language that would have enabled them to understand what their horse was trying to communicate to them.

Although "unintentional dismounts" were rare, once in a great while one of Deep Hollow's sweet old trail horses would buck its rider off. It was the only way the horse—or any horse, for that matter—could get its human to stop the unnecessary and painful pulling of the reins and the metal bit in its mouth.

It had nothing to do with whether or not the horse "liked" the rider. In fact, if the horse could have spoken, it might have simply said, "You seem like a pretty nice human. But every time I push my head down and pull the reins out of your hands to tell you that the way you're pulling on the bit in my mouth is hurting me, you don't stop; instead, you pull harder. That's why I have 'suggested' that you get off my back."

Having fun and being safe with horses does not mean that one needs to learn how to stay on a horse if it suddenly bucks. It means knowing that a horse will always let you know when it's thinking about bucking by doing something else with its body first. In fact, horses communicate with both horses and humans using sequential phases of body language that increase with physical intensity.

What begins as a symbolic physical gesture readily understood by every horse and/or any human fluent in equine communication will, if ignored, escalate into direct bodily contact, with physical "discomfort" being the intended goal. Before they bite, they'll pin their ears. Before they kick, they'll lift their leg. Before they buck, they'll drop their head down close to the ground.

Here's a piece of old cowboy wisdom: Good horsemanship is knowing what happens before what happens happens. Then you can respond appropriately before it "suddenly" happens.

During the years I worked at both the Idaho and the New York ranches, people would frequently ask me if I was riding my own horse. Each time, they seemed surprised when I said no. I knew, however, that I could learn the most about horses if I spent time with as many different ones as possible.

I used to say that it was similar to the value of dating before one got married. If a man married a woman he thought was wonderful without being able to compare her with other women, the validity of his judgment and his opinion would be extremely limited and often could be disappointingly inaccurate.

How could he know if she was someone of long-lasting compatibility in all the vital areas necessary for a good partnership? How could anyone know, for instance, what would make a good friend until one had experienced having both a good friend, who was reliable, honest, and thoughtful, and a lousy one, who wasn't?

The same is true for horses. How would you know what it felt like to ride a horse that instantly stopped the moment you only thought "stop" if you had never ridden one that could? And wouldn't knowing whether this was even possible be helpful when trying to decide which horse was best for you?

Although I knew it made sense to experience many different horses before I committed to one, the truth was that there was an additional factor in my waiting to make a commitment. It was called perfectionism. For years, it had caused me to feel anxious about making a mistake when it came time to come to a final decision about pretty much anything.

What I failed to remember was that even though I had spent time with and ridden vast numbers of horses, finding the perfect equine partner would be no different from finding the perfect woman. To the dismay and disappointment of countless men and women there is no such thing as the perfect partner, human or equine.

At first this realization caused me to fearfully project spending years with a horse in a less-than-ideal relationship. Many times one of my students had said, "My horse is perfect except for _____." However, as I thought more about it, I realized that even if there were such a thing as a perfect horse, having one that wasn't perfect could possibly lead to something more valuable than having one that was.

The moment one accepts the nonexistence of perfection, acceptance, tolerance, patience, forgiveness, understanding, and compassion become possible for oneself, for others, for all humans, for all horses. Is not the acceptance of imperfection a cornerstone of realistic healthy love? This is what eventually happened to me with a horse named Austin.

Although New York City was a fascinating, exhilarating, and one-of-a-kind town to be born and raised in, it was not the first place one would go when looking for a horse. For almost the entire twentieth century, there were only three places one could find horses in the borough of Manhattan: Central Park, the stables of the NYPD's Mounted Unit, and the Claremont Riding Academy.

The Claremont Riding Academy had been built in 1892 on Eighty-ninth Street and Columbus Avenue. It became the only place in Manhattan where one could rent and ride a horse. However, this changed dramatically in 1997 with the opening of the Chelsea Equestrian Center. CEC, as it was known, was an exclusive, members-only forty-thousand-square-foot, state-of-the-art equine facility. It was located at Pier 63 on the banks of the Hudson River, near the intersection of West Twenty-third Street and the West Side Highway.

CEC offered its members a 180-by-75-foot indoor arena, a

150-by-65-foot outdoor arena, fifty box stalls, two wash stalls, a tack room, massage rooms, a glassed-in lounge, and fifty school horses, most of which were Thoroughbreds and warmbloods named after cities of the world: Paris, Boston, Boulder, London, Burlington, and so on. However, there was one eight-year-old chestnut gelding quarter horse. His name was Austin.

For four years, from CEC's opening in 1997 until it closed in 2001, I taught natural horsemanship classes to its members three days a week. And just as I had with the ranch horses I'd worked with in Idaho and Montauk, I gradually began to learn the different personalities of all the CEC horses.

Both humans and horses have distinctive personalities, and as time went on, my students' personality traits would also become apparent to me during their lessons. Every time a new student arrived for a class, I'd allow them to choose the horse they wished to work with. Remarkably, the student's personality would be almost identical to that of the horse they chose.

Anxious people chose spooky horses, confrontational people chose challenging horses, shy people chose timid horses, light-hearted people chose playful horses, and so on. People recognize in others, often unconsciously, that which seems most familiar and, therefore, usually something that exists in themselves. It seemed like the unconscious human desire to choose what's familiar when picking a human partner also existed when picking a horse. In either case, it could provide a sense of emotional comfort at the start of a relationship.

Since I already knew the personality of every horse, the moment a student picked her favorite, I discovered, I could accurately predict the more prominent characteristics of her personality. When I would ask my students why they chose a particular horse, many would say something like "I don't know why, but there was something about that horse that I liked."

However, what they couldn't see seemed obvious to me. They were being drawn to horses that behaved in a manner that reminded them of themselves. As my work at CEC continued, I, too, found myself being continually drawn to one horse: Austin.

Although this was many years ago, I still remember that Austin had a look in his eyes that reflected awareness, approachability, and kindness. At that time, even though I thought I had fairly good self-esteem, I don't think I would have had the emotional security to actually choose those adjectives in describing myself.

One of Austin's most appealing personality traits first became apparent when I'd go into the barn to see him. I'd walk up to his stall and silently look at him. He seemed so peaceful, calm, and content. Even when he was facing the other way, he could always sense that someone was there and would immediately turn in my direction. When he saw me, he'd make licking and chewing motions with his mouth, as if he were eating.

When a horse licks its lips and makes a chewing motion with its mouth, it's communicating feelings of relaxation, understanding, acceptance, and trust. This symbolic gesture is derived from a hardwired natural need of baby horses.

Equine relationships are established and maintained with body language. Both threats of and eventually actual displays of kicking and biting are used to establish the more dominant horse. This, in turn, determines the herd's pecking order and its accompanying perks, such as who eats first.

In order to protect its little two-hundred-pound body from getting bitten or kicked by a twelve-hundred-pound stallion or mare, both male and female foals, in their first year of life, signal their youthful vulnerability by licking, chewing, and moving their mouths in a manner that replicates the behavior of nursing on their mother. If one were to translate this equine body language into human English language, it might be something like "Look, I'm just a little baby horse, please don't hurt me."

When a horse grows up, it no longer needs to communicate youthful vulnerability. An adult horse that licks and chews is making a purposeful choice to communicate feelings of relaxation, understanding, acceptance, and trust toward whoever—horse or human—has entered its personal space.

Having Austin repeatedly do this when I came to visit not only felt good, it felt significant. Even though he wasn't my own horse, I decided I would take the time to create a meaningful relationship with him.

When my last class ended, at nine P.M., I'd take Austin to the outdoor arena and we'd do groundwork exercises for about thirty minutes. Then I'd saddle him up and ride under the thousands of sparkling lights glowing and shining down from the massive New York City skyscrapers. The image this created was utterly phantasmagorical, and just like getting to know a person, I began to learn a lot about Austin.

Austin was playful, cautious, and overly sensitive. He would startle easily but was always gentle and friendly. He could, however, often be aloof. I believe it was his way of communicating that he needed a little extra time to relax and get comfortable each time we got together.

Another way to say this is that gaining Austin's trust required a bit more time and effort than it might have with some other horse. One day, after describing all these traits to one of my friends, I realized: Austin was just like me.

By this time in my own personal development, I had had enough therapy to identify some of the individual traits I had acquired as a direct result of growing up in my dysfunctional family, with an alcoholic father.

I knew I was hypervigilant, painfully sensitive, and always treated others kindly as a way to hide my lack of trust. I wanted people to like me and became enormously anxious if I thought I had made someone angry.

When I thought someone was mad at me, I would immediately try to find out whether they actually were. And even if I was unsure, I'd go to great lengths to be either friendly or funny, hoping I could make them laugh.

This is what I'd done as a child to feel safe when my parents were fighting. I would try to distract them by doing or saying something funny, hoping it would cause them to stop. I thought that if I could get them to stop, they'd like each other again, not get divorced, and not leave. Like a horse who knows he'll be safer with a herd, I knew I'd be safer with two parents.

As a hypervigilant child, I had an overreactive startle response. Today I still jump and unintentionally make a sound ("Oh!") when someone enters my personal space before I've noticed their presence. I can't specifically remember what I was afraid of as a child—most likely, being hit, yelled at, embarrassed, or shamed. In any case, I still startle easily. This was and is the same with Austin.

All horses are capable of being startled. After a horse feels safe and has emotionally acclimated to his barn, as well as everyone in it, he will usually turn and look if he hears someone approaching, but he won't startle. But when Austin hears someone approaching him in his stall, he will almost always startle and jump before he looks to see who it is.

I don't know if Austin's startle response is genetic or, like mine, a result of some past traumatic experience. It really doesn't matter. To be a good friend and partner, I must make him comfortable with understanding, tolerance, and acceptance.

The vast majority of the time, Austin was a kind and easy horse to be with. The more time we spent together, the more I appreciated and was enormously grateful for his calm, gentle, and reliably good-natured personality.

I remember thinking that if I could help him become a little less sensitive, a little more confident and trusting, he would be the perfect horse. It didn't occur to me that, just like another person, whether a family member, friend, or anyone else in my life, that was just the way he was and might possibly always be: perfectly imperfect.

As I've said, this mirroring dynamic from horse to human was also apparent with my students and their horses. In fact, some of the difficulties students encountered with their horses turned out to be the same difficulties they experienced in other areas of their life, especially with their interpersonal relationships. And as it happened, the principles of natural horsemanship not only improved relationships between humans and horses; it did so with all human relationships.

Where these students got stuck with their horses was usually where they got stuck with people. When I suggested that they try a different approach with their horse and it worked, some of them would have little epiphanies: "Maybe if I was a little more patient with my girlfriend like I need to be with my horse, she might also be easier to get along with."

Sometimes it was easier to see the change a student needed to make with a horse than it was for me to see the change I needed to make with Austin. I remember being struck with this realization while riding Austin one evening in the outdoor arena. It was a perfect example of "we teach what we need to learn."

As usual, I was feeling incredibly happy and excited to be doing this in the middle of Manhattan. As we moved into a canter, Austin began to go faster than I wanted to. One of Austin's traits was a tendency to become impulsive—to go faster than the speed requested by the rider.

I never liked it when Austin became impulsive, but I had always thought it was an inherent character trait that I might need to continually correct. I came to a stop, sat for a moment, and thought about what I had been telling one of my students who'd had a similar problem earlier that evening.

I'd told her if she was feeling anxious when she was riding, her horse would know it from the tightness in her body. This, in turn, would cause her horse to feel anxious, and that would cause him to go faster. If her horse could talk he might say, "I can feel your body tensing up, which tells me you're anxious and not relaxed. If you're anxious about something, then maybe I should be anxious, too, and if so, let's go as fast as we can, get the hell out of here, and stay alive."

Suddenly, like one of my students, I had my own epiphany. Austin was behaving in an excitable way because I was feeling excited. The problem was, he didn't know that my excitement came from feeling happy and not because I was anxious. For all he knew, I was excited because I was fearful of something.

When a person is happy and excited, he breathes faster and his body tightens. The same physical symptoms occur when a person feels anxious. Horses therefore can't tell the difference between when their rider is happy and excited and when he is anxious and excited. There's a wonderful example of how this can be demonstrated in human terms.

If you were looking down at the street from the top of the Empire State Building and someone threw hundreds of dollar bills out a window, you'd see lots of people the size of ants running in different directions, trying to get the money. They'd most certainly be running while feeling excited and happy.

In the same situation, if someone threw a bomb out the window, you would also see lots of people the size of ants running in different directions. However, they would be running while feeling excited and terrified. From the top of the building, both situations would look exactly the same. You would be unable to distinguish whether the people were running because they were happy or because they were terrified.

By the same token, if my body tightened and my breathing rate increased, what was being physically expressed as my joy of riding could inadvertently feel like anxiety and, therefore, an indication of danger to my horse.

Since survival is always the most important factor in a horse's life, if he believes his rider is anxious about something, he logically thinks he should be anxious, too. When a horse feels even the least bit of anxiety, he will always move his feet to make sure they're sound and working, in case he needs to run for his life.

If he's already moving his feet and he becomes anxious, he'll move them faster. Austin was going faster because he thought I was anxious about something. My next thought was "If I want Austin to change his behavior, first I need to change my behavior."

At the time, this sounded like something I had read in a book about marriage or relationships on how to get your partner to change. The premise was that the behavior you're complaining about in your partner might be caused by something you're doing. If you focus on yourself and stop trying to make your partner act different, they will begin to respond to you differently, and eventually they will change as if it were their idea.

It was the same with horses. Instead of trying to fix or change another's behavior, which never feels good to either a human or a horse, I needed to do something that would cause them to change because it seemed like a good idea to them. It was what Tom Dorrance and Ray Hunt used to tell me: I needed to cause my idea to become the horse's idea.

Once a horse or a human thinks that doing something is their idea, they don't feel like they're being forced and they're happy to do it. This simple idea has become one of the most helpful lessons I've learned from horses.

I sat quietly on Austin for a few more minutes, then asked him to move forward at a walk and gradually transition into a lazy trot. I was excited at the thought of moving up into a canter, but now I knew that feeling excited, even though I was happy, could cause Austin to become impulsive.

As we began to canter, I took deep breaths, exhaled slowly, focused my thoughts on physically letting go, and immediately felt my body get softer in the saddle. We continued and rode past a place in the arena where in the past Austin had often increased his speed, which would then cause me to gently lift my reins to ask him to slow down.

As we continued, I realized that Austin had not become impulsive or increased his speed and that I hadn't needed to lift my reins to ask him to slow down. When I'd changed what I was doing, Austin had immediately changed what he was doing.

I asked him to stop, we both took a long rest, and I gently stroked his neck. Allowing Austin to rest the moment he'd stayed relaxed at the canter was my way of rewarding and motivating him to repeat this behavior the next time. One of the most meaningful rewards a rider can give his horse is simply to let him rest.

Whether it's a dressage rider practicing a piaffe or a Western reiner working on a slide stop, if a rider wants to perform better, the moment their horse shows even the slightest improvement, they should stop and rest. This is so important to the horse.

If you could translate its thoughts, you might hear, "Wow, this feels good. I'm going to remember exactly what I did before my rider let me rest so I can do the same thing again next time." A horse knows whether you care more about him than his performance. If you do, he'll always give you his best.

I walked Austin back to his stall and gave him some hay. As he lowered his head to eat, it occurred to me that Austin had not only taught me an invaluable lesson; he had become my teacher.

The cost of operating a state-of-the-art equestrian facility in New York City was enormous, and each year the red ink just kept piling up. CEC was situated only a short distance from the

World Trade Center towers, and after the traumatic events of September 11, the problems of keeping it going became insurmountable.

In the late fall of 2001, almost four years to the day of its opening, Chelsea Equestrian Center closed its doors. It was the end of a remarkable New York City anomaly. A week after it closed, I bought my first horse: Austin—my friend, my partner, my teacher.

There are any number of ways a horse can let us know that we're important to them. Austin let me know one summer at an elaborate fund-raising event for a children's therapeutic riding organization. It happened at the annual benefit gala for Hillcrest Stables, near the fashionable East End of New York's Long Island. The affair included cocktails, dinner, a charity auction, and a forty-five-minute natural horsemanship demonstration provided by Austin and me.

Hillcrest had about fifty horses, all of which had been put inside the barn for the evening. Outside there were enormous white canvas tents, one for the grand dinner, the other for a fund-raising auction. Opposite the dinner tent was a sixty-foot round pen where Austin and I would perform our demonstration. It was also where I had "parked" Austin for the evening with some hay and water, allowing me time to mingle with the guests before and after our presentation.

The event was well attended, and an hour before Austin and I were to begin our demonstration, I was asked to move my truck and horse trailer. I had parked close to Austin's pen, in a parking area that was now needed to accommodate more guests. As I started to back up my truck and trailer, Elaine, one of the barn staff, came running up to my window, yelling for me to stop.

She said, "Your horse is going crazy. I think he thinks you're leaving." I looked over at Austin; moments ago, he had been peacefully eating hay. Now he was running back and forth, head held high, looking at me over the fence and frantically whinnying.

I glanced left and right, searching for anything that might have caused Austin to become anxious and upset. Nothing had changed. Everything was exactly as it had been before I had started to move my truck.

I thought, "Elaine is right. Austin sees me driving away, he thinks I'm leaving him behind, and that's upsetting him. He doesn't want me to leave him alone in a strange place with strange things and strange people." Our relationship was such that anytime we went anywhere new, Austin always made sure he could see me. He might eat a little hay, but periodically he'd lift his head and scan his surroundings to see where I was.

Austin had watched me get into the truck and start driving away with his horse trailer. Now he was calling to me, trying to get my attention, telling me to stop and not leave him alone. What happened next told me that this theory was correct.

I made a U-turn, drove back to Austin's pen, pulled up alongside, and parked. The moment I turned the truck around and even before I arrived at the round pen, Austin stopped pacing up and down the fence and he stopped whinnying.

I got out of the truck, walked into the pen and over to my friend. I could see the tension in his body: his muscles were tight, and his head was still elevated. But he had stopped running, and he was quiet. I got close and slowly started stroking his neck. It reminded me of rubbing my son's back when he was a little boy and had had a bad dream. Austin lowered his head, his muscles relaxed, he sighed and licked his lips. I lowered my head next to his and felt him exhale his sweet, warm breath into my face.

I have never felt a more unmistakable expression of loving connectedness from a horse than I did that night. There is a moment in a human love relationship when you can look into the eyes of your partner and communicate a thought or feeling without having to speak. That summer night my partner was a horse . . . Austin.

In March 2014, Austin turned twenty-five and I turned sixty-nine. In the horse-to-human age equation, we're in about the same place. We've been friends for more than seventeen years and partners for thirteen. We've traveled many miles teaching, learning, making new friends, and having fun.

People come to watch us and are awed and inspired by our relationship and the love, trust, and respect we have for each other. But no matter how much I talk and share with people what I've learned from horses, the truth is that at the end of the day . . . everyone wants to meet Austin. He's got that special something. And just as I had done years ago, people instantly fall in love with him.

11

THE EVOLUTION OF HORSEMANSHIP

There has always been more than one method of training horses. Historically, the method most often used throughout the world involved controlling and training a horse with force or the threat of force. Due to countless centuries of its continued practice, this method could rightly be referred to as "traditional horsemanship."

This method creates a relationship between horse and rider that is primarily physical. Force is used as the principal motivator and means of communication. For example: you kick the horse to make him go; if he doesn't, you kick harder. You pull on the bit in the horse's mouth to make him stop; if he doesn't, you pull harder.

Ultimately, pain and the fear of pain often become the tools that are used to control the horse and to "show 'im who's boss." Since the vast majority of the time this method has been effective, other methods have usually been of little interest.

Natural horsemanship is an alternative method of training

that replaces force with communication derived from natural equine herd dynamics. Control is achieved with leadership by replicating the same methods horses use with other horses to become the herd leader.

Training is always begun on the ground. The possibility of safer, more effective, and more harmonious riding is greatly increased when the rider has already established his leadership on the ground. Utilizing the psychology of natural horse behavior, the rider creates a relationship that includes and relies on a horse's mental and emotional characteristics, as well as its physical attributes. A rider may have physical control, but without knowing how to influence and control the horse's thoughts and feelings, he will ultimately lose that physical control the instant the horse spooks and becomes overwhelmed by fear.

Once a horse feels safe and unafraid, it is highly motivated to seek physical comfort. It is therefore able to control the behavior and movement of other horses in the herd by either providing them with comfort or taking it away. The horse that does this best becomes the herd leader, or alpha horse.

Using the same method of motivation as the herd leader, the rider can also control the movement of his horse and become the leader. By replicating equine communication that uses body language, touch, and feel, the rider is then willingly granted his request by causing what he wants his horse to do to feel comfortable, and causing the horse to feel uncomfortable if it refuses. This also allows the horse the dignity to choose its own response.

In natural horsemanship, using leadership to physically control, train, and cause a horse to move could be described as "dominance." Using force or the threat of force or pain to physically control, train, and cause a horse to move could be described as "intimidation."

Comparing synonyms from a thesaurus immediately helps us distinguish the difference between the two terms:

Intimidate: coerce, scare, threaten, bully
Dominate: lead, govern, direct, control

Here's an equine example: To establish its superiority, horse A will communicate with horse B using body language to "suggest" that B move away. Horse A will begin by pinning his ears. If B does not move away, A will lift its leg. If B still doesn't move, then A will kick B's personal space. Finally, if B has still not moved, A will kick and make bodily contact with B. This will usually cause B to move away. The next time A wants B to move, he may only need to pin his ears and B will respectfully take off.

Herd-dominance contests are carried out until every horse knows its place in the pecking order. This enables horses to create and maintain exceptionally complex functioning herds while remaining socially harmonious.

Natural horsemanship simply means what is natural for horses, as opposed to what is natural for humans. Horses control each other using physical dominance administered with minimal contact, without violence, abuse, or injury.

Humans can replicate this with groundwork, using tools such as halters, ropes, and round pens. And just as with an alpha horse, human leadership is created on the ground by establishing mutual respect, trust, acceptance, tolerance, and compassion. The round pen is perhaps the tool most widely associated with natural horsemanship today.

In its natural environment, the horse survives as a prey animal by outrunning potential predators first and investigating second. The natural flight distance of a wild or untamed horse is a quarter of a mile, or about thirteen hundred feet. This is about two hundred feet farther than the chase distance of its predator enemies—chiefly mountain lions, wolves, and bears—who run out of steam at about eleven hundred feet. At thirteen hundred feet, the horse will usually stop and safely investigate to see what it was running from and either take off again or relax and conserve its energy for its next escape.

Today, because of the human desire for breeds with specific abilities, horses' natural flight distances can drastically vary. Thoroughbreds, for example, are bred to run for up to two miles and sometimes more before stopping.

The round pen allows the horse the freedom to run as far as it wants to without going anywhere. When gentling a wild or untamed horse that has not been socialized with humans (predators), a trainer can quietly stand in the middle and allow the horse to freely run in a circle for its entire flight distance of approximately thirteen hundred feet (about eight or nine laps around a fifty-foot-diameter round pen) or longer. When the horse reaches the point at which it would naturally investigate, it sees that its human predator is miraculously still where he was originally but is not attempting to capture or eat it. The trainer can then begin to communicate with body language, allowing the horse to gradually feel safe and comfortable with its human.

The body language used by the trainer to communicate with the horse is similar to that which would be exhibited by another horse seeking to be the more dominant horse or leader. The trainer will begin to step closer to the horse until the horse turns his head, looks at him, and acknowledges him. Stepping toward the horse creates emotional discomfort and is referred to as putting "pressure" on the horse. The moment the horse acknowledges the trainer by looking at him, the trainer looks away and takes a step back, which stops the pressure and brings the horse relief, or emotional comfort.

The trainer is, in effect, rewarding the horse for acknowledging him. Using body language to control the movement of the horse by administering and relieving pressure establishes the trainer as the alpha, or the leader of the two. The trainer continues this process, rewarding the horse with the removal of pressure each time the horse moves closer to him. This eventually leads to the horse allowing himself to be touched by the trainer and thus begins the process of being gentled and then "started," or what used to be referred to as being "broken."

A green domestic horse (usually two years old) that has not been started also benefits from the emotional comfort of the round pen. (A "green domestic" horse has been born and raised with humans, is not fearful of them, is gentle, and can be started. A "green wild" horse has never be with humans, is afraid of them, and needs to be gentled before it is started.)

Although comfortable around humans, the green domestic horse needs to be introduced to other unnatural things. It must become comfortable with blankets, saddles, bridles, bits, and, eventually, a human on its back.

The round pen allows the green domestic horse the freedom to run and move about until it's satisfied that these strange objects are not going to hurt or eat him. When it is time for its first ride, both the horse and its human benefit from being in a safer, more controllable small enclosed space. The horse is free to move until it becomes comfortable and desensitized. The lack of corners in a round pen prevents the horse from "hiding" or getting stuck in a corner.

In order to communicate with a horse in a round pen using body language, one must first learn the different body movements that have meaning for the horse. Often this can be achieved by first communicating via a twelve-foot lead line and a four-foot stick fitted at the end with a flag as an extension of one's body, in what has already been referred to as groundwork. Controlling the movement of a horse with groundwork establishes one's leadership by creating mutual trust and respect.

Being connected with a lead line enables one to control the movement of the horse as well as preventing it from escaping and running away. If a trainer starts in a round pen before he has established his leadership, a green domestic horse may engage him in a game of horseplay called "you can't catch me" and simply keep running away. If the horse isn't clear that the trainer is the leader, working a horse in a round pen is nothing more than unstructured exercise. Everyone eventually gets tired, and it's meaningless to the horse.

In traditional horsemanship, though the trainer often uses a round pen to break a horse, he will nevertheless continue to control the horse's movements using methods of force and intimidation, as opposed to its natural equine behavioral characteristics. With natural horsemanship, control is achieved with the trainer replicating the dominant body language of another horse.

Force and intimidation have been used for thousands of years for primarily two reasons: expediency and lack of knowledge. Force can and does obtain results. It is also easier and faster to teach than the natural equine communication of body language, touch, and feel. Additionally, anyone using a different, or *nontraditional,* method was often thought of as controversial and usually scoffed at.

Generally speaking, humans usually prefer the easier, faster way of doing most things. When it comes to doing something for the first time and without asking any questions, so as not to appear unintelligent, humans often just do what they hear or see others doing.

A person may have no idea what they're doing or why and may, in fact, be doing something that is completely unnecessary or counterproductive. Often they will pass on this "knowledge" to anyone who asks for help: "Horses are simple. Just kick 'em to go and pull 'em to stop."

Years ago, on a Colorado horse ranch, a savvy old horseman named Pat gave me his view of how most people learn how to train horses. He said it was much like the way his wife, Margaret, had learned to make meat loaf.

He said, "One night I was sitting in the kitchen, watching Margaret make a meat loaf. Just before she put it in the pan she took a knife and cut off about one inch from each side. I figured it had something to do with the recipe, y' know, to make it taste better, so I asked her. She said no, it was just the way her mother had taught her to do it.

"The next week her mother came over for dinner, and I asked her if cutting one inch off the sides made the meat loaf taste better. Her mother said no, it was just the way she had been taught by her mother to make meat loaf. That really stuck in my head, and when Thanksgiving came around, I sat down next to my wife's grandma and asked her if she remembered why she used to cut one inch off the sides of her meat loaf before she put it in the pan to cook.

"She said, 'Well, Pat, unlike your wife Margaret's spacious new pan, the one I had back then was much smaller. I just cut the sides off the meat loaf so I could get it to fit into the pan. I have no idea why she does it that way.'"

Communication is sophisticated and requires the knowledge and use of language. Force is simple; you either get what you want or add more force until you do. Since horses don't speak English, French, German, or any other human language, historically it seemed logical to control a huge, powerful, dangerous creature like the horse with force, fear, and intimidation.

However, even if it didn't end up with the horse or rider getting hurt, force almost always had some degree of negative impact on their relationship. Not only was it usually hurtful and cruel for the horse, it could have a lasting and often damaging effect on how the horse felt about his rider. Because horses are hardwired to be enormously tolerant, forgiving, and basically prefer to get along with others, most riders were, are, and continue to be unaware of this reality.

For thousands of years, probably the most influential and contributing factor to the continued use of traditional horsemanship training was war. As men discovered that they were stronger, faster, and more lethal warriors when mounted on horseback, it wasn't long before the prevailing armies of the world were those with cavalry.

However, it quickly became apparent that it would be difficult to create an army of a hundred thousand soldiers on horseback when many of those soldiers had never even been on a horse before. People therefore opted for the easier, faster, and less complicated methods of traditional horsemanship.

Even though it was not as practical or as expedient for training mass numbers of cavalry soldiers, the principles of natural horsemanship—the art and technique of creating a relationship of mutual love, trust, and respect between human and horse—did exist and were not completely lost. In fact, the leaders of these massive armies and some of history's most revered military generals became legendary as magnificent horseman.

When one traces the origins of natural horsemanship, it is widely acknowledged that the first written account of what would be considered this method was found in *The Art of Horsemanship,* written by the Greek soldier Xenophon and published in 350 B.C. This manuscript of equine eloquence contains Xenophon's most famous quote: "What a horse does under compulsion he does blindly, and his performance is no more beautiful than would be that of a ballet-dancer taught by whip and goad."

From that time and throughout history, the most successful and victorious armies of the world had the greatest cavalries, and the greatest cavalries were led by superior horsemen riding extraordinary horses: Genghis Khan and Naiman, Alexander the Great and Bucephalus, Napoleon and Marengo.

Though the vast majority of their soldiers were schooled as expeditiously as possible with traditional horsemanship techniques, these heroic generals and their noble horses were all deeply bonded in unique and extraordinary relationships that were created over many years with love and dedication.

With every step, at any gait, in any direction, horse and rider constantly shared a life-or-death reality. Both required a partnership that encompassed the highest confidence, unwavering trust, and a fervent mutual desire to succeed as brave and victorious warriors.

For thousands of years, great soldiers on horseback, whether Roman, Greek, Chinese, or French, needed their horses to maneuver with lightning reflexes at any speed and in all six directions—up, down, left, right, forward and back—in order to win and survive.

Their horses needed to remain calm, cool, and collected in the heat of battle. They needed to be confident, brave, focused, and have total faith in their rider and his requests. Horse and rider needed to act together as one unit. They needed to be in total communication with each other mentally, emotionally, and physically. They needed to look out for and protect each other. This was the art of horsemanship at its highest level and is the origin of today's natural horsemanship.

As wars ended, master horsemen, many of them former military generals in countries such as France, Germany, England, Spain, and Austria, opened riding academies and wrote books. They wanted to pass on what they knew from battle to be the principles of great riding, or what was known as "the art of horsemanship."

Since that time, riders of all disciplines have continued to study and learn from the books of François Baucher and General Decarpentry of France, Waldemar Seunig of Germany, Henry Wynmalen of England, and Colonel Alois Podhajsky of the Austrian army and director of the Spanish Riding School in Vienna, Austria.

In time, the high-level equine communication and athletic maneuvers, which were taught in the schools of these magnificent war generals, became known as "classical dressage." The

French word *dressage* is typically translated to mean "training," and as an equine reference it usually implies the highest level of training.

Though the study of these maneuvers was originally limited to people of status and wealth, gradually its popularity became more cosmopolitan and its method of training, with its accompanying performance, became known simply as dressage. Today it is one of the most popular international equine disciplines in both noncompetitive and competitive events, including the Olympic Games.

Groundwork, or "work in hand," as it is referred to in dressage, is an integral part of establishing natural communication between horse and rider. It precedes riding and is most often the beginning of high-level horsemanship in any discipline.

To control and train a horse by interacting and communicating on the ground, before one gets on its back, is and has always been the most effective method of establishing oneself as a trusted and respected leader, for the simple reason that it's the same way horses naturally control each other. Horses don't ride other horses.

In fact, groundwork is the principal foundation in the curriculum of the Spanish Riding School. Originally founded in 1572, the school is still considered by many to be the finest riding academy in the world. If a person is accepted into its prestigious program, they are not allowed to ride until they have first created a relationship with their horse on the ground. Remarkably, the time allotted for this is four years! It is only then that the student begins to ride. Graduation is celebrated at the end of eight years, after four years of groundwork and four years of riding.

Although some of the great schools of horsemanship are still in existence—in addition to the Spanish Riding School, France's

Le Cadre Noir, for instance—the vast majority of horse training in Europe and America is most often done through the less costly, more expedient methods of traditional horsemanship.

In America, the philosophical origins of natural horsemanship can be traced back a few hundred years to the Native Americans. America's "first people" lived with the philosophy and understanding that the earth was a shared resource for all creatures. Horses, like all animals, were treated with kindness and respect, as were all other living things that shared the planet.

Native chiefs, like the European army generals from hundreds of years before, were also brilliant horsemen and led some of the most revered tribes; two of the best known are Crazy Horse, of the Lakota Sioux, and Geronimo, of the Apache. Chief Joseph of the Nez Perce tribe, in his desire to have the greatest war ponies, created and bred the Appaloosa, today one of our country's most popular breeds; its name evolved from the Palouse River, in the Pacific Northwest, which ran through the tribe's land.

The relationships between the great native chiefs and their horses, like those of their European counterparts, were also created and bonded with mutual love, trust, and respect. How else could a Native American warrior fearlessly ride at top speed without a saddle and without holding the reins as he aimed and shot his arrows with deadly accuracy?

The end of the Native American civilization, as it was being vanquished by the white settlers, was also the end of America's original natural horsemen. Almost nothing about the Native Americans' methods was written down or passed on. All that remained is what we see in movies: Cowboys rode with saddles. Indians rode bareback.

During the twentieth century, in America as well as in Europe, the horse as a means of transport for military, agricultural, and personal use gradually became obsolete, replaced by machines. Supported by one of man's favorite adages—"If it ain't broke, don't fix it"—horse training and horseback riding continued to use the easier, faster, and simpler methods of traditional horsemanship.

The American military, like the forces of other countries, became motorized, disbanding most of its cavalry. However, unlike its European counterparts, it did not have renowned military generals who were also master horsemen who then opened schools, wrote books, and passed on their training methods in the art of horsemanship. In this country, the fact that there was another way, one that produced enormously better results and was far more beneficial for both horse and rider, was for the most part, and until recently, lost.

Although lacking in the schools and teachers of master-level horsemanship that were found in Europe, America had something else. Something that would bond horse and rider in a true partnership; something unique that could give horses a sense of purpose similar to the one they felt when carrying their soldiers into battle. That something was the American cowboy.

High-level horsemanship, which requires partnership, harmony, finesse, and athleticism, though no longer necessary for outmoded cavalry generals, was found to be quite useful and efficient when controlling the millions of cattle that grazed the lands of the American West.

However, most ranchers and cowboys were traditional horseman. To acquire the most sophisticated skills, to improve the speed, accuracy, desire, and agility of their working cow horses and to control and manage thousands of head of cattle, a cowboy would need to go outside his own environment and seek out a nontraditional way to achieve these higher levels of finesse and communication between horse and rider.

In pursuit of improving their own horsemanship but having no ancient American sources to turn to, a small handful of cowboys began to read the books and study the methods of some of Europe's master horsemen. Fortuitously, the same equine maneuvers that had helped these great generals become victorious in war began to bring greater success and vast improvements to the way cowboys managed their livestock.

When looked at side by side, there are striking similarities in the equine maneuvers that evolved over the ages: from the generals of ancient civilizations to the European classical dressage masters to the American cowboy and, eventually, to the natural horsemanship clinicians of today.

Executing a lateral movement with his horse that helped to protect a soldier in battle looked as magnificent when performed as a half-pass in a dressage competition. And both looked remarkably similar to a cowboy side-passing his horse up to a fence while out working his cattle.

The ancient war horse that could instantly turn 360 degrees on his hind legs to empower his general to do battle from all sides looked almost identical to a competitive high-level dressage horse performing a "turn on the haunches." And both war horse and dressage horse moved and looked remarkably like a working cow horse that had to swiftly spin on his hind legs in order to charge after a runaway steer.

It is no coincidence that a Western rider performing a lightning-fast competitive 360-degree spin in the equine event of reining looks remarkably similar to an English-style rider executing a competitive "pirouette" in an upper-level dressage event. In fact, reining has often been referred to as "dressage with speed."

The American cowboy most often acknowledged and recognized as the father of today's natural horsemanship is the late Tom Dorrance. Tom grew up in a large northeastern Oregon ranching family during the 1920s. One of his many brothers, Bill Dorrance, also went on to achieve his own status as a master horseman and helped carry the natural horsemanship training message.

Tom was often asked what drew him to the methods of natural horsemanship. His answer was not only simple; it turned out to be identical to one of the naturally hardwired survival characteristics of the horse. Tom said he had always just wanted to get along with others. He confessed, "I wanted to do whatever I could to avoid trouble."

Tom was physically small, which, he said, added to his aversion to confrontation and fighting. Like all cowboys, he had seen the time-tested traditional ways of dealing with horses, which relied on force, fear, and intimidation. But being who he was, he just couldn't follow that path, so he set out to understand and relate to horses by considering their point of view. Over the years, he became affectionately known as "the horse's lawyer."

Tom Dorrance never took credit for any of the breakthroughs or insights he had with horses. He always gave the credit to the horse. Some of Tom's most well-known concepts, which I so often quote and credit him for in my own teaching, were simple sentences expressed in his book *True Unity: Willing Communication Between Horse and Human*: "The horse is never wrong"; "Fix it up and let him find it"; "Cause your idea to become his idea"; "Feel, timing, and balance are the keys to riding with true unity"; "Feel for each other, feel of each other, then feel together."

Of all the wisdom Tom was able to share with others, his concept of "feel" was one of the most profound. For the most part, horses communicate silently with each other using body language, touch, and feel—for example, though mutual grooming, nuzzling, pinning ears, swishing tails, threatening to bite or kick, and actually biting and kicking. They have to be careful when they communicate vocally because it can identify their location to predators and thereby prove fatal.

Because they communicate using touch and feel, they are physically hypersensitive; a horse can easily feel uncomfortable when, say, a fly lands on his leg. Therefore when they feel uncomfortable, physically or emotionally, they respond negatively (they stamp their leg). When something feels comfortable, physically and emotionally, horses respond positively (they stand relaxed).

Long ago, Tom's number one disciple, Ray Hunt, expressed Tom's most valued principle of horse training. Though it is often used today by many teachers and clinicians of horsemanship, it was Ray Hunt who originally said, "Make the wrong thing difficult and the right thing easy." Today the words "difficult" and "easy" could be replaced with "uncomfortable" and "comfortable."

What Tom meant was that when a human asks something of their horse, they need to set up a situation that requires the horse to make a choice. If the horse chooses what the human is requesting, it will lead to a feeling of comfort. If the horse chooses to refuse what the human has requested, it will lead to a feeling of discomfort.

For example: If a rider goes to mount her horse and instead of standing still the horse slowly starts to walk forward before she can sit in the saddle, the rider will not continue mounting.

Back on the ground, she will quickly turn the horse in three tight circles to the right and to the left, stop, and let the horse stand and think about what just happened. The rider will do this every time she attempts to mount and the horse doesn't stand still.

What the rider is communicating to the horse is: I need you to accept and respect my leadership and comply with my requests. If I ask you to stand still and you decide to move, I will let you move. However, as your leader I will decide for how long and in what direction you will move. Instead of slowly moving forward, you will have to move quickly in tight, monotonous circles.

At some point, the horse will realize what is going on and decide that it is more comfortable to stand completely still and not walk forward than to quickly turn in six tight circles. Instead of using force, the rider has given the horse the option of choosing between two things: one that feels comfortable and another that feels uncomfortable. The rider has caused her idea to become the horse's idea and allowed the horse the dignity of choice. The rider has made the wrong thing difficult and the right thing easy.

Tom Dorrance passed away in 2003, at the age of ninety-three, leaving behind a legacy of what is now globally referred to as natural horsemanship. Long before Tom departed, he passed all his teachings on to legendary horseman Ray Hunt. Ray, in turn, went on to mentor master horsemen Buck Brannaman and Pat Parelli, as well as many other gifted teachers of natural horsemanship. Some credit Pat Parelli with coining the term "natural horsemanship."

I was honored to have met Tom and blessed to have spent a few precious days with him. Someone once asked me if I knew how Tom felt about causing such a phenomenal worldwide shift in how humans treat and train horses. I said I didn't know but I believed he probably would have said, "I am glad people are helping the horse get a better deal."

During the nineteenth century in both America and Western Europe, equine specialists known as horse tamers rehabilitated horses that, although born in captivity, had become dangerous. They behaved like wild horses, were often extremely violent, and in some cases were known to have actually killed their previous owners.

When possible, *horse tamers* would make these rogue horses safe for horse trainers. *Horse trainers* prepared domestic horses (those born and raised in human environments) to perform any number of different skills, whether for work, sport, or show.

Equine history has given the world centuries of men and women endowed with unique and remarkable abilities to tame, train, and transform horses into creatures of unsurpassed athletic performance who participate in unequaled work partnerships and become lifelong friends. But defining what it takes to have this magical gift with equines has never been stated more eloquently then by Dennis Magner, who is acknowledged as one of the original group of nineteenth-century American horse tamers responsible for giving rise to the term "horse whisperer."

In his 1887 work *Standard Horse and Stock Book*, Magner stated that, unlike other professions where one can become successful by being proficient in only one area, the horse tamer must have not only a combination of talents but a very rare combination of them. Magner wrote, "He must have the delicacy of touch and feeling of a woman, the eye of an eagle, the courage of a lion, and the hang-on pluck of a bulldog."

The last three of these four talents would most certainly be included in any accurate description of a gifted horseman. But it is "the delicacy of touch and feeling of a woman" that makes this statement so unique, as it astutely identifies the one and probably most significant ingredient found in not only the legendary horse whisperers of the 1800s but in today's most successful teachers of natural horsemanship.

It was the ability to override his macho hardwiring when confronted by a dangerous and aggressive horse that helped imbue the horse whisperer with his gift. Instead of reacting with frustration, anger, and violence, these men were able to respond with patience, kindness, and compassion.

The earliest accounts of what became referred to as horse whispering go back to County Cork, Ireland, at the start of the nineteenth century. It was here, in secret, behind closed barn doors, that horse tamer Daniel Sullivan was known to mysteriously tame and rehabilitate the most dangerous horses. However, what was hidden from the public was nothing more than a simple and unexceptional dominance technique. Sullivan would cause the horse to become immobile by tying up one of its legs with a soft rope.

Standing on only three legs and being unable to either kick or run from its tamer, the horse was swiftly rendered vulnerable and completely submissive. At this point, Sullivan would gently pet and stroke the horse and, in a calm, reassuring voice, softly speak words of kindness and affirmation.

Sullivan quickly established himself as the herd leader, or alpha horse, by controlling the ability of the other horse to either move or not move, without using the force, fear, intimidation, or pain of a traditional horse trainer and thus preventing the possibility of traumatizing the horse. By combining his human dominance with kindness and a soothing voice, Sullivan could do something remarkable: when the rope was untied and the horse could move again, Sullivan would open the barn door and, to the amazement of his audience, lead the previously dangerous horse out into the paddock like a puppy.

By not letting his spectators see what he was doing, Sullivan was able to build a magical reputation, performing what was truly a life-or-death encounter with a dangerous horse. He could also charge admission, which created a highly profitable business.

Although the attending crowds were unable to see what Sullivan was doing behind the barn doors, they could often hear his soft, gentle voice speaking to the horse in what sounded like a whisper. From that moment on, people naturally assumed that the dramatic change in the horse's behavior was the mysterious result of the horse tamer's whispers.

Sullivan was not the only renowned horse whisperer of that period. In fact, he was the inspiration for some of America's best-known horse tamers: John Rarey of Ohio, Oscar Gleason of New Hampshire, Willis Powell of New York, and Dennis Magner of Ireland and Pennsylvania.

There were great similarities in both the philosophies and the methods of all four of these trainers. They all stressed the importance of kindness, patience, gentleness, and perseverance. They all utilized the same methods of body language, touch, and feel that horses use to communicate with other horses. They were all able to control the horse's movement without using force, fear, intimidation, or pain.

For years, these gifted horsemen amazed countless others with their ability to tame not only problem horses but horses who had actually killed their previous trainers. Equally impressive was that any one of these horsemen could accomplish this miraculous transformation in such a limited amount of time. Some wrote of their methods in books; others traveled extensively, demonstrating their equine expertise.

Instead of using force, they would cause undesirable behavior to be uncomfortable and desirable behavior to be comfortable and allow the horse to make the choice. And, finally, they would establish themselves as the leader by maintaining total control over the horse's feet and their movement.

Horse whispering had nothing to do with whispering. It was the knowledge that one could control and train a horse with kindness, understanding, and communication by simply using the mental, physical, and emotional evolutionary nature and psychology of the species. Today this is referred to as natural horsemanship.

12

RIDING HOME

Not everyone likes horses. They're also not a silver bullet solution for healing every deep emotional or physical wound any human has. But there is scientific, psychological, biological, and experiential evidence that some of today's equine therapeutic programs are, and have been, making a profound difference by helping thousands of men, women, and children achieve life-altering emotional breakthroughs. The awareness and insights that a person can attain from simply interacting with a horse can create a psychological transformation, without which emotional recovery from a traumatic event is often difficult and sometimes impossible.

Everyone knows someone who needs help: a husband, a wife, a child, a friend, a troubled teenager, a war veteran with PTSD, someone with autism or an addiction or an eating disorder, a victim of sexual trauma—basically, anyone in emotional pain or who has lost their way. Helping one of these people on a personal level is undoubtedly important, but it is also vitally important on a societal level.

There is no cure for autism. Loving, raising, and coping with an autistic child can crush the very heart of a parent, condemning some to living in an endless state of fear and sadness. This is what Lynn, the mother of a seven-year-old autistic girl named Rachel, felt when she took her daughter to a horse farm as a last resort for healing.

In equine therapy, Rachel, for the first time in her life, felt acknowledged and accepted simply as a child, not as a child with autism. The fact that this acceptance came from a horse named Alfie made no difference to her. Alfie helped Rachel learn that she could trust another being and feel comfortable with herself; and by doing this with Alfie, she learned that she could do it with people.

After two years of ineffective talk therapy, fourteen-year-old Kyle Wilson finally saw his problem reflected back to him from a horse. Equine therapy provided a previously unavailable self-awareness that finally enabled him to perceive that the origin of what had become his painful and self-destructive life was himself.

The nonverbal rejection expressed to him in the behavior of a horse helped Kyle recognize his own inability to express his feelings of hurt and anger at his parents. He could thus understand that by not expressing these feelings that had been produced when his parents divorced, he had been self-destructively, though unconsciously, acting them out with his family, his friends, and his acquaintances at school, as well as by using drugs.

Unlike Kyle, Francis Kirkson did well in high school and was eager to do something meaningful with her life. She joined the

United States Marines, became a sergeant, and chose to go to the war in Iraq. She thought she could make a positive difference. She thought it would give her a sense of purpose and self-worth. She had no idea of how war devastates the very essence of everything that makes one human. But it wasn't the war; it was coming home from the war that almost killed her.

Her last traditional therapist had begun to feel hopeless and had considered giving up when Sergeant Kirkson, as if through providence, met a horse. The unconditional love and nonjudgmental acceptance Kirkson felt from establishing a relationship with a horse created a physical, mental, and emotional shift, enabling her to finally begin a meaningful recovery from her PTSD.

It is by no means an exaggeration to say that the simple experience of interacting with a horse created a transformation that not only helped save Francis Kirkson's life, it enabled her to build a new and rewarding one.

A twenty-three-year-old gang member from Los Angeles named Morris was serving fifteen to twenty-five years in a Colorado prison for killing another twenty-three-year-old, a man from a rival gang. Morris came from a world where all he knew was violence. He might have finished his sentence, left prison, gone back to his old life, and more than likely been sent back to prison for a new crime, had he not tried to tame a horse.

During this process, Morris saw that, just like him, though the horse was acting violently, he was in fact terrified. For the first time in his life, Morris felt something he had never known existed . . . compassion.

For a young man whose prospects for a rich and productive life were severely limited by his nearly nonexistent interpersonal skills, this was a transformational breakthrough. Seeing himself mirrored back by a horse was the beginning of an emotional healing for Morris. By establishing a positive relationship with this four-legged animal, Morris would dramatically increase his chances of creating positive human relationships and a meaningful life when he eventually returns to society.

Whether it's a man in prison for his uncontrollable violence, an autistic child who has never spoken a word, a high school dropout arrested for smoking marijuana, or a decorated war veteran ripped apart from PTSD and unable to care for himself or his family, many of society's wounded men, women, and children are recovering from deeply painful afflictions through the simple love, understanding, and acceptance that comes from establishing a relationship with a horse.

I believe that creating such a relationship has the power to do even more. Discovering who one is, how one fits into the world, and connecting with one's own humanity can begin long before a person is wounded or subjected to life-damaging traumas.

Most emotionally wounded men, women, and children are not born that way. Could spending time with a horse be an invitation to stop, even if just briefly, our addictive, compulsive, technologically driven lifestyle and remember that we, too, are just a speck in a miraculous world of nature that silently exists in an infinite universe?

In his landmark book, *Last Child in the Woods,* author Richard Louv describes a growing modern illness and its impact on children; he calls it "nature-deficit disorder." It is a real disorder, with symptoms such as diminished use of the senses, attention difficulties, and higher rates of physical and emotional illnesses.

In one study, when a fourth-grader was asked why he preferred to play indoors and not outside, he answered, "That's where all the electrical outlets are."

Today's technological brilliance brings great rewards to our children but, paradoxically, it fosters in them even greater loss. Recent studies have discovered correlations between children with attention deficit/hyperactivity disorder (ADHD) and the amount of time spent indoors watching television or using a computer or some other technological toy. Millions of children and their parents struggle not only with the difficulties of ADHD and depression but even more with the painful side effects of Ritalin or Adderall, as well as other chemical remedies prescribed by their doctors.

Louv reports that recent studies have suggested that exposure to nature may actually reduce the symptoms of ADHD. In remembering his own childhood he says, "The woods were my Ritalin. Nature calmed me, focused me, and yet excited my senses."

He adds, "For children, nature comes in many forms. A newborn calf; a pet that lives or dies . . . whatever shape nature takes, it offers each child an older, larger world separate from parents. Unlike television, nature does not steal time; it amplifies it. Nature offers healing for a child living in a destructive family or neighborhood."

I believe that being outside to interact with horses is one of the most powerful ways to prevent and eliminate nature-deficit disorder. Horses are nature in one of its finest forms. They help and inspire children to learn, grow, and become healthy, functional adults.

In her groundbreaking book *Animals in Translation,* Dr. Temple Grandin says, "People were animals, too, once, and when we turned into human beings we gave something up. Being close to animals brings some of it back." She ends her book with: "I wish more kids could ride horses today. People and animals are supposed to be together. We spent a long time evolving together, and we used to be partners. Now people are cut off from animals unless they have a dog or a cat."

What if more children could spend time interacting with horses? Could horses help empower these young folks with both the self-worth and the sense of values necessary to overcome some of society's compulsive obsessions with power, materialism, and celebrity?

Stephanie Lockhart believes they can. She has created Natural Horsemanship for Children, one of the first equine programs that utilizes the relationship-building skills of natural horsemanship to empower children with more authentic self-worth and compassion, as well as a stronger sense of ethics and morality. Learning the textbook-perfect social skills of the herd dynamics of horses profoundly increases a child's ability to develop healthier human relationships.

Natural Horsemanship for Children introduces children of all ages to horses and teaches them how to safely interact and create equine relationships. This enables these children to acquire the same love, trust, respect, and compassion that is naturally inherent in the herd dynamics of horses and then utilize these abilities with their parents, their friends, and in all of their other human relationships.

Stephanie Lockhart is the founder and program director at the Center for America's First Horse, in Johnson, Vermont. (For more information about the Center for America's First Horse, see the Appendix.)

For reasons that are both unique yet now comprehensible, a relationship with a horse can remarkably change a human from the inside out. Horses help us discover hidden parts of ourselves, whether we're seven or seventy. They model relationships that demonstrate acceptance, kindness, honesty, tolerance, patience, justice, compassion, and forgiveness. Learning to practice these qualities, which occur naturally in equine relationships, is available to all children, regardless of their family of origin.

Horses cause all of us to become better people, better parents, better partners, and better friends. And this amazing ability of horses to heal by teaching us about ourselves is accessible to anyone.

The equanimity of the horse, which naturally exists in equine society, is identical to something that has been known by and taught to humans for centuries. Stated simply, in order to survive and flourish, horses are born with a natural ability to know how to treat each other the exact way they want to be treated. Though written about, preached, and often taught to humans by their parents and others over countless generations, this "Golden Rule" has largely been lost or forgotten in the world we live in today.

Horses have supported and contributed to the survival of humans more than any other animal. And today, when war, addictions, shattered families, and technological advancements all conspire to depersonalize twenty-first-century humans, the horse yet again comes to our rescue.

This remarkable creature can not only continue to serve humanity but can help heal our wounded, remind us of our connectedness to others, and ground us with love for ourselves and for all living things. The power of the horse will not be found by sitting on its back. It will be felt on the ground from its heart.

It is the hope of this author that anyone, adult or child, who wishes to take a break from what they already know and reach out to something new or different, something that may bring feelings of self-awareness, joy, wonder, humility, and peace of mind, as well as anyone who needs help in healing their emotional wounds, whether derived from painful families or parenting, the hopelessness of incarceration, the PTSD of war, or the debilitating effects of autism, will now know that there's another way.

Welcome to the healing power of the twenty-first-century horse.

ACKNOWLEDGMENTS

Sitting down to write a book, especially one's first book, is daunting. Although it is only you, your thoughts, and the ever-intimidating blank pages, you do not accomplish it alone. When I think about the people who helped me in ways large and small, I am deeply moved and profoundly grateful. They have all come from different parts of my life. They are all important. They are all somewhere in these pages.

ROBERT REDFORD

Thank you for your kind and generous words. Your heartfelt support is of tremendous help in guiding men, women, and children to the love and remarkable healing power of horses. For many years I have greatly admired your transformative contributions to film, Native Americans, and our environment. Thank you for everything you have given to our world. I am forever grateful.

THE LITERARY PROFESSIONALS

To be represented by a literary agent is enormously rewarding. For him to be one of the most accomplished and respected in the New York City world of publishing has been an unexpected privilege. Thank you, Al Zuckerman and Writers House, for believing I had something worthwhile to say.

Thanks to everyone at St. Martin's Press and a special thank-you to my editor, Daniela Rapp. Your gifts and skill in helping shape my manuscript were invaluable. To be recognized and published by you and St. Martin's Press has not only been amazing, it has been an honor. A thank-you to Lisa Davis and Bonnie Thompson for your editing prowess and for protecting me from all of my misplaced modifiers and dangling participles. And thank you, Elisa Rivlin, for your thoughtful and gentle guidance in all matters legal.

Thank you, Tom Martin, for introducing me to your uncle Bill Martin, and thank you, Bill Martin and Beverly Zwerling of Agent Research & Evaluation. Bill, your wisdom, your generous heart, and your lifelong dedication to helping others was the inspiration that led me to focus my book on the healing power of horses. Beverly, your talents as an editor as well as an accomplished and successful author were unparalleled in helping me prepare my manuscript proposal. Thank you, Colin Harrison of Scribner and Jennifer Gates of Zachary Shuster Harmsworth, for your kindness and encouragement.

Years ago, I told my friend the esteemed literary agent Loretta Barrett how I had discovered horses and how they had changed my life. She immediately urged me to write a book about it. If it hadn't been for Loretta, I don't know if this journey would have begun. I will always be profoundly grateful for all her time, efforts, guidance, and support.

THE HUMAN STORIES

This book would not exist without the real-life men, women, children, and families who unflinchingly revealed to me some of their most personal and often painful life experiences. I am profoundly grateful to all of them. Each one allowed me the privilege of conveying to others the extraordinary healing they each experienced by simply interacting and creating a relationship with a horse.

To the incomparable brave souls of our American military. To the people who hit a wall of hurt in their life and needed to find another way. To those born with an additional physical or emotional challenge in their ability to realize or to obtain self-love, happiness, and peace of mind. I thank you all for sharing your courage, your honesty, your love, and your service to humanity. And although you may never know who they are, there will be many others who will be deeply grateful to you for your loving and selfless contributions to this book.

THE HORSE AND HUMAN HEALERS

A thank-you to Temple Grandin, your brilliant work, your remarkable discoveries, and all that you have contributed to help people, animals, and the world of autism.

Multiple thank-yous to Taylor Dawson, Kyle Martin, Shauna Smith, and the Wounded Warrior Project for everything you do for our veterans and for helping me with this book; to Liz Adams, Barbara Abrams, and everyone at the High Hopes therapeutic riding programs for all your help and generosity; to Hearts and Horses and, especially, to Tamara Merritt for your time, effort, and invaluable help into the world of equine healing.

Thanks to Jean Desranleau, Mary Willmuth, Roger Gibbons, Jo Guerrieri, and everyone else at CHAMP's equine therapeutic program at Good Hope Farm for all your help, and to Katie Kilcommons-McGowan, Jamie Thomas-Martin, and everyone else at HorseAbility Center for Equine Facilitated Programs. A thank-you to Ellen Lear and everyone at Pal-O-Mine Equestrian, Inc.

Many thanks to the Center for America's First Horse and its entire staff: Stephanie Lockhart, Mary Anne Machis, Elsie M. Brennan,

Deirdre O'Malley, Janis Cooper, and Cher Feitelberg, for all you do with horses and children; to In Balance Ranch Academy and all that you do to heal humans with horses; and to Wyatt Webb and the unique gift you have created with the Equine Experience at Miraval.

THE RANCHERS, THE COWBOYS, THE HORSEMEN

If it weren't for Linda and Kyle Hesthag, Okie and Misty McDowell, and their horse Spot, I would never have discovered my connection to horses. I am forever grateful to all of them and for bringing me to the Joseph Black & Sons cattle ranch and the Black families of Idaho: Jay, Penny, Mark, and Scott; Chris, Dixie, Joseph, Justin, and Bridget; as well as cowboys Joel Herrmann and Jeremy Mink.

The Blacks: with their ranches, their horses, and their kindness and generosity, not only did they allow me to work and live as a cowboy, they showed me a way of life that is as right, true, and loving as any I have ever known.

Thank you, Rusty and Diane Leaver of Deep Hollow Ranch of Montauk, New York. The many years I spent working with you, your horses, and your magnificent ranch added greatly to my understanding of the relationship between horses and humans.

Thank you to Brian Hardin and to everyone else from the Wild Horse Inmate Program and the U.S. Bureau of Land Management. The work and achievements you produce with horses and humans are magical and a gift to all of those you help.

I have been extremely fortunate to have befriended and learned from the master horsemen who gave rise to what is known in the twenty-first century as natural horsemanship: the late Tom Dorrance, the late Ray Hunt, Larry Mahan, Pat Parelli, Buck Brannaman, Mark Rashid, Dr. Robert Miller, Jack Brainard, Richard Shrake, and David Ellis. Thank you all for all your wisdom and your unparalleled knowledge of the horse. You not only showed me how the horse could help me become a better human, you have all made the world a better home for the horse.

THE FRIENDS

I have been blessed with lifelong friends who gave me their time and loving support and helped me create a book that could be published: Gus Waite and his family, Meaghen Lewis Damato, Cynthia and Patrick O'Neal, Richard and Diane Robbins, David Frankel, Jim Miller, Peter Emerson, Gerry Cooney, Brian Decubellis, Christopher and LuAnne Hormel, Gary Gatza, Dan Solin, Nancy Rosanoff, Emily Kyzok, and especially my dear friend Donna Kail, who, along with a brilliant Joyce Deep, graciously helped in bringing a magnanimous, one-of-kind foreword to this book. I also want to thank Carl Bernstein, a special friend, an American hero, and a Pulitzer Prize–winning writer, who graciously guided me in reporting my first story from the Wild Horse Inmate Program in Cañon City, Colorado. And, last, my entire journey would not have been possible without the wisdom, love, and service of Bill Wilson and Dr. Bob Smith.

THE FAMILY

Horses can't survive without their herd, and I could not have made it without the incredible love and support of my family. My love and infinite gratitude goes out to my son, Dr. Richard Hayes, for loving me with all my annoying fatherly clichés, and to my amazing brothers and their families: Dennis and Marta Hayes, Chris Hayes, Kerry, Maggie, Ali, Zoe, and Piper Hayes. Much love to my dear cousins the Grabar-Sage family for always being there for me—thank you, Nick, Jen, Henry, Olivia, and Margaret.

Most important and special has been the support and contributions of my fiancée and life partner, Stephanie Lockhart, and her one-of-a-kind daughters, Tori and Eliza. It is with Stephanie that I have finally found the love I have searched for my whole life. It is the same remarkable love that horses give to each other and that I have written about in these pages.

Last but not least, I want to thank my teacher, my partner, and my friend Austin. It was Austin who taught me that to be a better human I just needed to be a better horse.

THE WRITING PLACES

This entire book has been written on a laptop in many different public settings. I never write at home; it's too distracting. I have always felt more comfortable writing in rooms with other people who are writing or reading. I am deeply grateful to the following places, which over time have provided me with peaceful havens for writing: the Writers Room and Poets House of New York City; Steve Truso and the Green Mountain Inn of Stowe, Vermont; the libraries of East Hampton, Bridgehampton, and Southampton, New York, and the Johnson State College and Morrisville libraries of Vermont; the Lovin' Cup Café of Johnson, Vermont; and, last but not least, the Starbucks locations everywhere, and to the company's brilliant creator Howard Schultz for his compassionate donation to U.S. veterans suffering with PTSD as well as for all things that make the world a better place for humans.

APPENDIX

EQUINE RESOURCES IN THE UNITED STATES

The following organizations (listed alphabetically) are available to help people connect with a wide range of equine programs, including not only equine-assisted therapy but also programs for self-discovery, personal growth, and reconnection with the natural world. Contact any of these organizations for assistance or to locate a program or branch in your area.

American Hippotherapy Association (AHA)
www.americanhippotherapyassociation.org
877-851-4592

AHA is part of the international community that provides education, facilitates research, and promotes equine-assisted therapy as an effective treatment strategy for improving the quality of life for individuals with disabilities.

Autism Society
www.autism-society.org
301-657-0881 or 800-328-8476

The Autism Society exists to improve the lives of all people affected by autism. It increases public awareness and provides the latest information regarding treatment, education, research, and advocacy.

Autism Speaks
www.autismspeaks.org
888-288-4762 or 212-252-8584

Autism Speaks is the world's largest autism advocacy organization. It sponsors autism research and conducts awareness and outreach activities aimed at families, governments, and the public. It is a resource for equine-assisted therapy programs that work with children with autism.

The Center for America's First Horse—Natural Horsemanship for Children Session
www.centerforamericasfirsthorse.org
802-730-5400

Equine Assisted Growth and Learning Association (EAGALA)
www.eagala.org
877-858-4600

EAGALA is an international nonprofit association that provides education, standards, innovation, and support for addressing mental health and human development needs in the fields of equine-assisted psychotherapy and equine-assisted learning. EAGALA has more than four thousand members in forty-nine countries.

Horses for Heroes
www.horsesforheroes.org
505-798-2535

Horses for Heroes fosters recovery for wounded veterans, including those suffering from PTSD. Information is available from the following three organizations:

PATH International Equine Services for Heroes
http://www.pathintl.org/resources-education/path-intl-equine-services
-for-heroes
800-369-7433

U.S. Department of Veterans Affairs
http://www.va.gov/health/NewsFeatures/20110106a.asp
800-827-1000

Wounded Warrior Project
www.woundedwarriorproject.org
877-832-6997

Miraval and the Equine Experience
www.miravalresorts.com
800-825-4000

National Association of Therapeutic Schools and Programs (NATSAP)
natsap.wordpress.com
301-986-8770

NATSAP serves as a resource for programs and professionals assisting
young people beleaguered by emotional and behavioral difficulties—or
"Youth at Risk." Members include more than one hundred fifty U.S. therapeutic and residential treatment schools, as well as wilderness, outdoor
therapeutic, young adult, and residential programs. A large number of
NATSAP's members offer programs in equine therapy.

**National Wild Horse and Burro Program, U.S. Bureau of Land
    Management**
http://www.blm.gov/wo/st/en/prog/whbprogram.html
866-468-7826

**Professional Association of Therapeutic Horsemanship (PATH)
    International**
www.pathintl.org
800-369-7433

PATH International members, instructors, and centers serve children and adults with a range of physical, emotional, behavioral, and cognitive challenges, through a variety of equine-assisted activity and therapy programs. The following is a very short list of conditions and challenges addressed every day through PATH International.

- Amputation
- At-risk behavior in youth
- Attention-deficit and other hyperactivity disorders
- Autism
- Cerebral palsy
- Developmental delay
- Down syndrome
- Emotional and behavioral difficulties
- Family dysfunction
- Grief
- Learning disabilities
- Multiple sclerosis
- Muscular dystrophy
- Paralysis
- Post-traumatic stress disorder (PTSD)
- Reactive attachment disorder
- Spina bifida
- Spinal cord injury
- Stroke
- Substance addiction and abuse
- Terminal illness
- Traumatic brain injury
- Visual and auditory impairment
- Weight-control disorder

Wild Horse Inmate Program (WHIP)
https://www.coloradoci.com/serviceproviders/whip/
800-685-7891

The following treatment centers, therapeutic riding venues, and equine therapy organizations (all listed alphabetically) are members of either PATH International or NATSAP. They were invaluable in providing their time and contributions for the creation of this book and can be contacted directly for information and support.

BraveHearts Therapeutic Riding and Educational Center
www.braveheartsriding.org
815-943-8226

Caron Treatment Centers for Trauma and Addiction
www.caron.org
800-854-6023

CHAMP (Champlain Adaptive Mounted Program) at Good Hope Farm
http://www.vtchamp.org/boarding.html
802-372-4087

Hearts and Horses Therapeutic Riding Center
www.heartsandhorses.org
970-663-4200

High Hopes Therapeutic Riding Inc.
www.highhopestr.org
860-434-1974

HorseAbility, Center for Equine Facilitated Programs
www.horseability.org
516-333-6151

In Balance Ranch Academy
www.inbalanceranch.com
877-304-3329

The Meadows Treatment Center for Trauma and Addiction
www.themeadows.com
800-632-3697

Onsite (treatment center for trauma and addiction)
https://onsiteworkshops.com
800-341-7432

Pal-O-Mine Equestrian, Inc.
www.pal-o-mine.org
631-348-1389

Pegasus Therapeutic Riding Academy
www.pegasusridingacademy.com
215-742-1500

GLOBAL EQUINE RESOURCES

Therapeutic riding and equine therapy organizations are also available globally. They include the following:

GLOBALLY

EAGALA Around the World
www.eagala.org/Global
801-754-0400

Professional Association of Therapeutic Horsemanship (PATH) International
www.pathintl.org/path-intl-centers/find-center
800-369-7433

AUSTRALIA, NEW ZEALAND, NEW GUINEA, AND ASIA PACIFIC ISLANDS

Equine Assisted Growth and Learning Association (EAGALA)
www.eagala.org/Australasia
0448-762-184

CANADA

Autism Speaks Canada
www.autismspeaks.ca
416-362-6227

Equine Assisted Growth and Learning Association (EAGALA)
www.eagala.org/Canada
613-489-5294 or 403-934-3046

Wounded Warrior Project Canada
woundedwarriors.ca/contact-us
888-706-4808 or 905-430-9419

IRELAND

Equine Assisted Growth and Learning Association (EAGALA)
www.eagala.org/Ireland
353(0) 87-6822093

NETHERLANDS

Equine Assisted Growth and Learning Association (EAGALA)
www.eagala.org/Netherlands
31 650 278895

SOUTH AFRICA

Equine Assisted Growth and Learning Association (EAGALA)
www.eagala.org/SAfrica
084-500-0672

UNITED KINGDOM

Equine Assisted Growth and Learning Association (EAGALA)
www.eagala.org/UK
07956 448777

The National Autistic Society
www.autism.org.uk
+44 (0) 20 7833 2299

Strength in Horses Equine Assisted Therapy
www.sihequinetherapy.org.uk
07532 207198

NOTES

Discussions in this book of the WHIP inmates; of the Equine Experience participants at Miraval; of program personnel, therapy patients, and their families; and of the various equine therapeutic sessions are all based on the experiences of individuals who generously shared their stories with me in personal interviews. While I have placed my accounts at real therapeutic centers and facilities, and have reported stories based on what I observed or learned of these programs, I have in no instances been given any patient information by these centers or facilities.

In conveying these accounts, I have changed names and other identifying details, and in some instances have created a composite character. What has not been changed or altered are the actual personal breakthroughs, transformations, and emotional healings that occurred as a result of the relationships created by these individuals with their horses.

Research sources for this book have included books, journals, magazines, newspapers, organizations, institutions, and websites. These are given here, broken down by chapter and tied to a key phrase in the text. All online information was retrieved on December 20, 2013.

1. WILD HORSES—WILD MEN

8   **The Wild Horse Inmate Program was originally set up:** "Colorado Wild Horse Inmate Program," Bureau of Land Management, Colorado, U.S. Department of the Interior, http://www.blm.gov/co/st/en/BLM_Programs/wild_horse_and_burro/Wild_Horse_Inmate_Program_Colorado.print.html.

9   **Cañon City, Colorado, prisons, as well as other BLM WHIP programs:** A current list of WHIP programs can be found at "Prison Wild Horse Training Programs," Mustangs4Us, http://www.mustangs4us.com/Adopt%20Section/prisonhorses.htm.

19   **within three years of their release:** Information on U.S. rates of prison recidivism is from "U.S. Prisons Overcrowded and Violent, Recidivism High," InfoPlease database, http://www.infoplease.com/ipa/A0933722.html.

20   **recidivism rate for inmates from the Wild Horse Inmate Program:** Alysia Patterson, "At Colo. Prison, Wild Horses Tame the Inmates," Associated Press, March 12, 2009, http://www.utsandiego.com/news/2009/mar/12/taming-mustangs-taming-prisoners-031209/all/?print; and *Colorado Correctional Industries,* brochure, https://www.coloradoci.com/bin-pdf/CCibrochure.pdf.

2. THE NATURE OF HORSES—THE NATURE OF HUMANS

21   **we must first know the horse:** The works of Stephen Budiansky and Dr. Robert M. Miller often overlap in their equine history and research. For many years, they have been invaluable sources of equine knowledge; I called on both these books throughout this chapter: Stephen Budiansky, *The Nature of Horses* (New York: Free Press, 1997); and Robert M. Miller, *The Ancient Secrets of the Horse's Mind* (Neenah, WI: Russell Meerdink Co., 1999).

37   **in 1890, Oscar Gleason:** Oscar Gleason, *Practical Treatise on the Breaking and Taming of Wild and Vicious Horses* (Scranton, PA: Prof. O. R. Gleason, Printer and Publisher, 1890).

37 **"The two controlling passions of a horse's nature":** Gleason is quoted in Emily Kilby, "Secrets of the Horse Tamers," *Equus Magazine,* June 1998, p. 43.

54 **"The horse is never wrong":** Quoted in Robert M. Miller and Rick Lamb, *The Revolution in Horsemanship* (Guilford, CT: Lyons Press, 2005), p. 27.

3. HORSES HEALING HUMANS . . . BODIES AND MINDS

57 **Miraval . . . offers what it calls the Equine Experience:** For information on Miraval and its creator, see "Wyatt Webb: Creator of the Equine Experience" and "The Miraval Equine Experience: Immersion with Wyatt Webb," both at http://www.miravalresorts .com/plan_your_stay/specialists/wyatt_webb.

60 **the only "therapeutic" use of horses I knew was . . . hippotherapy:** Allen C. Bowling, "Hippotherapy and Therapeutic Horseback Riding," *Neurology Care* (blog), April 27, 2011, http://www .neurologycare.net/hippotherapy-and-therapeutic-horseback -riding.html.

62 **equine-assisted therapy, or . . . equine therapy:** A good synopsis of the transition from hippotherapy to equine-assisted therapy can be found in Carol O'Connor, "The Silent Therapist: A Review of the Development of Equine Assisted Psychotherapy," which appears on the Capital Area Therapeutic Riding Association's website, at http://www.catra.net/info/silent.html.

66 **"focusing" or using a "felt sense":** Eugene Gendlin, *Focusing,* 2nd ed. (New York: Bantam Books, 2007), pp. 58–74. For more information on focusing, see also Ann Weiser Cornell, *The Radical Acceptance of Everything* (Los Angeles, CA: Calluna Press, 2005), p. 13; and Ann Weiser Cornell and Barbara McGavin, *The Focusing Student's and Companion's Manual, Part One* (Los Angeles, CA: Calluna Press, 2008).

72 **a horse is a mirror of one's own personality:** Information of mirroring is from D. M. Romano, "A Self-Psychology Approach to

Narcissistic Personality Disorder: A Nursing Reflection," *Perspectives in Psychiatric Care* 40, no. 1 (2004): 20–28, http://onlinelibrary .wiley.com/doi/10.1111/ppc.2004.40.issue-1/issuetoc.

76 **Mirror neurons reside in the brain:** Information on mirror neurons is from Giacomo Rizzolatti and Laila Craighero, "The Mirror-Neuron System," *Annual Review of Neuroscience* 27 (2004): 169–92, http://www.annualreviews.org. I also consulted Christian Keysers, "Mirror Neurons," *Current Biology* 19, no. 21 (2009): R971–973, http://www.sciencedirect.com/science/article/pii/S09609822090 16005.

4. HORSES DON'T GET DIVORCED . . . TODAY'S YOUTH AT RISK

Information on divorce in this chapter comes from Cynthia Harper and Sara S. McLanahan, "Father Absence and Youth Incarceration," *Journal of Research on Adolescence* 14, no. 3 (2004): 369–97, http://www.gwu.edu/~pad/202/father.pdf. I also consulted sources that dealt with the absence of fathers and its effect on their children: Wayne Parker, "Statistics on Fatherless Children in America," About.com, http://fatherhood.about.com/od/fathersrights/a/father less_children.htm; and "Life without a Father: Does It Really Matter?" PreventingDivorce.com, http://www.preventingdivorce.com /life_without_father.htm. Studies and research on divorce and its effects on children appear on the website for Americans for Divorce Reform, www.divorcereform.org.

94 **Recent U.S. government statistics report:** See Matthew Lynch, "High School Dropouts: More Than Loss of Money," *Education Futures* (blog), *Education Week*, October 28, 2013, http://blogs .edweek.org/edweek/education_futures/2013/10/high_school _dropouts_more_than_loss_of_money.html?qs=high +school+dropouts; Matthew Lynch, "High School Dropout Rate: Causes and Costs," *Education Futures* (blog), *Education Week*, November 6, 2013, http://blogs.edweek.org/edweek/education_futures /2013/11/high_school_dropout_rate_causes_and_costs.html

?qs=high+school+dropouts; "Fast Facts: Dropout Rates," Institute of Education Sciences, National Center for Education Statistics, http://nces.ed.gov/fastfacts/display.asp?id=16; "High School Drop-out Statistics," Statistic Brain, http://www.statisticbrain.com/high -school-dropout-statistics/; and website for the Alliance for Excellent Education, all4ed.org.

94 **The United Nations has defined Youth at Risk:** "Definition of Urban Youth at Risk," UN-Habitat, United Nations Human Settlements Program, http://ww2.unhabitat.org/programmes/safercities /uyr.asp.

95 **in 2011, there were 24,718,000 children:** "Children in Single-Parent Families," Kids Count Data Center, Annie E. Casey Foundation, http://datacenter.kidscount.org/data/tables/106-children-in -single-parent-families?loc=1&loct=2#ranking/1/any/true/867/any /430.

99 **a term coined by the eminent British psychoanalyst . . . our "false self":** Information on the "false self" is from D. W. Winnicott, *The Maturational Process and the Facilitating Environment: Studies in the Theory of Emotional Development* (New York: International Universities Press, 1965), pp. 140–52.

6. THE WALKING WOUNDED—HORSES FOR HEROES

Information about post-traumatic stress disorder and the *DSM-5* criteria for PTSD in this chapter was accessed from "What Is PTSD?" PTSD: National Center for PTSD, U.S. Department of Veterans Affairs, http://www.ptsd.va.gov/public/pages/what-is-ptsd .asp; and "DSM-5 Diagnostic Criteria for PTSD Released," PTSD: National Center for PTSD, U.S. Bureau of Veterans Affairs, http:// www.ptsd.va.gov/professional/pages/diagnostic_criteria_dsm -5.asp.

147 **In 2013 . . . between 300,000 and 400,000 veterans in the United States:** The 2013 statistics on the number of veterans with PTSD and their suicide rates were retrieved from "Shocking PTSD, Suicide Rates for Vets," Face the Facts USA, George Washington

University, June 5, 2013, http://www.facethefactsusa.org/facts/the
-true-price-of-war-in-human-terms; and "Who We Serve," Wounded
Warrior Project, http://www.woundedwarriorproject.org/mission
/who-we-serve.aspx.

147 **In 2011, the *New York Times* reported that . . . drugs for treating veterans:** Information on ineffective drugs and their side effects for veterans with PTSD from Benedict Carey, "Drugs Found Ineffective for Veterans' Stress," *New York Times,* August 2, 2011, http://www.nytimes.com/2011/08/03/health/research/03psych.html.

7. HORSES, HUMANS, TRAUMA, AND PTSD

149 **What is diagnosed as PTSD in today's military is not new:** The brief history of PTSD from Thomas C. Weiss, "Post-Traumatic Stress Disorder (PTSD) Facts and Treatment," *Disabled World News,* updated September 16, 2010, at http://www.disabledworld.com/disability/types/psychological/ptsd.php#ixzz2JyFMMkVj.

150 **In 2013, the American Psychiatric Association published the fifth edition:** Information on diagnostic criteria for PTSD from "DSM-5 Diagnostic Criteria for PTSD Released," PTSD: National Center for PTSD, U.S. Department of Veterans Affairs, http://www.ptsd.va.gov/professional/pages/diagnostic_criteria_dsm-5.asp.

151 **children walking around in the bodies of grown-ups:** Dr. Tian Dayton, "What Is an ACoA?," *Huffington Post,* February 13, 2011, http://www.huffingtonpost.com/dr-tian-dayton/what-is-an-acoa_b_822493.html. See also Dr. Tian Dayton, "Adult Children of Alcoholics ACoAs: Qualities and Traits," *Huffington Post,* September 25, 2009, http://www.huffingtonpost.com/dr-tian-dayton/adult-children-of-alcohol_b_300572.html.

151 **The symptoms of PTSD can be experienced throughout childhood:** For further reading, an excellent source of information on PTSD in children and adolescents is Raul R. Silva, *Post-Traumatic Stress Disorders in Children and Adolescents: Handbook* (New York: W. W. Norton, 2004).

153   **similar to what occurs when a combat veteran hears a car engine backfire:** Bessel A. van der Kolk, "Post Traumatic Childhood," *New York Times,* May 10, 2011, http://www.nytimes.com/2011/05 /11/opinion/11kolk.html.

153   **Painful childhood feelings that remain unconscious:** The work of John Bradshaw proved very useful. For many years, I've found his book *Homecoming: Reclaiming and Championing Your Inner Child* (New York: Bantam Books, 1990) an invaluable source of information on healthy parenting and healing one's wounded childhood.

154   **Whether the original wound is caused by a raging father or a roadside bomb:** Eamon McCrory, "Maltreated Children Show Same Pattern of Brain Activity as Combat Soldiers," University College London, *UCL News,* December 5, 2011, http://www.ucl.ac.uk/news /news-articles/1112/111205-maltreated-children-fMRI-study.

154   **horses are able to initiate the healing of PTSD:** Levine's trauma research is in Peter A. Levine, *Waking the Tiger: Healing Trauma* (Berkeley, CA: North Atlantic Books, 1997).

155   **three options: fight, flight, or freeze:** Thwarted physical energy and the surge of brain chemicals is in Daniel Goleman, "A Key to Post-Traumatic Stress Lies in Brain Chemistry, Scientists Find," *New York Times,* June 12, 1990, http://www.nytimes.com/1990/06 /12/science/a-key-to-post-traumatic-stress-lies-in-brain-chemistry -scientists-find.html?pagewanted=all&src=pm.

8. "I WISH PEOPLE HAD EARS LIKE HORSES"

Information in this chapter on the autism spectrum is from "Autism: Symptoms, Causes and Treatment—an Interview with Glenn S. Hirsch, M.D.," AboutOurKids.org, NYU Child Study Center, http://www.aboutourkids.org/articles/autism_symptoms_causes _treatment.

164   **One difficult symptomatic behavior . . . is called "stimming":** "What Autistic People Do to Feel Calmer," *Ouch* (blog), BBC

News, June 4, 2013, http://www.bbc.co.uk/news/blogs-ouch-2277 1894.

165 **Emergency foster care parents are specialists:** "Emergency Foster Care," Adoption.com, http://www.fosterparenting.com/foster-care /emergency-foster-care.html.

165 **Foster children range in age from infants to teenagers:** "Too Many Children Are Trapped in Foster Care," Facts About Foster Care, Children's Rights.org, http://www.childrensrights.org/issues -resources/foster-care/facts-about-foster-care; "Facts for Foster Parents," Indiana Department of Child Services, http://www.in.gov/dcs /files/DCS_FosterFactsSheet09-07.pdf.

165 **might be suffering from RAD, or reactive attachment disorder:** "Definition: Reactive Attachment Disorder," Diseases and Conditions, The Mayo Foundation for Medical Education and Research, http://www.mayoclinic.com/health/reactive-attachment -disorder/DS00988.

166 **thought to be symptoms of reactive attachment disorder:** For information on discriminating between reactive attachment disorder and autism, see "Discriminating Reactive Attachment Disorder from Autism Spectrum Disorder: Key Symptoms and Clinical Characteristics," International Meeting for Autism Research, International Society for Autism Research, https://imfar.confex.com /imfar/2011/webprogram/Paper9121.html; and "Reactive Attachment Disorder (RAD): Signs & Symptoms," The Child Study Center, New York University, http://www.aboutourkids.org/families /disorders_treatments/az_disorder_guide/reactive_attachment _disorder/signs_symptoms.

173 **now considered the fastest-growing developmental disability in the United States:** "Facts about Autism," Autism Speaks, http:// www.autismspeaks.org/what-autism/facts-about-autism; and "Facts and Statistics," Autism Society, http://www.autism-society.org /about-autism/facts-and-statistics.html.

174 **Dr. Temple Grandin:** Temple Grandin and Catherine Johnson, *Animals in Translation* (New York: Scribner, 2005). For more on Temple Grandin, see Christine Hamilton, "On Horses and Autism:

Temple Grandin, Ph.D., Uses Her Autism to Gain Insights into Equine Behavior," *America's Horse Daily,* March 22, 2011, http:// americashorsedaily.com/on-horses-and-autism.

174   **"I have had a number of parents tell me":** Grandin quoted in Tara Parker-Pope, "Healing Autism with Horses," *New York Times,* April 14, 2009, http://well.blogs.nytimes.com/2009/04/14/healing -autism-with-horses.

175   **She refers to them both as being "hyperspecific":** Temple Grandin and Catherine Johnson, *Animals Make Us Human: Creating the Best Life for Animals* (New York: Houghton-Mifflin Harcourt, 2009). An excerpt from Chapter 4, "Hyper-Specific Fear Memories and How to Handle Them in Horses," is from http://www .grandin.com/inc/animals.make.us.human.ch4.html.

175   **fear is the main emotion in both autistic people and prey animals:** Temple Grandin, "Thinking the Way Animals Do," *Western Horseman,* November 1997, pp. 140–45, http://www.grandin.com /references/thinking.animals.html.

177   **Andrew Solomon's brilliant *Far from the Tree*:** Andrew Solomon, *Far from the Tree: Parents, Children, and the Search for Identity* (New York: Scribner, 2012); see especially Chapter 5, on autism, pp. 221–94.

178   **"autism spectrum disorder" as a neurodevelopmental disorder:** *Diagnostic and Statistical Manual of Mental Disorders,* 5th ed. (Arlington, VA: American Psychiatric Publishing, 2013); see esp. p. 62.

9. WHAT DRAWS HUMANS TO BE WITH HORSES?

185   **Buck Brannaman was one of these horsemen:** *Buck,* directed by Cindy Meehl, Cindy, Sundance Selects, 2011. Quotes from Buck Brannaman are from Christopher Middleton, "The Horse Whisperer: My Dad Taught Me to Understand Fear," *Telegraph,* April 17, 2012, http://www.telegraph.co.uk/culture/tvandradio /9206938/The-horse-whisperer-My-dad-taught-me-to-understand -fear.html.

190 **There are approximately sixty million horses in the world:** From a March 2013 study by the Food and Agriculture Organization of the United States, reported by the Ultimate Horse Site, http://www.ultimatehorsesite.com/info/horsequestions/hq_number ofhorses.htm.

193 **According to a 2012 . . . Equine Industry Survey:** C. J. Stowe, "Results from 2012 AHP Equine Industry Survey: American Horse Publications," http://www.americanhorsepubs.org/news_updates /9578.asp.

196 **"hypermasculinity" was coined to describe . . . "macho":** Donald L. Mosher and Silvan S. Tomkins, "Scripting the Macho Man: Hypermasculine Socialization and Enculturation," *Journal of Sex Research* 25, no. 1 (1984): 60–84, http://www.beyondutopia .net/leadership-lectures/tomkins-1.pdf.

198 **cites endless examples of the . . . need to trust one's intuition:** Malcolm Gladwell, *Blink: The Power of Thinking Without Thinking* (New York: Little, Brown, 2005).

198 **creativity, compassion, and intuitiveness . . . originates in the right:** From Daniel H. Pink, *A Whole New Mind: Why Right-Brainers Will Rule the Future* (New York: Riverhead Books, 2005).

199 **"Intuition becomes increasingly valuable":** John Naisbitt, *Megatrends: Ten New Directions Transforming Our Lives* (New York: Warner Books, 1982).

199 **"the intuitive mind is a sacred gift":** Albert Einstein quote from GoodReads.com, http://www.goodreads.com/author/quotes/9810 .Albert_Einstein.

199 **"That which is most personal is most common":** This quote is often attributed to Carl Jung. According to the C. G. Jung Center of New York, there is no record of Dr. Jung having written or said this. They have suggested that over the years it may have been confused with a quote from another well-known psychologist, Dr. Carl R. Rogers, from his book *On Becoming a Person: A Therapist's View of Psychotherapy* (New York: Houghton Mifflin Company, 1961). On page 26, Dr. Rogers wrote, "What is most personal is most universal."

10. AUSTIN

200 **"I spent my youth looking for the perfect woman"**: I have added the two cowboys, "Tom" and "Dave," to this story, which I originally found in Rick Fields et al., *Chop Wood, Carry Water* (New York: Jeremy P. Tarcher/Putnam, 1984), p. 35.

203 **hardwired necessity of the human brain to give meaning**: Walter J. Freeman, "How and Why Brains Create Meaning from Sensory Information," *International Journal of Bifurcation and Chaos* 14 (2004): 513–30, http://escholarship.org/uc/item/1fs73030.

11. THE EVOLUTION OF HORSEMANSHIP

221 **Comparing synonyms from a thesaurus**: The distinction between *intimidate* and *dominate* is from http://thesaurus.com.

227 **"What a horse does under compulsion he does blindly"**: The quote is from Xenophon, *The Art of Horsemanship* (Mineola, NY: Dover, 2006), p. 61.

229 **the principal foundation in the curriculum of the Spanish Riding School**: Further information on the school is available at http://www.srs.at/en.

229 **France's Le Cadre Noir, for instance**: Further information on the school is available at http://www.cadrenoir.co.uk.

233 **The American cowboy most often acknowledged**: For information on Tom Dorrance and natural horsemanship, see Tom Dorrance, *True Unity: Willing Communication Between Horse and Human* (Tuscarora, NV: Give-It-a-Go-Enterprises, 1987). See also Robert M. Miller and Rick Lamb, *The Revolution in Horsemanship* (Guilford, CT: Lyons Press, 2005), pp. 7, 27.

234 **"Make the wrong thing difficult and the right thing easy"**: Ray Hunt, *Think Harmony with Horses: An In-Depth Study of Horse/Man Relationship* (Tuscarora, NV: Give-It-a-Go Books, 1978), p. 87.

236 **"He must have the delicacy of touch and feeling of a woman"**: Dennis Magner, *Standard Horse and Stock Book* (New York: Saalfield Publishing Company, 1887), p. 50.

237 **The earliest accounts of what became referred to as horse whispering:** Emily Kilby, "Secrets of the Horse Tamers," *Equus Magazine,* June 1998, pp. 33–45.

12. RIDING HOME

243 **author Richard Louv ... calls it "nature-deficit disorder":** Richard Louv, *Last Child in the Woods: Saving Our Children from Nature-Deficit Disorder* (Chapel Hill, NC: Algonquin Books of Chapel Hill, 2005), pp. front matter, 7, 10.

244 **Millions of children and their parents struggle:** Daniel J. De-Noon, "Depression Drugs' Risks to Kids Kept Secret," WebMD Health News, April 22, 2004, http://www.webmd.com/depression /news/20040422/depression-drugs-risks-to-kids-kept-secret?last selectedguid=%7b5FE84E90-BC77-4056-A91C-9531713CA348 %7d.

244 **the painful side effects of Ritalin:** L. Alan Sroufe, "Ritalin Gone Wrong," *New York Times,* January 29, 2012, http://www.nytimes .com/2012/01/29/opinion/sunday/childrens-add-drugs-dont-work -long-term.html?_r=0.

244 **"People were animals, too, once":** Temple Grandin and Catherine Johnson, *Animals in Translation* (New York: Scribner, 2005), pp. 5, 307.

BIBLIOGRAPHY

BOOKS AND PERIODICALS

Bradshaw, John. *Homecoming: Reclaiming and Championing Your Inner Child*. New York: Bantam Books, 1990.

Budiansky, Stephen. *The Nature of Horses*. New York: Free Press, 1997.

Carey, Benedict. "Drugs Found Ineffective for Veterans' Stress." *New York Times*, August 2, 2011, p. A13.

Cornell, Ann Weiser. *The Radical Acceptance of Everything*. Los Angeles, CA: Calluna Press, 2005.

Cornell, Ann Weiser, and Barbara McGavin. *The Focusing Student's and Companion's Manual, Part One*. Los Angeles, CA: Calluna Press, 2008.

Dorrance, Tom. *True Unity: Willing Communication Between Horse and Human*: Clovis, CA: Give-It-a-Go-Enterprises, 1987.

Fields, Rick, et al. *Chop Wood, Carry Water*. New York: Jeremy P. Tarcher/Putnam, 1984.

Freeman, Walter J. "How and Why Brains Create Meaning from

Sensory Information." *International Journal of Bifurcation and Chaos* 14 (2004): 513–30.

Gendlin, Eugene. *Focusing.* 2nd ed. New York: Bantam Books, 2007.

Gladwell, Malcolm. *Blink: The Power of Thinking Without Thinking.* New York: Little, Brown, 2005.

Gleason, Oscar. *Practical Treatise on the Breaking and Taming of Wild and Vicious Horses.* Scranton, PA: Prof. O. R. Gleason, Printer and Publisher, 1890.

Goleman, Daniel. "A Key to Post-Traumatic Stress Lies in Brain Chemistry, Scientists Find." *New York Times,* June 12, 1990, p. C1.

Grandin, Temple, and Catherine Johnson. *Animals in Translation.* New York: Scribner, 2005.

———. *Animals Make Us Human: Creating the Best Life for Animals.* New York: Houghton Mifflin Harcourt, 2009.

Grandin, Temple. "Thinking the Way Animals Do." *Western Horseman,* November 1997, pp. 140–45.

Hamilton, Christine. "On Horses and Autism: Temple Grandin, Ph.D., Uses Her Autism to Gain Insights into Equine Behavior." *America's Horse Daily,* March 22, 2011. Online edition.

Hunt, Ray. *Think Harmony with Horses: An In-Depth Study of Horse/Man Relationship.* Bruneau, ID: Give-It-a-Go Books, 1978.

Keysers, Christian. "Mirror Neurons." *Current Biology* 19, no. 21 (2009): R971–73.

Kilby, Emily. "Secrets of the Horse Tamers." *Equus Magazine,* June 1998, pp. 33–45.

Levine, Peter A. *Waking the Tiger: Healing Trauma.* Berkeley, CA: North Atlantic Books, 1997.

Louv, Richard. *Last Child in the Woods: Saving Our Children from Nature-Deficit Disorder.* Chapel Hill, NC: Algonquin Books of Chapel Hill, 2005.

Magner, Dennis. *Standard Horse and Stock Book.* New York: Saalfield Publishing Company, 1887.

Miller, Robert M. *The Ancient Secrets of the Horse's Mind*. Neenah, WI: Russell Meerdink Co., 1999.

Miller, Robert M., and Rick Lamb. *The Revolution in Horsemanship*. Guilford, CT: Lyons Press, 2005.

Mosher, Donald L., and Silvan S. Tomkins. "Scripting the Macho Man: Hypermasculine Socialization and Enculturation." *Journal of Sex Research* 25, no. 1 (1984): 60–84.

Naisbitt, John. *Megatrends: Ten New Directions Transforming Our Lives*. New York: Warner Books, 1982.

Parelli, Pat, with Kathy Kadash. *Natural Horse-Man-Ship*. Fort Worth, TX: Western Horseman Publications, 1993.

Parker-Pope, Tara. "Healing Autism with Horses." *New York Times*, April 14, 2009. Online edition.

Pink, Daniel H. *A Whole New Mind: Why Right-Brainers Will Rule the Future*. New York: Riverhead Books, 2005.

Silva, Raul R. *Post-Traumatic Stress Disorders in Children and Adolescents: Handbook*. New York: W. W. Norton, 2004.

Solomon, Andrew. *Far from the Tree: Parents, Children, and the Search for Identity*. New York: Scribner, 2012.

Sroufe, L. Alan "Ritalin Gone Wrong," *New York Times*, January 29, 2012, p. SR1.

Winnicott, D. W. *The Maturational Process and the Facilitating Environment: Studies in the Theory of Emotional Development*. New York: International Universities Press, 1965.

Xenophon. *The Art of Horsemanship*. Mineola, NY: Dover, 2006.

WEBSITES AND ARTICLES BY CATEGORY

Information was retrieved on December 20, 2013.

ADHD and Prescription Drugs

DeNoon, Daniel J. "Depression Drugs' Risks to Kids Kept Secret: Unpublished Studies Show Most Antidepressants Risky, Ineffective in Children, Teens." WebMD Health News, April 22, 2004. http://www.webmd.com/depression/news/20040422/depression-drugs-risks-to-kids-kept-secret?lastselectedguid=%7b5FE84E90-BC77-4056-A91C-9531713CA348%7d.

Sroufe, L. Alan. "Ritalin Gone Wrong." *New York Times,* January 28, 2012. http://www.nytimes.com/2012/01/29/opinion/sunday/childrens-add-drugs-dont-work-long-term.html?_r=0.

Adult Children of Alcoholics

Dayton, Dr. Tian. "Adult Children of Alcoholics: ACOAs, Qualities and Traits." *Huffington Post,* September 25, 2009. http://www.huffingtonpost.com/dr-tian-dayton/adult-children-of-alcohol_b_300572.html.

———. "What Is an ACOA?" *Huffington Post,* February 13, 2011. http://www.huffingtonpost.com/dr-tian-dayton/what-is-an-acoa_b_822493.html.

Autism

"Autism: Symptoms, Causes, and Treatments: An Interview with Glenn S. Hirsch, MD." Langone Medical Center. The Child Study Center. http://www.aboutourkids.org/articles/autism_symptoms_causes_treatment.

"Facts about Autism." Autism Speaks Inc. http://www.autismspeaks.org/what-autism/facts-about-autism.

"Facts and Statistics." The Autism Society. http://www.autism-society
.org/about-autism/facts-and-statistics.

Parker-Pope, Tara. "Healing Autism with Horses." *New York Times,*
April 14, 2009. http://well.blogs.nytimes.com/2009/04/14/healing
-autism-with-horses.

Autism: Stimming

"Stimming: What Autistic People Do to Feel Calmer." *Ouch* (blog),
BBC News, June 5, 2013, http://www.bbc.co.uk/news/blogs-ouch
-22771894.

Buck Brannaman

Buck. Film directed by Cindy Meehl. http://buckthefilm.com.

Middleton, Christopher. "The Horse Whisperer: 'My Dad Taught Me
to Understand Fear.'" *The Telegraph,* April 17, 2012. http://www.tele
graph.co.uk/culture/tvandradio/9206938/The-horse-whisperer-My
-dad-taught-me-to-understand-fear.html.

Disadvantaged Children

Annie E. Casey Foundations. www.aecf.org.

Divorce

American Divorce Reform. www.divorcereform.org.

Divorce: Father Absence

Harper, Cynthia C., and Sara S. McLanahan. "Father Absence and
Youth Incarceration." *Journal of Research on Adolescence* 14, no. 3
(2004): 369–97. http://www.gwu.edu/~pad/202/father.pdf.

Parker, Wayne. "Statistics on Fatherless Children in America." About.com. http://fatherhood.about.com/od/fathersrights/a/fatherless_children.htm.

Equine-Assisted Therapy

O'Connor, Carol. "The Silent Therapist: A Review of the Development of Equine Assisted Therapy." Capital Area Therapeutic Riding Association, Inc. http://www.catra.net/info/silent.html.

Foster Care

"Emergency Foster Care." Adoption.com. http://www.fosterparenting.com/foster-care/emergency-foster-care.html.

"Facts about Foster Care: Too Many Children Are Trapped in Foster Care." Children's Rights. http://www.childrensrights.org/issues-resources/foster-care/facts-about-foster-care.

"Facts for Foster Parents." Brochure. Indiana Department of Child Services. http://www.in.gov/dcs/files/DCS_FosterFactsSheet09-07.pdf.

Temple Grandin

Grandin, Temple. "An Excerpt from Chapter 4: Horses." From *Animals Make Us Human*. New York: Houghton Mifflin Harcourt, 2009. http://www.grandin.com/inc/animals.make.us.human.ch4.html.

———. "On Horses and Autism." *America's Horse Daily*, March 22, 2011. http://americashorsedaily.com/on-horses-and-autism.

———. "Thinking the Way Animals Do." *Western Horseman*, November 1997, pp. 140–45. http://www.grandin.com/references/thinking.animals.html.

Hippotherapy

Bowling, Allen C. "Hippotherapy and Therapeutic Horseback Riding." *Neurology Care* (blog), April 27, 2001. http://www.neurologycare.net/hippotherapy-and-therapeutic-horseback-riding.html.

Horse Statistics and Facts

"AHP Releases the 2012 Equine Industry Survey Results to the General Equine Public." Press release. American Horse Publications, September 23, 2012. http://www.americanhorsepubs.org/news_updates/9578.asp.

The Ultimate Horse. http://www.ultimatehorsesite.com/info/horse questions/hq_numberofhorses.htm.

The Human Brain

Freeman, Walter J. "How and Why Brains Create Meaning from Sensory Information." *International Journal of Bifurcation and Chaos* 14 (2004): 513–30. http://escholarship.org/uc/item/1fs73030.

Hypermasculinity

Mosher, Donald L., and Silvan S. Tomkins. "Scripting the Macho Man: Hypermasculine Socialization and Enculturation." *Journal of Sex Research* 25, no. 1 (February 1988): 60–84. http://www.beyond utopia.net/leadership-lectures/tomkins-1.pdf.

Miraval and Wyatt Webb

"The Miraval Equine Experience: Immersion with Wyatt Webb." Miravalresorts.com. http://www.miravalresorts.com/The-Experience /Miraval-Specialists/Wyatt-Webb.

Mirroring

http://onlinelibrary.wiley.com/doi/10.1111/ppc.2004.40.issue-1 /issuetoc.

Mirror Neurons

Annual Reviews. http://www.annualreviews.org.

Keysers, Christian. "Mirror Neurons." http://www.sciencedirect.com /science/article/pii/S0960982209016005.

Post-Traumatic Stress Disorder

"DSM-5 Diagnostic Criteria for PTSD Released." http://www.ptsd.va
.gov/professional/pages/diagnostic_criteria_dsm-5.asp.

"Maltreated Children Show Same Pattern of Brain Activity as Combat Veterans," *UCL News,* December 5, 2011. http://www.ucl.ac
.uk/news/news-articles/1112/111205-maltreated-children-fMRI
-study.

"Post Traumatic Stress Disorder (PTSD): Facts and Treatment." *Disabled World.* http://www.disabledworld.com/disability/types/psychological
/ptsd.php#ixzz2JyFMMkVj.

van der Kolk, Bessela A. "Post-Traumatic Childhood." *New York Times,* May 10, 2011. http://www.nytimes.com/2011/05/11/opinion
/11kolk.html.

"What Is PTSD?" U.S. Department of Veterans Affairs. http://www
.ptsd.va.gov/public/pages/what-is-ptsd.asp.

"Who We Serve." Wounded Warrior Project. http://www.wounded
warriorproject.org/mission/who-we-serve.aspx.

Post-Traumatic Stress Disorder and Brain Chemistry

Goleman, Daniel. "A Key to Post-Traumatic Stress Lies in Brain Chemistry, Scientists Find." *New York Times,* June 12, 1990. http://
www.nytimes.com/1990/06/12/science/a-key-to-post-traumatic
-stress-lies-in-brain-chemistry-scientists-find.html?pagewanted=all&
src=pm.

Post-Traumatic Stress Disorder and Medication

Carey, Benedict. "Drugs Found Ineffective for Veterans' Stress." *New York Times,* August 2, 2011. http://www.nytimes.com/2011/08/03/health
/research/03psych.html.

Post-Traumatic Stress Disorder and Suicide

"Shocking PTSD, Suicide Rates for Vets." Face the Facts USA. George Washington University. http://www.facethefactsusa.org/facts/the-true -price-of-war-in-human-terms.

Prison Recidivism

Colorado Correctional Industries. Brochure. https://www.coloradoci .com/bin-pdf/CCibrochure.pdf.

Patterson, Alysia. "At Colo. Prison, Wild Horses Tame the Inmates." Associated Press, March 12, 2009. http://www.utsandiego.com/news/ 2009/mar/12/taming-mustangs-taming-prisoners-031209/all/?print.

"U.S. Prisons Overcrowded, Recidivism High." Info Please. http:// www.infoplease.com/ipa/A0933722.html.

Reactive Attachment Disorder

The International Society for Autism Research. "Discriminating Reactive Attachment Disorder from Autism Spectrum Disorders: Key Symptoms and Clinical Characteristics." International Meeting for Autism Research, May 13, 2011. https://imfar.confex.com/imfar/2011 /webprogram/Paper9121.html.

"Reactive Attachment Disorder: Definition." Mayo Clinic. http:// www.mayoclinic.com/health/reactive-attachment-disorder/DS00988.

"Reactive Attachment Disorder (RAD): Signs & Symptoms." The Child Study Center. New York University. http://www.aboutourkids .org/families/disorders_treatments/az_disorder_guide/reactive_attach ment_disorder/signs_symptoms.

Riding Schools

Le Cadre Noir, the French National Riding School. http://www.cadre noir.co.uk.

Spanish Riding School. http://www.srs.at/en.

Wild Horse Inmate Program

Colorado Wild Horse Inmate Program. Bureau of Land Management. U.S. Department of the Interior. http://www.blm.gov/co/st/en/BLM_Programs/wild_horse_and_burro/Wild_Horse_Inmate_Program_Colorado.print.html.

Prison Wild Horse Training Programs, Mustangs4Us.com, http://www.mustangs4us.com/Adopt%20Section/prisonhorses.htm.

Youth at Risk

Alliance for Excellent Education. http://www.all4ed.org.

"Children in Single-Parent Families." Kids Count Data Center. Annie E. Casey Foundation. http://datacenter.kidscount.org/data/tables/106-children-in-single-parent-families?loc=1&loct=2#ranking/1/any/true/867/any/430.

"Definition of Urban Youth at Risk." UN Habitat. United Nations Human Settlements Programme. http://ww2.unhabitat.org/programmes/safercities/uyr.asp.

"Fast Facts: Dropout Rates," National Center for Education Statistics, http://nces.ed.gov/fastfacts/display.asp?id=16.

"High School Dropout Statistics." Statistics Brain. http://www.statisticbrain.com/high-school-dropout-statistics.

List of articles on high school dropouts, *Education Week,* http://www.edweek.org/search.html?qs=high+school+dropouts.

INDEX